Flight Lessons 1. Basic Flight

How Eddie Learned the Meaning of it All

James Albright

Copyright © 2015 James Albright
All rights reserved.
ISBN-10: 0986263001
ISBN-13: 978-0-9862630-0-2

Acknowledgments

Thanks to Chris Manno for over thirty years of trading aviation stories, writing techniques, and for permitting my blatant grand larceny of his artwork without complaint. Thanks also to Chris Parker for all the fact checking, sense of grammar, and style pointers. If he's told me once, he's told me a thousand times to avoid hyperbole.

James' Lawyer Advises:

Always remember that James, when you get right down to it, is just a pilot. He tries to give you the facts from the source materials but maybe he got it wrong, maybe he is out of date. Sure, he warns you when he is giving you his personal techniques, but you should always follow your primary guidance (Aircraft manuals, government regulations, etc.) before listening to James.

Contents

Notes From Day One	5
1: Mechanics	7
2: Physics	16
3: Fluid Dynamics	23
4: Attitude Determines Altitude	28
5: UPT and ICE-T	35
6: Suck, Squeeze, Bang, Blow	43
7: Simulate	47
8: Aviate	52
9: Recover!	60
10: Charlie Brown	66
11: Getting Cross	74
12: Everybody has an Angle	79
13: In a Fix	84
14: Cooking With Gas	88
15: Go Around Burners!	93
16: Too Hot!	97
17: Hold	101
18: Critical	108
19: Decision	111
20: SERE	121
21: Unstable Aircraft	131
22: Unstable Pilots	140
23: Lost	149
24: Found	155
25: Limitations	163
26: Hands Full	170
27: The Leper Crew	181
28: A Practiced Calm	188
29: Magic	198
30: The Big Sky Theory	207

Notes From Day One

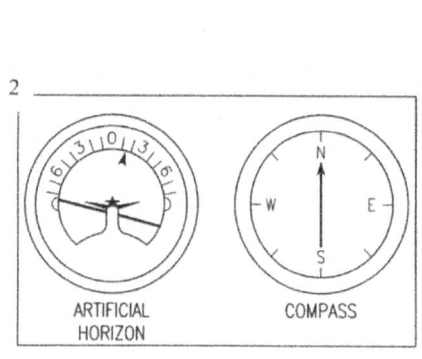 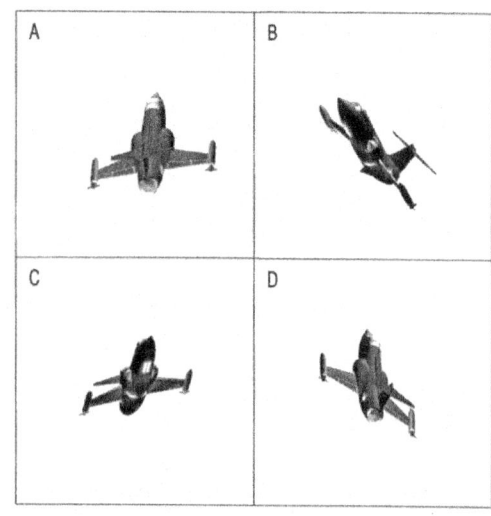

At seventeen, I had what some today might call attention deficit disorder. I recognized in myself what I then called a lack of focus, but today recognize as a lack of singular focus. I was interested in all things mechanical and that translated, in turn, to a zealous interest in bicycles, surfing, cars, airplanes, computer hardware, aeronautical engineering, computer software, flying, motorcycles, and finally, aviation. Yes, there is a recurring theme.

But that is hindsight. In the moment, in 1973, growing up in Hawaii, my sequential focus was moving from cars to the future Lovely Mrs. Haskel. As the Vietnam War was coming to an end and my U.S. Naval officer dad could not be home for my high school graduation, I needed to come up with a plan for college and to do my part as one-half of a married couple.

So I plodded off to take all the tests the military was handing out those days to prospective officer candidates. For some reason, I was presented with a bunch of pictures. There were all sorts of things to do. I had to match instruments with airplane drawings. I had to move an imaginary "stick" and rudder pedals to make the drawings react accordingly. At this point in my life I had zero interest in airplanes but I did understand auto mechanics. How hard could it be?

In a testament to how anyone with a logical brain can solve a poorly designed test, I got two ROTC scholarships and an appointment to the Air Force Academy. As is true with much of my life, as you will soon see, serendipity plays a big role in how things turn out. Purdue was the best choice for me and there I learned how to think, and that in turn taught me how to survive. All that I lacked was what I really wanted: the meaning of it all. So here we go . . . Volume One: Basic Flight.

Each chapter contains a story of the flight lesson as I learned it, followed by the flight lesson as it exists today, in the year 2015. The stories are as I would have written them at the time and the flight lessons are from today's perspective, with all the knowledge that has been added since.

Oh yes, the names. All of the names, even my own, have been changed.

1: Mechanics

Purdue University

West Lafayette, Indiana

1974

Purdue University (Erich Kirchubel - Creative Commons)

Day one for an Air Force Reserve Officer Training Corps (ROTC) cadet in 1974 began with a mountain of paperwork, a hill of uniforms, and barely a mention of the four years to come. The Air Force paid for the tuition, books, any lab expenses, and they threw in a cool one hundred dollars a month. In exchange I agreed to graduate in the allotted time and give back another four years as an officer. "Or else," I heard in what was offered as a joke.

"Or else what, sir?" I asked the guy on the other side of the table. He was dressed in dark blue slacks and a light blue shirt with five stripes sewn on each sleeve.

"First off, cadet," he said, "I am not a sir, I work for a living." He let that sink in and raised his gaze to mine. "I enlisted in the Air Force, I was not commissioned. You can address me as Sergeant Thompson, sergeant, or, hell, you can call me Marty. But I am not a sir. And the 'or else' has everything to do with that. You either become a 'sir' after Uncle Sugar pays for your next four years here at Purdue, or you will become an enlisted man, just like me. Got it?"

"Yes," I said, "sergeant." That task completed, I shuffled into the next line where I got two dark blue slacks and shirts, just like the sergeant's, but no stripes. Then came socks, belts, a hat, and other stuff that ended with a silver badge. "What's this, sergeant?" I asked, proud of myself being able to address the next enlisted person correctly.

"I am not a sergeant," she replied tersely, "I am an airman first class. You can call me airman. And these, cadet, are your wings. You are a pilot after all. At least that's what your paperwork says." How could I be a pilot, I thought, having never flown an airplane?

In the weeks to come I was to learn that Air Force ROTC Detachment 220 at Purdue University was one of the largest in the country. Our freshman class had about a hundred cadets of which thirty were on four-year scholarships and half that number wore cadet pilot wings. We were treated with extra care and attention and the non-pilots seemed to look upon us with a mixture of admiration and envy. But of we fifteen "pilots," I think only three had actual pilot's licenses.

Not to worry. Life as a freshman cadet meant a few hours of drill, a few hours of class, and an hour of counseling every month or so. We had to pass everything Purdue threw at us, after all, or our four years would be for naught. As a freshman aeronautical engineering student, I was immersed in introductory aero courses that taught me engineers don't design airplanes anymore, committees design airplanes. The math and physics courses made up for that disappointment, and I soon enjoyed an additional status to that of my so-called pilot's wings. I carried an ivory slide rule and book of math tables wherever I went. Purdue is an engineering school, yes, but most students study agriculture and other, less technical, professions.

For an eighteen-year old brought up in a Japanese house where humility was the highest virtue, I was being force-fed an ego from both my Air Force and engineering halves. In my quest to find "the meaning of it all," I wasn't sure about aviation yet, but the engineering somehow provided much of what I was looking for on how to think. Especially the study of mechanics...

Flight Lessons 1: Basic Flight

Position, starting with 2 dimensions

Mechanics

We can measure our position forward with positive numbers and backwards with negative numbers. The bike is at 0.

Speed (Average)

If we take two odometer readings, one at the start of the hour and another two hours later, our average speed is:

0	0	1	0	0	0

0	0	1	0	9	0

$$\text{Speed} = \frac{(1090 - 1000)}{2 \text{ hours}} = 45 \text{ mph}$$

Speed

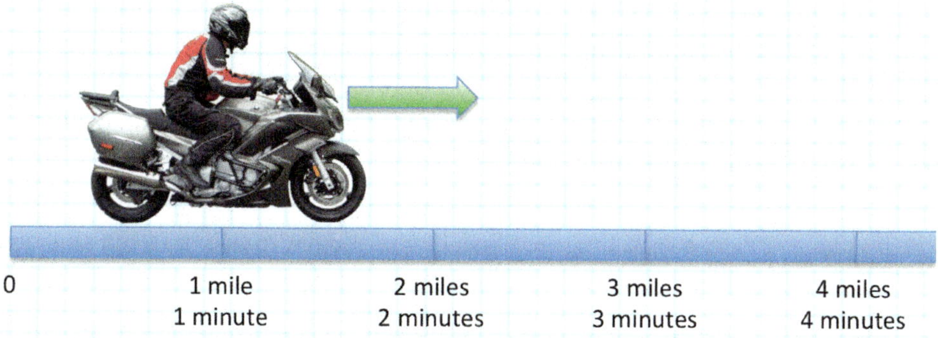

| 0 | 1 mile
1 minute | 2 miles
2 minutes | 3 miles
3 minutes | 4 miles
4 minutes |

If after 1 minute the bike has traveled 1 mile, we can say:

$$\text{Speed} = \frac{1 \text{ mile}}{1 \text{ minute}} = 1 \text{ mile/min}$$

Or, if we prefer a more standard measure:

$$\text{Speed} = \frac{1 \text{ mile}}{1 \text{ minute}} \times \frac{60 \text{ minutes}}{1 \text{ hour}} = 60 \text{ mph}$$

Velocity

Speed is a scalar quantity (it only has magnitude, no direction.)

Velocity is a vector quantity (it has magnitude and direction).

Direction is like angles on a grid, or on a compass. The bike is heading 30° north of east, or in pilot-speak: heading 060°

$$\text{Velocity } v = \frac{d}{t}$$

$$\text{Distance } d = vt$$

$$\text{Time } t = \frac{d}{v}$$

Consistent Units

We should keep the units consistent. Anything can be multiplied by one without changing the answer, so multiplying by a unit conversion keeps the answer true while making it more useful. 1 hour equals 60 minutes, for example. 1 hour divided by 60 minutes, therefore, equals 1. So multiplying something by 1 hour and then dividing by 60 minutes keeps the answer correct. In the example, 50 mph = 84 fps.

$$\left[\frac{50 \text{ miles}}{1 \text{ hour}}\right] \times \left[\frac{1 \text{ hour}}{60 \text{ mins}}\right] \times \left[\frac{1 \text{ minute}}{60 \text{ secs}}\right] \times \left[\frac{6076 \text{ feet}}{1 \text{ mile}}\right] = \left[\frac{84 \text{ feet}}{1 \text{ second}}\right]$$

$$\left[\frac{50 \cancel{\text{ miles}}}{1 \cancel{\text{ hour}}}\right] \times \left[\frac{1 \cancel{\text{ hour}}}{60 \cancel{\text{ minutes}}}\right] \times \left[\frac{1 \cancel{\text{ minute}}}{60 \text{ seconds}}\right] \times \left[\frac{6076 \text{ feet}}{1 \cancel{\text{ mile}}}\right] = 84 \text{ fps}$$

Some of the units cancel each other out. A "minute" divided by another "minute" equals 1 and disappears from the answer. In our example, every unit except feet and seconds disappear, yielding feet per second.

Flight Lessons 1: Basic Flight

Velocity on a Graph

You can also plot distance versus time to come up with a graphical representation of velocity. The slope of the distance change along any point of the line will show the velocity over that time span. Since our velocity is constant — neither accelerating or decelerating — any two points will yield a velocity of 84 fps

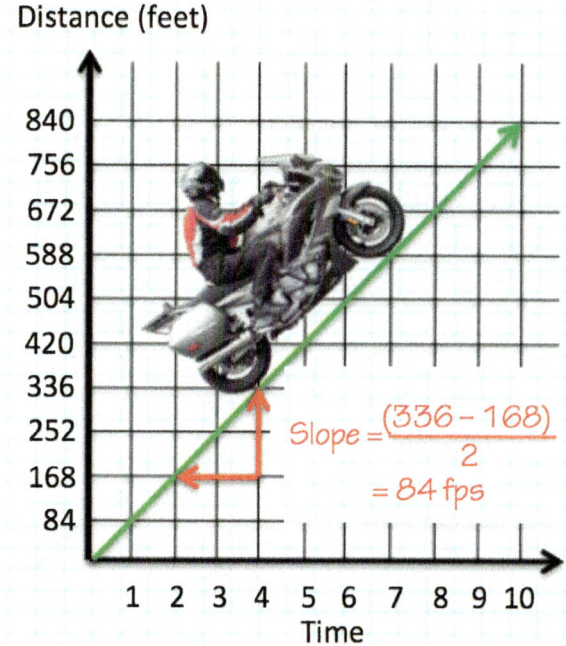

Acceleration

Change in velocity per unit of time

Δ symbol signifies change in values

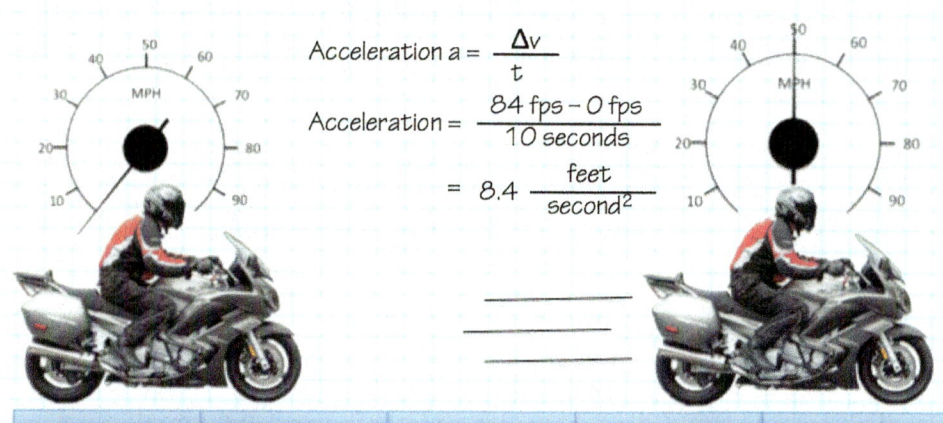

$$\text{Acceleration } a = \frac{\Delta v}{t}$$

$$\text{Acceleration} = \frac{84 \text{ fps} - 0 \text{ fps}}{10 \text{ seconds}}$$

$$= 8.4 \; \frac{\text{feet}}{\text{second}^2}$$

Acceleration on a Graph

The slope of the velocity change along any point of the line will show the acceleration over that time span. Since our acceleration is constant any two points will yield an acceleration of 8.5 fps².

Acceleration $a = \dfrac{\Delta v}{t}$

Where $\Delta v = v_1 - v_0$

Then: $v = at$

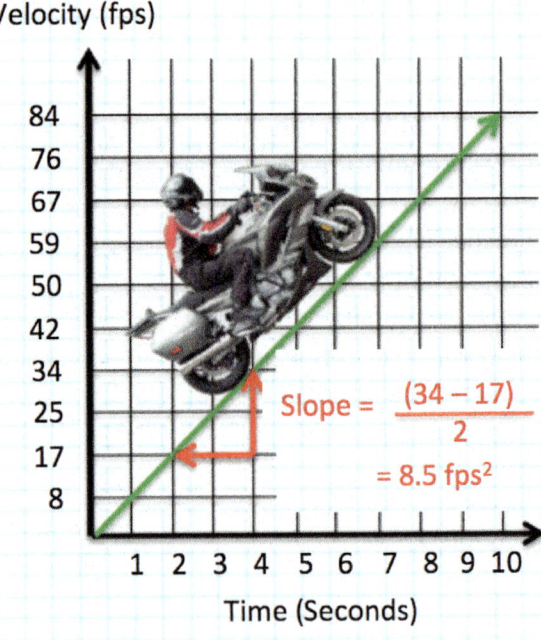

Slope = $\dfrac{(34 - 17)}{2}$ = 8.5 fps²

If $v_0 = 0$ (starting velocity) and
$v_1 = at$ (ending velocity)
Average velocity, $v_{average} = \frac{1}{2} at$
Since $d = vt$ that means $d = (\frac{1}{2} at)t$ and that means:
Distance, given constant acceleration: $d = \frac{1}{2} at^2$

Jerk

"Jerkiness" can be measured as the second derivative of position. If velocity is constant, acceleration is zero, if acceleration is constant, jerk is zero. If we go from 84 fps to a stop in 30 seconds:

Acceleration = $\dfrac{0 \text{ fps} - 84 \text{ fps}}{30 \text{ seconds}}$ = -2.8 $\dfrac{\text{feet}}{\text{second}^2}$

If we suddenly increase our deceleration to -5 feet/sec² in 5 seconds:

Jerk = $\dfrac{(-2.8 - (-5))}{5 \text{ seconds}}$ = 0.44 $\dfrac{\text{feet}}{\text{second}^3}$

In other words: Jerk: $j = \dfrac{\Delta a}{t}$

Now let's say our intrepid rider underestimates the amount of braking required. If he or she then decides to really clamp down on the brakes, then backs off, and then on again, the stop will be said to be "jerky."

Flight Lessons 1: Basic Flight

Why is jerk pertinent to a pilot? You can stop the airplane on a short runway using aggressive braking by applying your best guess of brake pedal and then holding the brakes steady. As the brakes heat up they become more effective and the deceleration will increase. But it will be done smoothly. Or you can apply some brake, a little less, a little more. Then the passengers will call you a jerk.

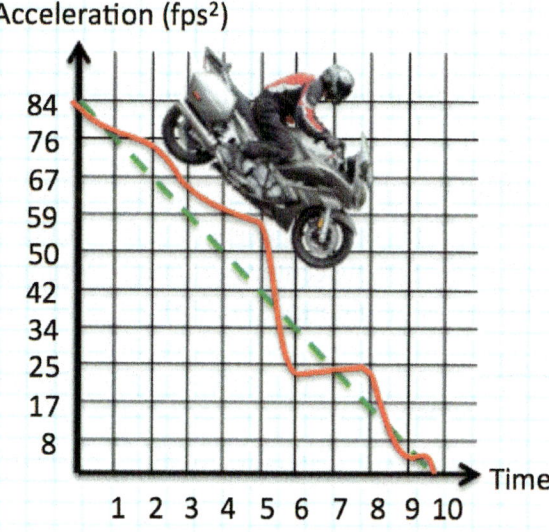

Gravity

Over the years we've come to realize that objects on earth fall at 32 ft/sec² which is 9.8 m/sec² for most of the world. When speaking of acceleration to earth — falling —, we substitute the term g for a so that:

Velocity under earth's gravity v = gt

And that means the distance resulting from earth's gravitational pull

D = ½ gt²

Mass

[Dole, pg. 6]

Mass is a measure of the amount of material in a body. Weight, on the other hand, is a force caused by the gravitational attraction of the earth, moon, sun, or other heavenly bodies. Weight will vary, depending upon where the body is located in space. Mass will not vary with position.

Weight (W) = mass (m) X acceleration of gravity (g)

W = mg

Rearranging: $m = \dfrac{W}{g} \quad \dfrac{lb}{ft/sec^2} = \dfrac{lb\text{-}sec^2}{ft}$

(Called a "slug")

Moments

[Dole, pg. 6]

Moments are measured by multiplying the amount of the applied force F by the moment arm l.

Moment: $M = Fl$

The moment arm is the perpendicular distance from the line of action of the applied force to the center of rotation. Moments are measured as foot pounds (ft-lbs) or as inch pounds (in.-lb).

Power

[Dole, pg. 9]

Power is defined as "the rate of doing work":

$$Power = \frac{Work}{time} = \frac{force \times distance}{time}$$

But distance / time = velocity, so: Power: Power = force X velocity

Friction

[Dole, pg. 10]

If two forces are in contact with each other, a force develops between them when an attempt is made to move them relative to each other. This force is called friction. Several factors are involved in determining friction effects on aircraft during takeoff and landing operations. Among these are runway surface material, condition of the runway, tire material and tread, the amount of brake slippage. All of these variables determine a coefficient of friction μ (mu). The actual braking force F_b is the product of this coefficient μ and the normal (squeezing) force between the tires and the runway:

Braking Friction: $F_b = \mu N$

where F_b = braking force, μ = coefficient of friction, N = normal force on wheels.

Flight Lessons 1: Basic Flight

Energy

Consider for a moment a metal ball traveling at a constant speed on a flat surface approaching a dip. We say the ball and the surface are both frictionless and there is no air resistance for the sake of this academic exercise. We know that as the ball goes down the dip in the surface, its speed will increase until it gets to the bottom where it will trade that extra speed to climb the ramp. When it ends up back at the original level it will again be at its original speed. Before it hits the slope, the energy of the ball can be described as the Kinetic Energy (KE) that comes from its motion and the Potential Energy (PE) due to its higher elevation.

Potential Energy: $PE = Wh$

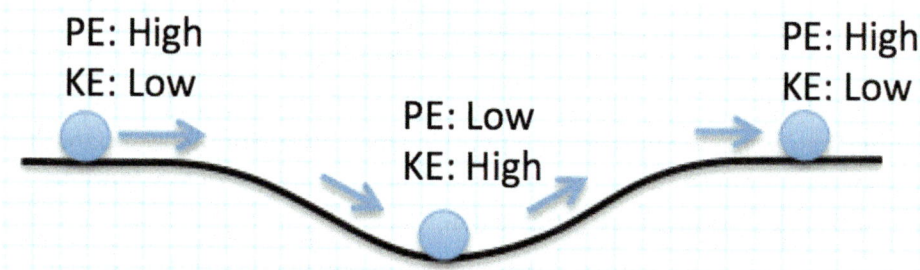

[Dole, pg. 8]

Kinetic energy requires movement of an object. It is a function of the mass m of the object and its velocity v:

Kinetic Energy: $KE = \frac{1}{2}mv^2$

[Dole, pg. 8]

The total mechanical energy of an object is the sum of its PE and KE:

Total Energy: $TE = PE + KE$

[Dole, pg. 8]

The law of conservation of energy states total energy remains constant. Both potential and kinetic energy can change in value, but the total energy must remain the same; "Energy cannot be created or destroyed, but can change in form."

2: Physics

Cessna 310 (Mark Jones - Creative Commons)

A Cessna 310! George was checked out in a 310! We crowded around Cadet George Daniel's new multi-engine pilot's license, a foreign piece of paper to most of us. But even to we mortals with no pilot's license of any kind, we knew this put George into the big leagues.

"So that's the best pilot's license there is," someone half asked, half stated. "Now you can fly any airplane, single-engine, twin-engine, even four-engine!"

"Sure can," George said, basking in his glory.

George had just turned nineteen, as was true with all of us in his shadow. Our ROTC class returned from summer break, about half strength. Most of the losses were due to grades, but some probably due to the end of the Vietnam War and the official suspension of the draft. We lost two guys on full scholarships but got two transfers, so we still had thirty guys on the full ride. We still had fifteen pilot candidates, but still only three had real pilot's licenses. George had the best license of them all.

"What about a 747," another voice asked. "Can you fly one of those?"

"Of course," he said, "the license says multi, doesn't it?"

Everyone nodded with the obviousness of it. I had to wonder. George was a good guy and he knew more about flying than anyone I knew. But I cringed at the thought of the Lovely Mrs. Haskel and I downstairs on a Boeing 747 with a nineteen-year old in the pilot's seat.

We fifteen were sitting in the armory lounge, waiting our turns to see Major Sawadee, the only pilot amongst our five cadre faculty members. He was also the sophomore cadet instructor, so we looked forward to more pilot war stories than military lessons this year in class. I waited for "A" to "G" to see the major and finally got my turn. Major Sawadee was satisfied with my grades the first year but wanted to know what I thought about aeronautical engineering. I told him about how much I was enjoying every aspect of engineering except the aero. "If you can't design an airplane, what's the point?"

"What is it," he asked, "that you are looking for?"

"I would like to know the meaning of it all," I said.

"You should be an industrial engineer," Sawadee said. "That fits your brain to a tee." He went on for quite a while but before he was done I was convinced. "So, Eddie," he asked, "anything else on your mind?"

"Yes sir," I said immediately, "I am wondering about pilot's licenses. What kind do you get when you get your wings?"

"You don't need a pilot's license at all to be an Air Force pilot," he said, "but most guys take a written test on the civilian rules and get a commercial, multi-engine pilot's license."

"Is that the best kind of license there is?" I asked, leaving aside the "commercial" bit for now.

"Well no," he answered, "the highest license would be the airline transport rating."

"Ah," I said. So there was someone else in our airliner's cockpit after all. "So that's what you need to fly a 747 then."

"Not exactly," he said, "if the airplane weighs over twelve thousand five hundred pounds you also need a type rating."

It was a lot more complicated than I knew. It was apparently more complicated than George knew too. On my walk home I pondered George's transgressions, his ignorance and mine. When the Lovely Mrs. Haskel came home from work I gave her every minute detail of the day and ended it all with, "George isn't so smart after all. He didn't know any of this."

"He didn't know what he didn't know," the Lovely Mrs. Haskel said, "that sounds like something you pilots should worry about. And so I started worrying about (YDK)[2].

The Lovely Mrs. Haskel thought industrial engineering was a marvelous idea and the next week I had a new major, a new class schedule, and a new outlook. As the fall turned to winter and the winter turned to spring, the Air Force decided it had too many pilots and three-quarters of every pilot candidate on full ride scholarships in the entire country got letters saying it was over. Take whatever education you had and have a good life. No commitment, no Air Force, and no pilot's wings. At Purdue the upper classes were decimated. Well, worse than decimated. Of eighty pilot candidates in the detachment, sixty were gone. In our sophomore class, fifteen turned to four. As one of the survivors, I started to want those pilot's wings more than just about anything. And not the fake ROTC pilot's wings, I started to covet the real thing.

At the end of year two, each cadet was sent off to boot camp for a month of drill, survival school, military discipline immersion, and the other fun raw recruits see on day one. As officer candidates we probably got less of each of those categories, but they still made a big deal of it. There were only two possible results, we were told, either we passed or we failed. But that wasn't true. We also had a day on the firing range where we could qualify for combat duty. All pilots had to pass. You can't very well be an Air Force pilot if you can't kill people and break things. (It is part of the creed, after all.)

The firing range was more than just combat qualification, however. If you did really well, you got a marksmanship ribbon that would follow you onto active duty. This was our only chance to start our lives as officers with more than just an empty chest where all the medals belong. I wanted that ribbon.

It was to be one hundred rounds with an Air Force drill sergeant in charge. We got two hours of instruction operating our M-16 rifles, an hour of range safety, and then an hour on the range. For someone who had never held a peashooter, much less an automatic rifle, the M-16 was an impressive weapon. I feared it. Intellectually, however, I thought I had the entire program wired. With a mechanical background in cars, an engineering background in school, I found myself understanding the rifle almost immediately. I was going to do this.

The first ninety rounds were carefully scripted: Ten rounds from the standing position, ten rounds while prone, ten rounds behind a barricade, ten rounds timed, and so on. They told us how they wanted the first ninety rounds.

Flight Lessons 1: Basic Flight

"The range is hot," the lead drill sergeant bellowed, "this will be ten rounds, prone. You have sixty seconds to fire all ten. You may fire at will."

Saw Gunners (Mark Stroud - Creative Commons)

I closed my left eye and placed the cross hair over the center of the bull's eye, 500-yards away. I was happy with the discipline of the sight, staying where I left it. I increased pressure on the trigger, "let it surprise you," the instructor said. A moment later I felt the recoil and imagined a spot dead center. And so it went for the next eighty-nine rounds, all ninety right in the bull's eye. So I had my combat qualification in the bag. Five more shots and I would have my marksman's ribbon.

The final ten rounds were from however we wanted: prone, standing, kneeling, behind a barricade, it didn't matter. But they had to be from our weak eye. I chose to kneel behind the barricade to steady my hand, closed my right eye, and proceeded to throw bullets into the straw either side of the target.

Well, you can only do so much. "All safe, all safe on the firing range." With our weapons safetied, we approached our targets and started the count. "Ninety-seven," I counted, "ninety-eight, ninety-nine, one-hundred. That can't be right." I counted again. ". . . one-hundred." I counted again.

The drill sergeant tapped me on the shoulder, "We got a problem, Kay-det?"

"Sergeant," I said, "I counted one-hundred."

"Congratulations," he said. "That makes you a marksman."

"But sergeant," I said, "I am certain I didn't hit the target one hundred times."

"I said you are a marksman, cadet," he said in the gruff voice issued to drill sergeants. "What part of that don't you understand?"

"I am a marksman, sergeant."

"That's what I thought you said." The sergeant marched off.

Another cadet tapped me on the shoulder, "What's the problem?"

I explained my situation and he smiled in recognition.

"You were two guys to my right," he explained, "you didn't see me because you are right handed and had your back to me." I nodded. "I'm right handed too, so I saw you and her. She was left handed."

The cadet explained that every time the middle cadet squeezed her trigger, she closed both her eyes. "Scared the hell out of me," he said, "but at least she made sure the rifle was pointed down range before she shot."

"So she hit my target ten times," I said, finally recognizing the source of my perfect score. "I need to report this."

"Don't bother," he said, "I already told them my score was bogus and was told to forget about it."

"How'd you do?" I asked.

"One-ten out of one-hundred," he said.

I sheepishly accepted my ribbon and marveled at how well my engineering had prepared me for everything except a weak left eye. I knew that a keen insight to physics would continue to serve me well . . .

Flight Lessons 1: Basic Flight

Physics

Newton's First Law

"A body at rest will remain at rest and a body in motion will remain in motion, unless acted upon by an unbalanced force."

The first law implies that bodies have a property called inertia. Inertia may be defined as the property of a body that results in its maintaining its velocity unchanged unless it interacts with an unbalanced force. The measure of inertia is what is technically known as mass.

Newton's Second Law

"If a body is acted upon by an unbalanced force, the body will accelerate in the direction of the force and the acceleration will be directly proportional to the force and inversely proportional to the mass of the body."

Acceleration is the change in motion (speed) of a body in a unit of time. The amount of acceleration a is directly proportional to the unbalanced force F and is inversely proportional to the mass m of the body. These two effects can be expressed by the simple equation:

$a = F / m$

or more commonly: Force: $F = ma$ and . . .
Weight: $W = mg$

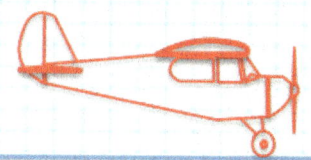

Newton's Third Law

"For every action force there is an equal and opposite reaction force."

A force is a push or a pull tending to change the state of a motion of a body.

Note: While most pilot training manuals use this Drag-Thrust / Lift-Weight diagram, there really is no such thing as forces called "lift" or "drag." The true forces are shown on the next page . . .

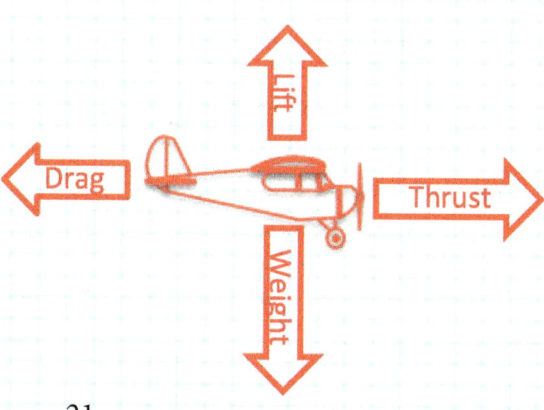

Aerodynamic Force

The true forces on an aircraft in level, unaccelerated flight are thrust (from the engines), weight, and aerodynamic force (from the wings and fuselage).

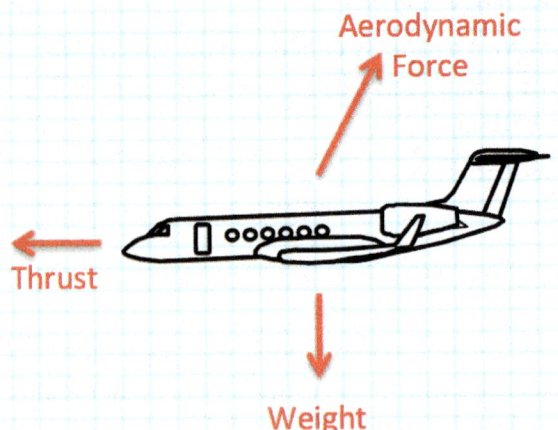

Aerodynamic force can be broken down into two components: one that is parallel to the relative wind and opposite thrust (called drag) and another that is perpendicular to that force and opposite weight (called lift).

Equilibrium Conditions

[Dole, pg. 6]

There are two requirements for a body to meet to be in a state of equilibrium: (1) There must be no unbalanced forces acting on the body. This is written as the mathematical formula $\Sigma F = 0$. Σ (sigma) is the Greek symbol for "sum of." (2) There must be no unbalanced moments acting on the body. Mathematically, $\Sigma M = 0$.

Moments at the fulcrum in [the figure] are 50 ft-lb clockwise and 50 ft-lb counterclockwise. So $\Sigma M = 0$. To satisfy the first condition of equilibrium, the fulcrum must press against the seesaw with a force of 15 lb. So, $\Sigma F = 0$.

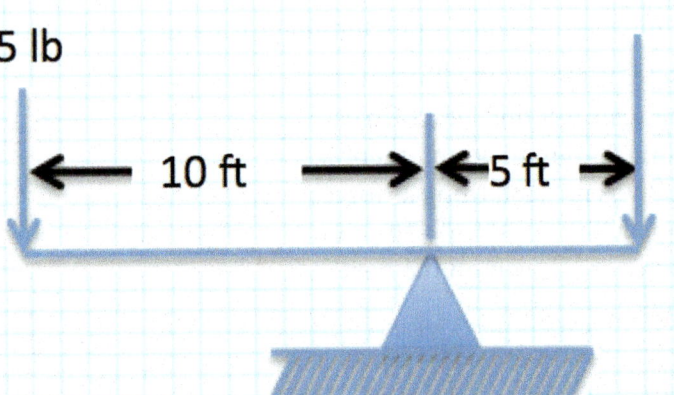

3: Fluid Dynamics

Purdue ROTC Patch (Eddie's Collection)

Year two ended with boot camp where I found myself as one of hundreds, neither distinguished nor vanquished. I wasn't a top graduate. I managed to be in the top half in every category, but in no way stood out from the crowd. Returning to Purdue, I knew, I would be competing with at least one or two who came back from their boot camp experiences as a top grad. There were four.

Year three is important, we knew, because now everyone remaining had signed on the dotted line to enter the Air Force as officers. The boys and girls who wanted to try it out just for fun were gone, now it was just us men and women. We were down to forty in total, but we gained five more pilots. Eight of us, if we graduated and got our commissions, would be headed for Air Force pilot training.

We gained one more thing, a new Professor of Aerospace Studies. He was an Air Force colonel charged with leading us through the four years on our way to the real Air Force. As a first and second year cadet I had very little contact with the PAS. Now as a junior I knew things would change. I noted his picture on the armory wall and shook my head.

"Shoe clerk," I heard from behind me. It was Cadet Daniels. "How can we have five officers in the detachment and only one a pilot?"

"Dunno," I said. We walked up the ramp to the second floor and gave the Reader's Digest version of our boot camp experiences. George was a top grad. Of course he was.

In our cadet lounge there was a crowd around the bulletin board. Everybody turned to face me. "So we have a new golden child," they said as one. The sea parted and I saw the reason for my new status. The PAS selected one cadet from each class to be his personal liaison with that class. For the third year cadets, the juniors, it would be me. I didn't know if that was good or bad.

"Bad, of course," George said. "You've got school work, you're married, you've got a cadet officer job, and now this." That was the consensus, at least of the group that morning. My first cadet officer job was as a flight commander, leading twelve freshman and sophomore cadets in their weekly drill. Easy enough. Now I also had an hour-long meeting with the PAS every month, starting with day one.

"Good to meet you Eddie," he said after returning my salute. "I guess you know why I picked you when you read my bio on the wall."

"Sir?" It was an inelegant betrayal of the fact I skipped the bio entirely. He either didn't notice or elegantly let it slide.

"We industrial engineers have to stick together, don't we Eddie?"

"Yes, sir." Ah so, I thought, the equation is solved. Colonel Bernard waxed poetic about the value of an industrial engineering degree and how it made the difference in his progress from cadet, to second lieutenant, and on to colonel. "Teaches you how to think, how to organize, how to get things done."

"The meaning of it all," I said.

"What's that?" he asked.

"Yes, sir," I said. "I hope it helps with being a pilot too."

"Oh it will," he said. "Have you taken advanced fluid dynamics yet, Eddie?"

"This semester, sir."

"Well that is going to set you apart from all the other pilots," he said, "you

Flight Lessons 1: Basic Flight

can bet on that."

We finished the talk with cadet corps matters and a little bit about the Lovely Mrs. Haskel and the need for me to set an example for the younger married cadets. The next morning there was a dusty, old manual in my cadet mailbox, a navy manual dated 1960 with the military sounding title "NAVWEPS 00-80T-80, Aerodynamics for Naval Aviators" written by a less than naval sounding guy named H. H. Hurt, Jr.

"Best book on fluid dynamics ever," the note said. The bottom of the note had a simple "CB" on it. Do colonels sign things like that? Colonel Bernard is "CB?" I finally read his bio. Colonel Charles Bernard had a degree in Industrial Engineering but spent most of his Air Force career in aircraft weapon systems procurement. It was all making sense. By the end of the semester I realized NAVWEPS-Whatever was the best book on fluid dynamics ever, assuming the fluid in question is air. As a pilot, the fluid in question usually is.

As the year progressed I became one of Colonel Bernard's favorite visitors. He was a bit aloof from outward appearances and didn't spend much time on the drill floor or our classrooms. But every now and then he would pop by the lounge and say, "Eddie, you got a minute?" and off I would go. Somehow the normal end of year debate on which senior year cadet would get the nod as cadet wing commander became moot.

Fluid Dynamics

Static Pressure

[Hurt, pg. 2]

The static pressure of the air at any altitude results from the mass of air supported at that level. At standard sea level conditions the static pressure of the air is 2,116 psf (or 14.7 psi, 29.92 in. Hg, etc.) The shorthand notation for the ambient static pressure is "p" and the standard sea level pressure is given the subscript "0" for zero altitude, p_0. The proportion of the ambient static pressure and the standard sea level pressure is assigned the standard notation of δ (delta).   Altitude Pressure Ratio: $\delta = p / p_0$

Density

[Hurt, pg. 2]

The density of the air is the mass of air per cubic foot of volume and is a direct measure of the quantity of matter. Air at sea level conditions weighs 0.0765 pounds per cubic foot and has a density of 0.002378 slugs per cubic foot. The shorthand notation used for air density is ρ (rho) and the standard sea level air density is then ρ_0. In aerodynamics it is convenient to consider the proportion of the ambient air density and standard sea level air density. This density ratio is assigned the shorthand notation of σ (sigma).

$\sigma = \rho / \rho_0$

A general gas law defines the relationship of pressure, temperature, and density when there is no change of state or heat transfer. Using the properties previously defined . . .

$$\frac{\rho}{\rho_0} = \left(\frac{P}{P_0}\right)\left(\frac{T_0}{T}\right)$$

Viscosity

[Hurt, pg. 4]

The coefficient of absolute viscosity is the proportion between the shearing stress and velocity gradient for a fluid flow. The viscosity of gases is unusual in that the viscosity is generally a function of temperature alone and an increase in temperature increases the viscosity. The coefficient of absolute viscosity is assigned the shorthand notation μ (mu). A more usual form of viscosity measure is the proportion of the coefficient of absolute viscosity and density. This combination is termed the "kinematic viscosity" and is noted by ν (nu).

Kinematic Viscosity: $\nu = \mu / \rho$

Flight Lessons 1: Basic Flight

Temperature

The absolute temperature of air is measured in degrees Kelvin, where 0°K is as cold as we think anything can get. Conversion:

°K = °C + 273

[Hurt, pg. 2]

The shorthand notation for the ambient air temperature is "T" and the standard sea level air temperature 288°K is signified by T_0. The more usual reference is the proportion of the ambient air temperature and the standard sea level air temperature. This temperature ratio is assigned the shorthand notation of θ (theta).

Temperature Ratio: $\theta = T / T_0$

Temperature Lapse Rate & the Troposphere

The standard atmosphere model reveals that the temperature decreases about 2°C every 1,000 feet. This is known as the temperature lapse rate. The lapse rate stops around 36,000 feet under standard conditions. Where the lapse rate exists is known as the troposphere and is where you will find most of our weather. Where the temperature is constant is the tropopause. Above that is the stratosphere.

ALTITUDE FT.	DENSITY RATIO σ	√σ	PRESSURE RATIO δ	TEMPERATURE °F	TEMPERATURE RATIO θ	SPEED OF SOUND a KNOTS	KINEMATIC VISCOSITY ν FT²/SEC
0	1.0000	1.0000	1.0000	59.00	1.0000	661.7	.000158
1000	0.9711	0.9854	0.9644	55.43	0.9931	659.5	.000161
2000	0.9428	0.9710	0.9298	51.87	0.9862	657.2	.000165
3000	0.9151	0.9566	0.8962	48.30	0.9794	654.9	.000169
4000	0.8881	0.9424	0.8637	44.74	0.9725	652.6	.000174
5000	0.8617	0.9283	0.8320	41.17	0.9656	650.3	.000178
6000	0.8359	0.9143	0.8014	37.60	0.9587	647.9	.000182
7000	0.8106	0.9004	0.7716	34.04	0.9519	645.6	.000187
8000	0.7860	0.8866	0.7428	30.47	0.9450	643.3	.000192
9000	0.7620	0.8729	0.7148	26.90	0.9381	640.9	.000197
10000	0.7385	0.8593	0.6877	23.34	0.9312	638.6	.000202
15000	0.6292	0.7932	0.5643	5.51	0.8969	626.7	.000229
20000	0.5328	0.7299	0.4595	-12.32	0.8625	614.6	.000262
25000	0.4481	0.6694	0.3711	-30.15	0.8281	602.2	.000302
30000	0.3741	0.6117	0.2970	-47.98	0.7937	589.5	.000349
35000	0.3099	0.5567	0.2353	-65.82	0.7594	576.6	.000405
*36089	0.2971	0.5450	0.2234	-69.70	0.7519	573.8	.000419
40000	0.2462	0.4962	0.1851	-69.70	0.7519	573.8	.000506
45000	0.1936	0.4400	0.1455	-69.70	0.7519	573.8	.000643
50000	0.1522	0.3902	0.1145	-69.70	0.7519	573.8	.000818
55000	0.1197	0.3460	0.0900	-69.70	0.7519	573.8	.001040
60000	0.0941	0.3068	0.0708	-69.70	0.7519	573.8	.001323
65000	0.0740	0.2721	0.0557	-69.70	0.7519	573.8	.001682
70000	0.0582	0.2413	0.0438	-69.70	0.7519	573.8	.002139
75000	0.0458	0.2140	0.0344	-69.70	0.7519	573.8	.002721
80000	0.0360	0.1897	0.0271	-69.70	0.7519	573.8	.003460
85000	0.0280	0.1673	0.0213	-64.80	0.7613	577.4	.004499
90000	0.0217	0.1472	0.0168	-56.57	0.7772	583.4	.00591
95000	0.0169	0.1299	0.0134	-48.34	0.7931	589.3	.00772
100000	0.0132	0.1149	0.0107	-40.11	0.8089	595.2	.01004

*GEOPOTENTIAL OF THE TROPOPAUSE

4: Attitude Determines Altitude

Cessna 152 (Joe Monster - Creative Commons)

As the fourth year and seventh semester began, so too began the Flight Instruction Program for the eight pilot cadets in the senior class. While the other seven were pouring over a flight text book and the Cessna 150 flight manual, I was busy meeting with the ROTC cadre and my cadet corps staff planning the year to come. It was not what I had in mind for the semester I had been looking forward to for three years.

As it turns out, being a cadet corps wing commander is a pretty silly job. At age twenty-one I still had a bit of a boyish face and at six-foot-one I weighed all of 150 pounds. Looking at the mirror I had to admit I didn't have the look of the title. And yet there I was, looking back in the mirror, dressed in a blue uniform with black shoulder boards and four silver stripes. All the Air Force cadets on campus knew to salute me. The other military cadets were not so sure. I once got a salute from a Navy lieutenant. I didn't bother explaining to him that I was not a real commissioned officer and that I owed him a salute, not the other way around. It seemed less embarrassing for everyone concerned to simply return the salute.

The job entailed holding a meeting every week with other cadets in the senior staff, standing in front of the 200 cadets every now and then during drills, and speaking to an audience of 200-plus every month. For some rea-

Flight Lessons 1: Basic Flight

son that last bit was the only part I enjoyed. No matter, I soon found time to fly.

The Air Force was going to pay for twenty hours in a Cessna 150 to see if I had what it takes, or so the story goes. I knew the real reason was to wash out those who had a natural fear of flying or a lack of desire. They said it cost a million dollars to put one candidate through Air Force Undergraduate Pilot Training and that if this Cessna 150 program washed just one candidate out it paid for itself. That wasn't going to be me.

I studied the Cessna 150 operating handbook the way I studied any engineering text. No, that's not right. I studied that handbook eagerly and as if my life depended on it. Because it did, I told myself. Lesson one was in the classroom with my very first flight instructor, Steve Belamy. He was a pure civilian out at Purdue Airport, just outside of West Lafayette, Indiana. Steve had no connection to the military other than the fact he was on the Air Force payroll every summer to get us cadets through this. He had long hair, wore polyester clothes, and had the swagger of the disco craze sweeping the country.

"Memorize this," he began lesson one on day one, "Power determines altitude and pitch determines airspeed."

I wrote the words down with the immediate realization that they were wrong. Even with zero hours in my logbook I knew that adding power made the airplane go faster and pulling up on the yoke makes you go higher. But I kept my mouth shut and finished the day looking forward to my first flight.

Sortie One was fun, as I knew it would be. Steve let me try a little bit of everything but my only gradable event for the day was keeping the airplane straight and level when asked to do so. "Power determines altitude," he repeated over and over, "keep the airplane in trim and you won't have to worry about the speed." I tried it his way. Though it worked, it seemed simpler to pull or push the yoke to make the altimeter behave.

I rushed to the library and picked up every book on primary flight instruction I could find. Steve's words were repeated in some of the very basic texts. It still made no sense at all. I was up there, flying the airplane. When I changed power the speed changed. And the altimeter reacted to the yoke. It was like George Daniels would always say, "Houses smaller," while pulling back on an imaginary yoke, "Houses bigger," while pushing forward.

Sortie One turned into Sorties Two, Three, Four and Five. The first cadet in our class soloed on Sortie Four. The next two on Sortie Five. I mastered each maneuver quickly, though I really wasn't doing the "power determines altitude" thing. As my grade book filled and all of the requirements for solo were met, Steve wouldn't let me take the airplane around the pattern on my own. I found myself in the humiliating position of being the only cadet yet to solo. Everybody knew I started last because of my cadet corps responsibilities, but soon they would know I was last because . . . well I'm not sure why.

I bore my frustration silently while going through the cadet wing commander motions. The colonel asked to see me one morning and wanted to talk about eye shadow. He didn't think female cadets should be allowed to wear blue eye shadow because it was unnatural. It was my job to ensure our cadets didn't wear blue eye shadow. When I reminded him that many people have blue eyes and perhaps it was natural after all, he emphasized the word was natural and there was natural blue and unnatural blue and my job was to determine the difference. Like I said, it was a silly job.

On my way out of the office I heard a cricket chirp, the telltale sign Major Sawadee wanted to see you. Sawadee was still the only pilot in our officer cadre but he still was teaching the sophomore cadets so I hardly ever saw him. "Sir?" I asked while poking my head into his office.

"How's it going, Eddie? How about shooting the breeze with a fellow pilot?"

"So you've heard," I said, "Sortie Five and I still haven't soloed." I explained how I was signed off on every maneuver but not for solo. Something just didn't add up.

"Some instructors are a bit skittish," the major explained, "just give him some time."

I explained how Steve Belamy signed me off for everything two flights ago, but just won't let me solo. I went over some of my complaints about Steve, starting with the "Power determines altitude and pitch determines airspeed" mantra.

"Well that's total bullshit," Sawadee said, "Attitude determines altitude. Period. Every military pilot knows that." He explained that with everything else constant on a simple propeller-driven airplane, there is a given airspeed for a given pitch. Civilians emphasize that as a way to hammer home the aircraft has to be trimmed for that airspeed.

"When you get to flying jets in the Air Force you are going to learn about the

Flight Lessons 1: Basic Flight

'control and performance' concept. But for now, do it your instructor's way." He sat quietly for a while and then looked me in the eye. "You are a typical engineer, Eddie, and that will help you in the cockpit in the long run. But in the short run it is hurting you. Your mental attitude, that's key."

"I've never had an attitude problem, sir."

"No," Sawadee admitted, "you haven't; just the wrong attitude. Being a pilot is more than stick and rudder, procedures and techniques. Being a pilot is about an inner faith in yourself. You have to believe you can do something before you can do it. You have to have the confidence. Don't strap into the aircraft. Strap on the aircraft, become a part of it. Don't push and pull the levers to coax the airplane into doing something you want, you make the airplane react to your will. You've got to have the pilot attitude."

"Cocky?"

"Yeah." Sawadee's eyes lit up. "Cocky and arrogant. That's what it takes. Why would a sane man get into a fighter and fly into a nest of surface to air missiles when the odds are against him? Because he believes he can beat them. He might be wrong, but he believes. You have to believe before you can do. There are times to be an engineer. But there are times to be a cocky SOB. It's all about attitude."

The next day I strapped on that Cessna 150 and flew it around the pattern like I owned the place. After my first landing Belamy pulled back on the throttle and said, "let's pull off the runway for a minute." I did as instructed and stopped on the nearest taxiway.

"You go up and give me three landings," he said while unfastening his seat belt, "then come pick me up."

I soloed on Sortie Six.

Control and Performance Concept

Procedure

[AFM 51-37, 1976, para 2.]

- Establish attitude and power settings on the control instruments which should result in the desired performance (make note of the settings).

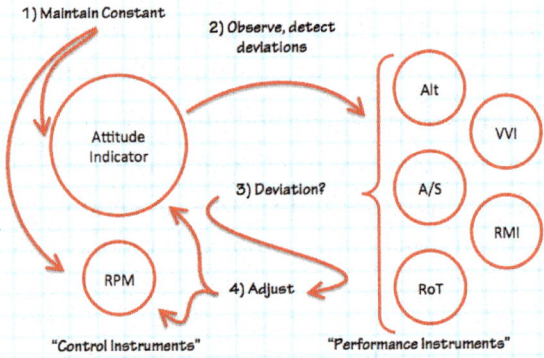

- Trim until control pressures are neutralized.
- Cross-check the performance instruments to determine if the established attitude or power setting is providing the desired performance.
- Adjust the attitude or power setting on the control instruments if a correction is necessary.

Notes:

- Pitch changes are made by moving the aircraft symbol on the attitude indicator to a new pitch attitude, trimming to neutralize pressures, and cross-checking altitude and airspeed. Subsequent changes are made in relation to the original pitch setting and that of the most recent change.
- Power control can be made by throttle alone, if the position of the throttle is noted before and after the change. Changes in increments of "knob widths" can be used to precisely control power, occasionally checking control instruments.
- An aircraft is trimmed by applying control pressure(s) to establish a desired attitude and then adjusting the trim so that the aircraft will maintain that attitude when the flight controls are released.
- You must be able to recognize when a change in attitude or power is required. By cross-checking the instruments properly, you can determine the magnitude and direction of the adjustment required.
- Cross-checking is a proper division of attention and the interpretation of the flight instruments. Attention must be efficiently divided between the control and performance instruments in a sequence that ensures comprehensive coverage of the flight instruments.

Going Forward

Purdue Airport Downwind (Creative Commons)

Our Purdue ROTC class graduated in May of 1978, forty of us with our four year-college degrees and commissions as second lieutenants in the United States Air Force. We were headed to specialty-specific training, eight of us to Undergraduate Pilot Training bases. During the height of the Vietnam War the Air Force had nine UPT bases spread throughout the southern half of the United States. Now they were down to five, one in Arizona, two in Oklahoma, two in Texas. Of those, only the Phoenix base was good and that's where I wanted to go: Williams Air Force Base, Arizona.

"You got Willy?" the other seven pilots seemed to ask as one.

"Yes I did," saying so proudly. This was the third year running that Purdue sent a cadet to Williams, something few ROTC detachments could say. It was the best base and most of the pilot candidates there came from the Air Force Academy. I thought it was a high achievement for somebody who soloed last.

"Lot's of luck," George Daniels said, "you'll need it!" The other six nodded.

"Why do you say that?" I asked.

"Because Willy has the highest washout rate in the country," George said, "everyone knows that. Why do you think no one else listed it on their dream sheets?"

Ah, the dream sheet. All cadets, pilots and non-pilots alike, had to submit an assignment request with our top three bases of preference. As pilot candidates, our choices were limited to the five UPT bases.

"Scurrilous rumors," I said, trying to make a joke of it all.

"You'll have fun in downtown Phoenix," another cadet said, "but fat lot of good that will do you if you end up behind a desk after a year."

I told myself that other pilots washed out, not me.

I was starting to think of myself as a pilot. I had twenty hours of time behind the yoke of a Cessna 150, I had four years of thinking aviation, but still no pilot's license. I also thought of myself as an engineer. I had a name-brand degree from a name-brand university, but I would never work as an engineer. Curiously, I had a difficult time thinking of myself as a military officer. The shiny gold bars on my shoulders said otherwise. How could a twenty-two year old kid from Hawaii, still in search for the meaning of it all, how could that kid be an officer?

5: UPT and ICE-T
Williams Air Force Base, Phoenix, Arizona
1979

Cessna T-37B (USAF Photo)

For four years I talked and dreamed aviation as a cadet. It was the institution's way of instilling the desire, the absolute hunger to slip the surly bonds. Intellectually I knew the reason behind it. It was the "pay it forward" concept the military treats all its warriors who are about to face battle for the first time. You instilled in those young warriors the concept that what they were doing was worth dying for, so they didn't show any fear when the time came. You showered them with hero status before they did anything heroic. You gave them titles and crowds of worshipers. And then, as the first spear was thrown, they would not dare chicken out.

I didn't care about any of that. It was January 1st, 1979, and I was signing into family quarters at Williams Air Force Base. The Lovely Mrs. Haskel watched as I wrote "2LT" next to my name on the form handed me. The quarters were certainly better than what we were accustomed. This was it, the big leagues. The game was afoot.

Then the day came. It was surreal: putting on the uniform, the light blue shirt, dark blue pants, and epaulets with the single gold bar on each shoulder. It was my first day in uniform since the day I was commissioned and my dad pinned those bars on my scrawny shoulders. Now I was walking into the flight room — my first flight room of many to follow — with seventy-six other officers, most of who were also second lieutenants. We looked like teenagers, too young to be officers.

Day one was spent at the base hospital. We had eye tests for our eyes, ear tests for our ears, cardio tests for our cardio, and a very large rubber gloved hand for . . . well I didn't know what that was for. In the end our 77 was pared down to 74. The flight surgeon started the process Williams was so famous for. We knew the historic washout rate would be high; at least a quarter of our numbers would not be around 48 weeks from this day.

They split our class into two flights, I was a part of "No Loss" and was issued four flight suits and four flight patches to sew on the right sleeve. On the right side of our chest we placed the Air Training Command patch and on the left, where the wings belonged, a plain blue patch with only our names. Our student flight commander was an ex-navigator captain with four years of surly bond slipping of his own, albeit from the back seat of an F-4. He knew what it was like out there.

"These blue uniforms are bullshit," Captain Ron Wilson said when we had our first meeting together, "pilots wear flight suits."

"Damned straight," we all said.

"Tomorrow we show up in the green bag," Ron continued, "to hell with regulations, to hell with instructions. You want to be pilots?" He let the question hang. "Then act like pilots!" So on day two, against all instructions, our flight showed up to class in green bags, ready to fly. We wouldn't touch an airplane for a month, but we were ready. Our instructor strolled in and somebody called the room to attention. From the corner of my eye I could see the instructor was surprised by our uniform choice, but he quickly recovered.

"Flying airplanes," the instructor began, "is one percent hands, ten percent brains, and ninety-nine-point-nine percent attitude." Perhaps his math was suspect, but we knew what he meant. You can't do this kind of flying without a large measure of attitude. "Today we start building on that ten percent brains, so get ready to memorize." He turned his back and wrote the first lesson: ICE-T.

Flight Lessons 1: Basic Flight

He explained that in the cockpit, the most important number to keep flying was airspeed. Of course, even on day one, we knew that. But that speed—Knots Indicated Airspeed (KIAS)—was only the beginning.

IAS—Indicated Airspeed (what we see on the instrument)

CAS—Calibrated Airspeed (IAS corrected for installation errors)

EAS—Equivalent Airspeed (CAS corrected for air compressibility)

TAS—True Airspeed (EAS corrected for air density)

"Your airspeed indicator gives you indicated airspeed," he said without a hint of humor, "it was built by the cheapest bidder and it wasn't built for the T-37. It was built for a generic airplane so you have to correct for that error. Turn to page A-2 of your dash ones."

We pulled out our brand new flight manuals, 1.T.O. T-37B-1, or simply "dash one." Mine was already removed from its plastic wrapper and placed into its binder with all the tabs correctly inserted. I skimmed the thing cover-to-cover overnight. The more macho in the group started to pull the plastic wrap from their untouched bundle of books.

In a few minutes we had the correct page.

"I wrote the 'C' slightly higher than the 'I' because it usually is slightly higher. As you can see from the chart, for most conditions the installation error is between zero and two."

I wrote down "installation error 0 - 2" as I heard some muffled laughter.

"Who gives a shit," I heard from a fellow stud. There was more laughter.

"Exactly right!" said the instructor. "You can't read 2 knots on the indicator, so who gives a shit? But the rest of those numbers? Your life depends on them so listen up boys and girls." Of course there were no girls in our class, but we all sat upright. This was important.

James Albright

CR-3 / CPU-26 (Computer Side)

Time / Speed / Distance

Given two, you can find the third. For example: 300 nm at 450 knots will take 40 minutes Procedure is identical on both computers.

Notice the ▲ is positioned at the "60" which is also "1 hour." This relationship allows computation for other items using "per hour" as a measure.

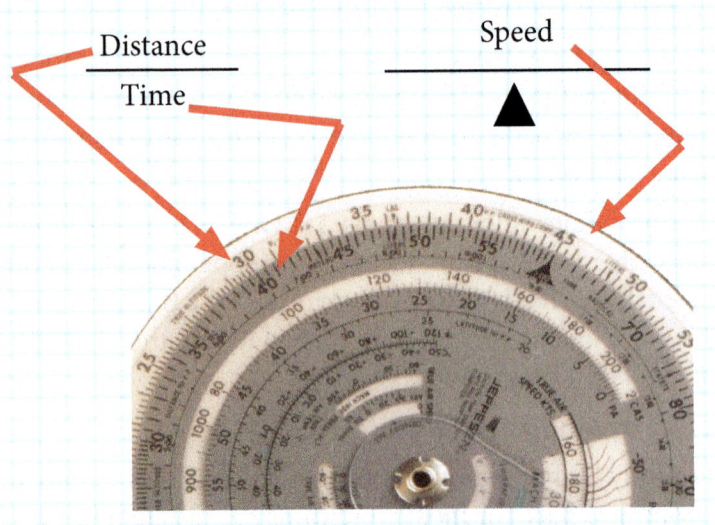

$$\frac{Distance}{Time} \qquad \frac{Speed}{▲}$$

Fuel / Time / PPH

Given two, you can find the third. For example: 450 PPH for 30 minutes will consume 225 pounds of fuel. Procedure is identical on both computers.

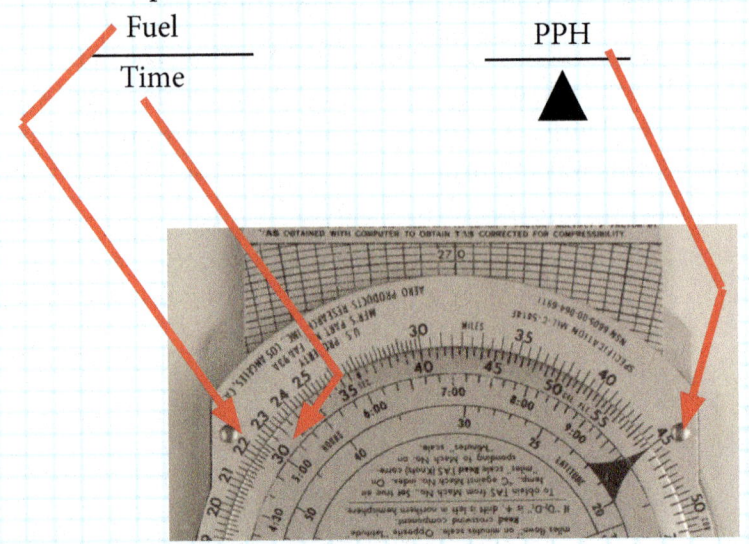

$$\frac{Fuel}{Time} \qquad \frac{PPH}{▲}$$

Nautical Miles / Statute Miles / Kilometers

Are found on one or both scales and are simply a matter of placing the "known value" under an index and looking for the "unknown value." (CR-3 and CPU-26 identical) For example, 100 nautical miles is equivalent to 115 statute miles and 185 kilometers.

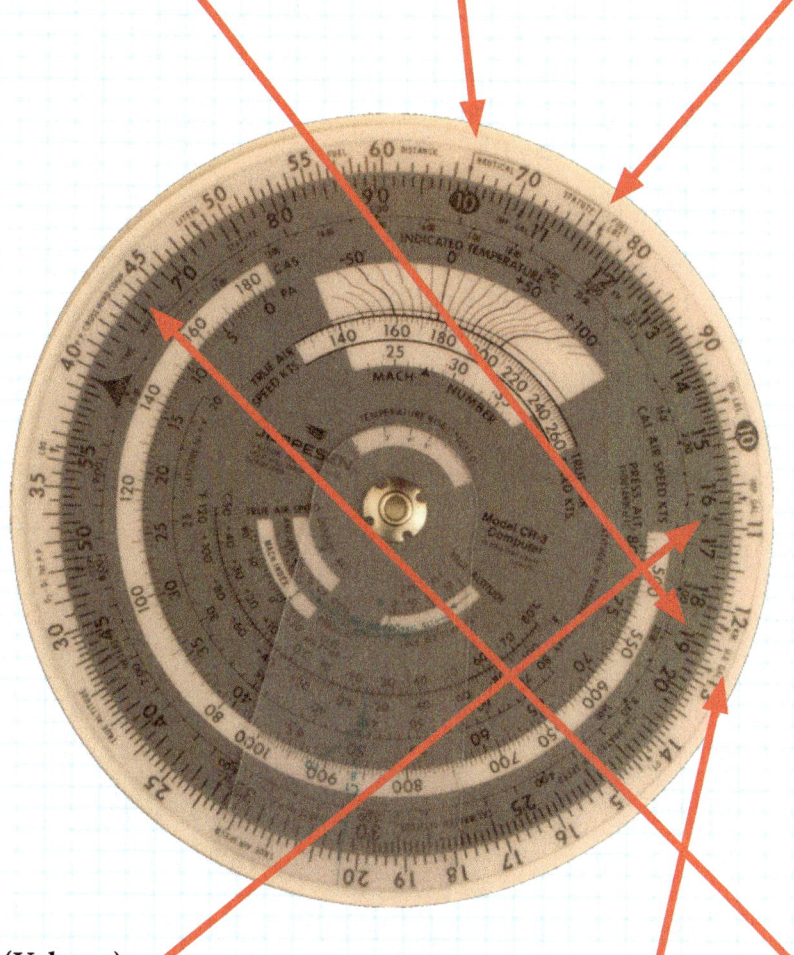

Fuel (Volume)

The CR-3 and CPU-26 both have good conversions for U.S. Gallons to Liters and to Imperial Gallons.

The "Fuel Lbs" will rarely work as expected because of density variations.

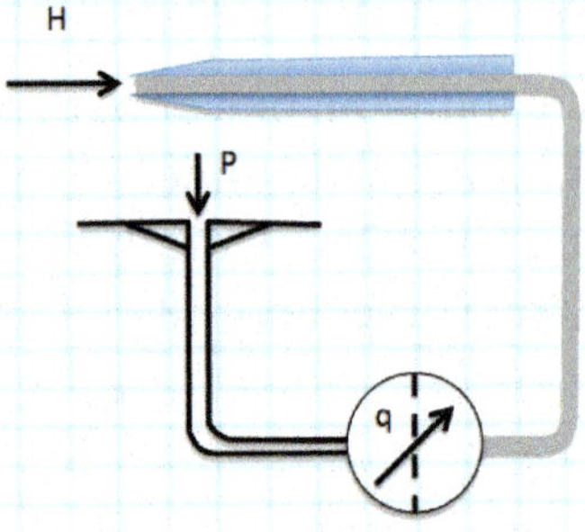

Indicated Airspeed (IAS)

Indicated airspeed is what is reported by the pitot tube, on most airplanes it is what the pilot sees on the indicator.

Indicated to True Airspeed.

To convert (I)ndicated airspeed to (T)rue airspeed you must first find (C)alibrated airspeed and (E)quivalent airspeed, problem known as "Ice-T"

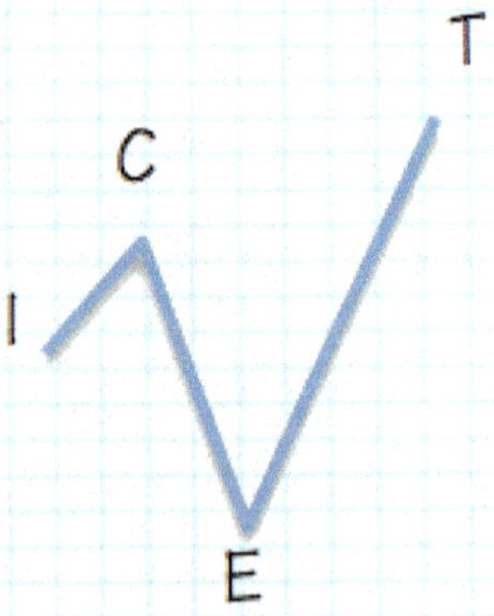

Equivalent Airspeed (EAS)

Equivalent airspeed is CAS corrected for air compressibility (the air gets compacted inside the pitot tube). It can be corrected by a flight manual chart or using a circular computer. The CPU-26 calls this "F-Factor."

In the example, 250 CAS at 20,000 feet yields an F-Factor of 0.98.

Place the "10" index (inner scale) opposite 250 (outer scale) and read the EAS answer opposite the F-Factor of 0.98. Answer: 245 EAS.

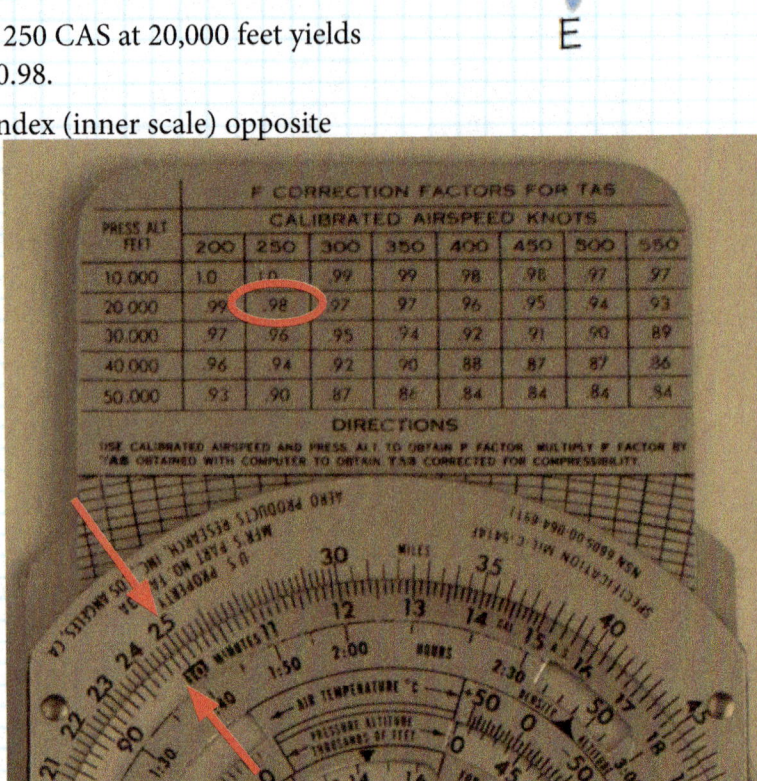

Note: this correction is considered automatically by the CR-3 computer

Flight Lessons 1: Basic Flight

True Airspeed (TAS)

True airspeed is EAS corrected for density altitude. It can be found mathematically:

$$TAS = EAS \frac{1}{\sqrt{\sigma}}$$

For our example, we'll assume standard temperature which is 15° minus 2° per 1,000' of altitude. (15° - 2(20)) = -25°C

Using the ICAO standard atmosphere table (extract shown), we figure:

$$TAS = 245 \frac{1}{\sqrt{0.5328}}$$

$$TAS = 336$$

ALTITUDE FT.	DENSITY RATIO σ
0	1.0000
1000	0.9711
2000	0.9428
3000	0.9151
4000	0.8881
5000	0.8617
6000	0.8359
7000	0.8106
8000	0.7860
9000	0.7620
10000	0.7385
15000	0.6292
20000	0.5328
25000	0.4481

EAS to TAS (CPU-26)

The CPU-26 converts EAS to TAS by first placing the pressure altitude opposite the air temperature. In our example, 20 on the inner window opposite -25°C.

The TAS is read on the outer ring opposite the EAS on the inner ring. In our example we see 245 EAS becomes 335 TAS.

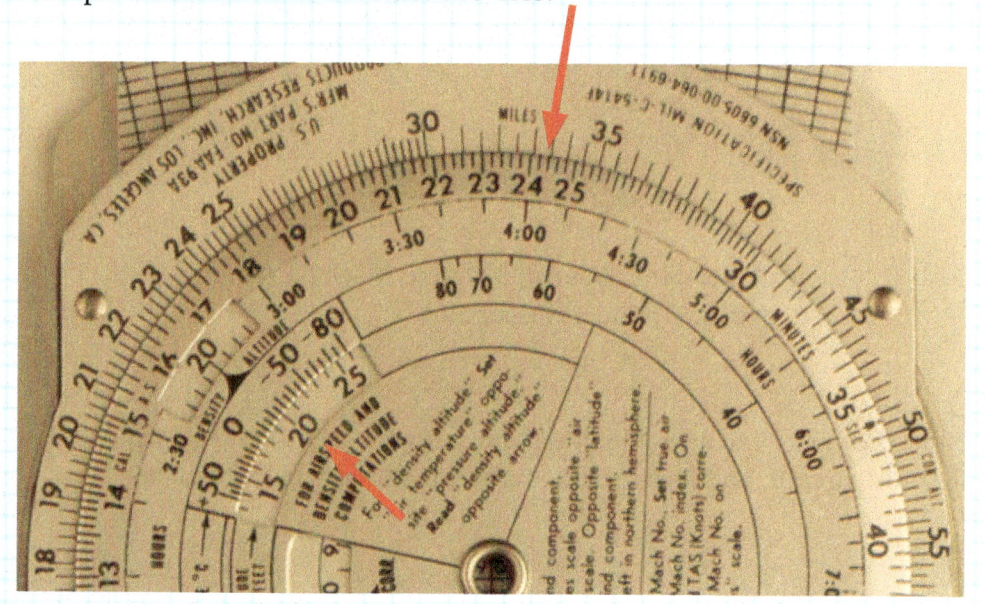

CAS to TAS and Mach Number (CR-3)

The CR-3 converts CAS to TAS without the need to consider compressibility effect.

1. Place the CAS (ex: 250) opposite the Pressure Altitude (ex: 20,000)

2. Move the cursor to where the temperature (ex: -25°C) intersects the line with the upward slope

3. Read the TAS (ex: 330) and Mach Number (ex: 0.53) under the cursor

Note: the cursor includes a temperature recovery coefficient, CT, which is 1.0 for most aircraft, but doesn't matter much at altitudes below 50,000'

6: Suck, Squeeze, Bang, Blow

"Sir," the petite airman said while pushing my knees together, "you need to hold your knees together or you are going to lose a kneecap when your body clears the canopy rail." Even when dealing with a gangly, uncoordinated second lieutenant, the airman was unfailingly polite and militarily courteous.

I nodded, trying better to remember my knees lest I lose a kneecap, as well as keeping my back pressed hard against the seat back lest I break it, and my head hard against the head rest lest I snap my neck, and my elbows in as I pull the hand grips lest I lose an arm, and so on and so on.

Ejection Seat Training (USMC Photo)

"The seat is live!" she yelled so all would stand clear. "Sir, eject, eject, eject!" I raised the handgrips and squeezed. Nine-G's and less than a second later I was ten feet up the rails, all limbs intact. The rest of the enlisted crew did whatever it was they needed to do and my seat was lowered and I unstrapped so the next stud – we were not allowed to call ourselves students – could get his chance at ejection seat qualification.

Every morning seemed to have some kind of non-classroom exercise, and every afternoon we sat in front of a chalkboard with the next morsel of information deemed absolutely critical before we got to touch our first airplane. Our half of the class, now down to 70 studs, got afternoon classroom time while the other got the mornings. Most of my peers were graduates of the Air Force Academy, three had ROTC backgrounds, and there were a handful of guys who were coming in from other parts of the Air Force.

Most of the Zooms, the Academy boys, gravitated to the back rows. That left me in the front row with whoever showed up late. Our first class about actual airplane stuff covered the engines and was taught by an instructor we hadn't seen before, Captain Fred Jenkins.

"The Continental J69-T-25 isn't much compared to most jet engines," the instructor began, "but at 1,025 pounds of thrust it has more power than any engine you have ever seen before." He scanned the room and noticed Captain Ron Wilson's navigator wings and added, "as pilots anyway."

"So here is a jet engine," Jenkins said while flipping the two-sided chalkboard end-over-end. Air gets sucked, squeezed, banged, and blowed." There were a few snickers in the class. "And it all happens thanks to some Italian guy named Isaac Newton."

"English," I said to myself.

"Damned right," I heard from the lieutenant to my right.

"Sir Isaac Newton," the instructor continued, "came up with a set of laws and it is the first law we are interested in."

"Second law," I said, quietly. Or so I thought.

"What's that?" the instructor asked, looking at the stud to my right.

"Sir," the innocent lieutenant said, "the first law of motion is about inertia, a body at rest and so forth. The second law is F = ma, a body accelerates in the direction of an unbalanced force."

"Well the textbook says that is the first law," the instructor said. His eyes scanned the class behind me, then his voice trailed off. I turned to see most of my peers shaking their heads side to side.

"Sir," I said, trying to make up for getting my wingman in trouble, "the third law also applies, for every action there is an opposite and equal reaction."

There was more silence. I turned and this time saw the crowd nodding their heads up and down.

"Well that's the one I was thinking about," he said finally, "so maybe the text is wrong. So let's call it the second and third laws. That okay with you, lieu-

Flight Lessons 1: Basic Flight

tenants?"

We both nodded our heads and the class got on with the subject at hand. During the next break I got a chance to apologize for getting my fellow stud in trouble.

"No sweat," he said, "there are so many errors in that text you would think it was written by a history major. I'm Roger, by the way, Roger Jeeter."

"Eddie," I said. We shook hands and traded engineering bona fides. Roger had a civil engineering degree from the Air Force Academy but got a healthy amount of aeronautical engineering on the way. "Industrial engineering," I said, "with the same dose of aero."

Captain Jenkins sped through the rest of the jet engine class, making a few more mistakes every thirty minutes or so. "The gas is lit by the combustion already taking place," Roger said at one point, "the igniters are only necessary for starting."

The instructor stopped, scanned the classroom of nodding heads, and shook his head. "Listen guys," he said, "I majored in psychology. I'm trying to teach this the way the syllabus is written. If any of you engineers want to rewrite the syllabus, then get your wings and come back as instructors."

I wasn't sure how to take that and it seemed neither did the rest of the class. But we got through it, each with a better understanding of what makes a jet engine "cook with gas."

Jet Engine 101

Centrifugal Jet Engine Basics

Air flow: air enters the intake and is compressed by compressor blades which accelerate it, raising its pressure and temperature. Fuel is sprayed into this airstream and ignited by the air just ahead of it. The mixture expands rapidly, shooting aft through turbine blades. These turbine blades are connected to the compressor, providing the necessary torque. The escaping gas goes through a narrowed nozzle, further accelerating it.

Principles of Propulsion

[ATCM 51-3, Pg. 105]

You can summarize how a jet engine works with two of Newton's Laws of Motion. Newton's second law can be written as: $F = ma$

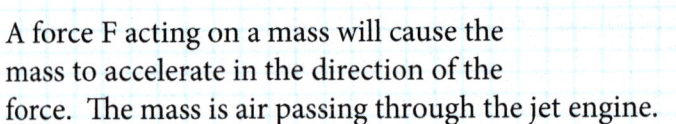

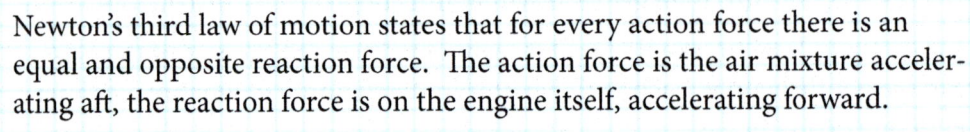

A force F acting on a mass will cause the mass to accelerate in the direction of the force. The mass is air passing through the jet engine.

Newton's third law of motion states that for every action force there is an equal and opposite reaction force. The action force is the air mixture accelerating aft, the reaction force is on the engine itself, accelerating forward.

Thrust

[Hurt, Pg. 116]

The turbojet engine is essentially a thrust-producing powerplant and the propulsive force is a result of the flight speed. The variation of available thrust with speed is relatively small and engine output is very nearly constant with flight speed. The momentum change given the engine airflow develops thrust by the following relationship:

$T_a = Q(V_2 - V_1)$

Where

T_a = thrust available, lbs.

Q = mass flow, slugs per sec.

V_1 = inlet or flight velocity, ft. per sec.

V_2 = jet velocity, ft. per sec.

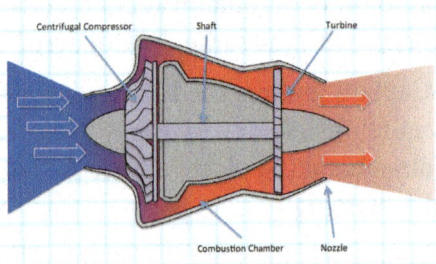

7: Simulate

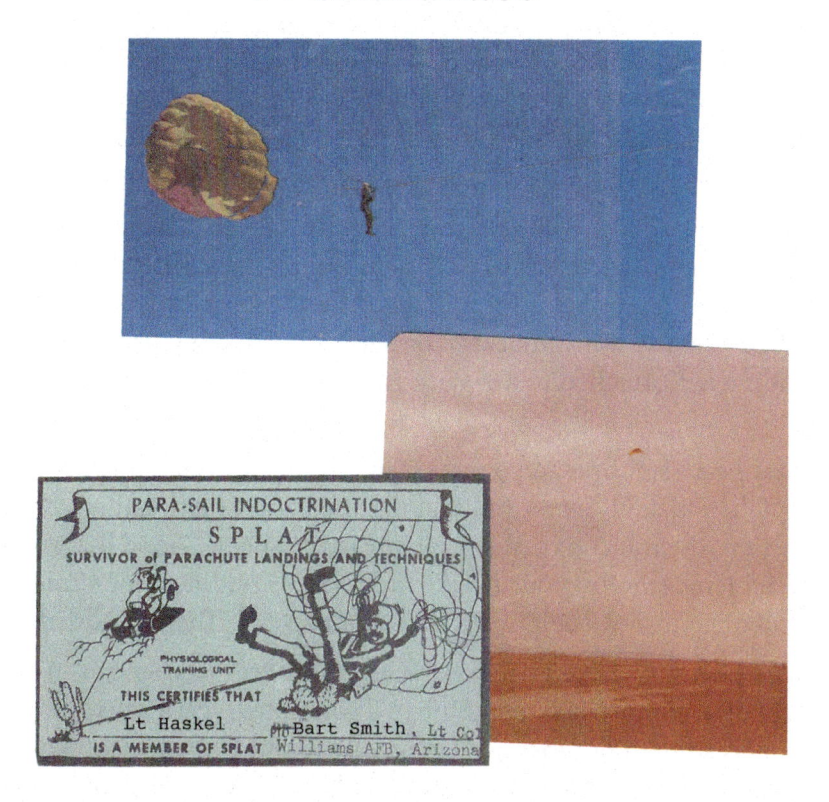

Haskel Falls Earthward (Eddie's Collection)

Week three saw our first sorties of many in T-37 simulators. These had cockpits just like the real thing and large screens up front that relayed what a computer put together with a camera mounted on a large terrain board. The simulator moved about on three axes plus just a little motion fore and aft, left and right. It was realistic, to be sure. It was a good chance to apply what we were learning in class, but not every day was spent in class.

Besides the ejection seat training, we also had to demonstrate the ability to fall gracefully once dropped to the ground at the hands of a military parachute. These were the ones packed to the bottoms of our ejection seats. They were steerable only by severing a few of the panels and the result was a landing hugely dependent on the wind. More than a few studs got hurt, so we needed to do this before they wasted any jet fuel on our training. They weren't about to risk us jumping out of airplanes; that was saved for the

Army where they expected a few fatalities along the way. Our plan was to strap on an unpacked parachute while tethered to a jeep. The jeep would accelerate until we were pulled off the ground and finally airborne. Then the jeep would floor it and we would have an express ride to the top floor, about 200 feet up. At that point we would disconnect from the tether and look for a spot to gently alight to the ground. At least that was the plan.

Before I could try that, I had to demonstrate I could flip myself right-side up if I ended up on my belly. As the rest of the class watched, I was dragged across the desert floor, face down, by four noncoms pulling at my parachute straps. I had to flip myself over and disconnect the risers to get a passing score. The exercise was important, because after ejecting from the airplane and landing still attached to a twenty-foot canopy, doing so would save my life.

"Lift your head, sir! Spread your legs, sir," the senior noncom yelled while pulling, "then kick." I did so and that did the trick. Still breathing hard from the exertion, the noncom handed me my grade sheet. "Good job, sir," he said, "please remember to lift your head. Uncle Sam is putting a lot of money into that skull of yours. We wouldn't want to damage it." Then he added, "Sir."

I thanked him and walked back to the assembly area to watch as my classmates followed in my footsteps. Due to a computer with a sense of humor I ended up as student number zero, zero, one in our class, which meant I got to experience every training exercise ahead of the class. I was done first. But I didn't get the benefit of watching others first. I think everyone who followed remembered to lift his head.

Once the last stud successfully lifted his head, spread his legs, kicked, and pulled the riser disconnects, we moved on to the jeep and the 200-foot rope. Everyone parted so student zero, zero, one could get tethered to the jeep. A sadistic looking NCO sat in the jeep, gunning the engine. Three others held the uninflated parachute behind me, ready to catch the wind. "Start walking," one of them yelled, and then, "Run!"

I did so and took another half step until I was off the ground. Then, just as promised, I shot straight up. I was nearing the tropopause when the line went slack. I slapped at the disconnect lever and found myself in a peaceful descent. No, that wasn't it at all. I was hurtling toward the desert floor at near terminal velocity. Yes, that's more like it. I pulled at the panel disconnect straps, shedding two lower panels of the parachute. It would speed my

Flight Lessons 1: Basic Flight

descent but it would also give the parachute forward velocity, allowing me to steer into the wind. I did all that and found myself headed for a large cactus tree. I know they don't grow as trees but this thing was bigger than a plant. With a firm tug of my right riser I missed the cacti and remembered to bend my knees and aim my butt for the impact: feet, calves, thighs, side, shoulders, roll.

"Good job, sir!"

"Thanks," I said, trying to hide the pain. One down, one to go. I had to demonstrate it again. The second landing was better but the climb skyward was terrifying. The first time I suspected it would hurt. The second time I knew it was going to hurt.

Our flight, No Loss, survived the physical ordeals with no losses and remained 34 strong. Our sister flight lost one to the ejection seat trainer – back injury – and two to the parachute – both were broken ankles – so we were sent to the flight line as a class of 65.

I was grouped with second lieutenants Kevin Davies, Roger Jeeter, and Marke Gibbs. Our instructor was first lieutenant Don Chesney. We four sat at one side of a table until Chesney showed up. We stood at attention and saluted. Chesney returned the salute and gestured to our chairs. "Be seated."

"So you are the four trouble makers," he began. We looked at each other with embarrassed grins. "I've heard you are the four engineers who have been questioning everything in class." Ah that was it. "Well don't worry, I'm an engineer too. We'll get along just fine."

Chesney spoke at length about the months to come, quizzed us on aircraft systems for a while, and said the honor of the first flight would be by draw of cards. It would be Marke and Kevin tomorrow morning, Roger then me after lunch. It was February but it was already hot in the Arizona afternoon. Roger and I would be prime candidates for the airsick bag that three-quarters of all studs had to use on flight one. We had a day to ponder that as we headed back to class.

CR-3 / CPU-26 (Wind Side)

Drift, Heading, Groundspeed (CPU-26)

The wind side of the CPU-26 easily computes drift, heading, and groundspeed given aircraft course and TAS and the wind speed and direction. In our example, we'll use 335 TAS, 300° true course, and winds of 240° / 60 knots.

1. Spin the wheel to place the wind direction (240°) under the True Index.

2. Place the slide so a convenient reading is under the grommet, we've used 100 in the example. Place an "X" spaced by the winds speed (60), 160 in our example.

3. Rotate the wheel to place the true course (300°) under the index.

4. You can read the drift directly from the slide (-9°), from which we determine our heading will be 300 – 9 = 291°

5. You can read the ground speed directly under the grommet (300 knots)

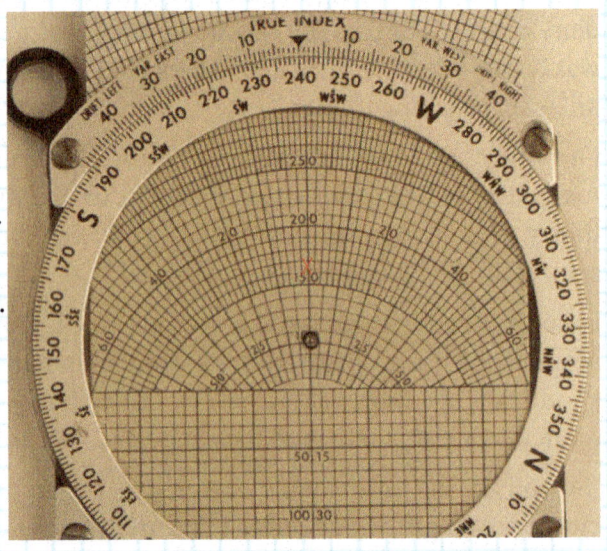

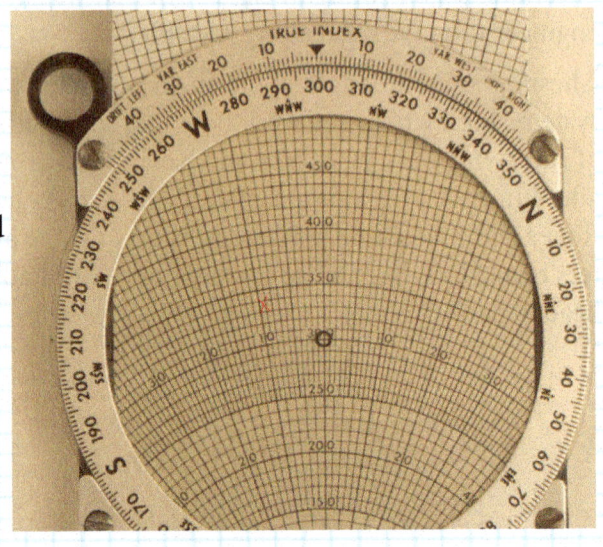

Flight Lessons 1: Basic Flight

Drift, Heading, Groundspeed (CPU-26)

The wind side of the CR-3 easily computes drift, heading, and groundspeed given aircraft course and TAS and the wind speed and direction. In our example, we'll use 335 TAS, 300° true course, and winds of 240° / 60 knots.

1. Set TAS (335) above TAS Index

2. Set True Course (300) above TC index

3. Find wind direction (240)

4. Draw a dot over wind direction/speed (240/60)

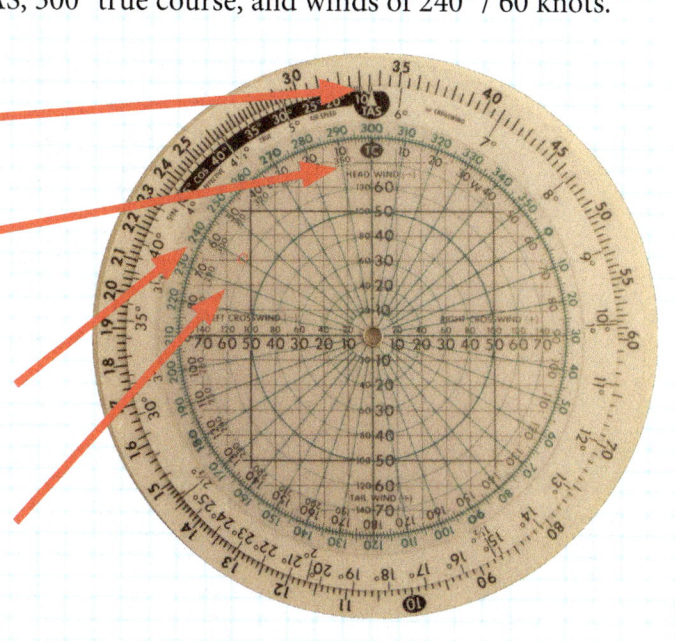

5. Draw vertical and horizontal lines from wind dot to determine headwind (30 knots) and crosswind (52 knots). Groundspeed is 335 − 30 = 305 knots

6. Enter outer scale with crosswind (52 knots) to read drift angle on inner scale (9°).

Heading is 300 − 9 = 291°

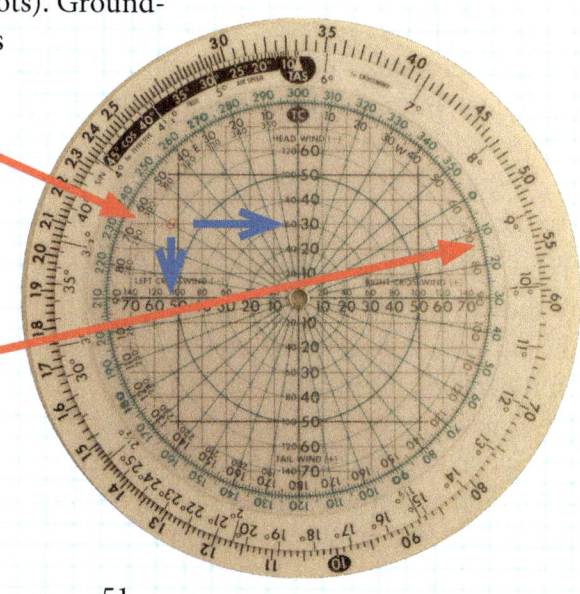

8: Aviate

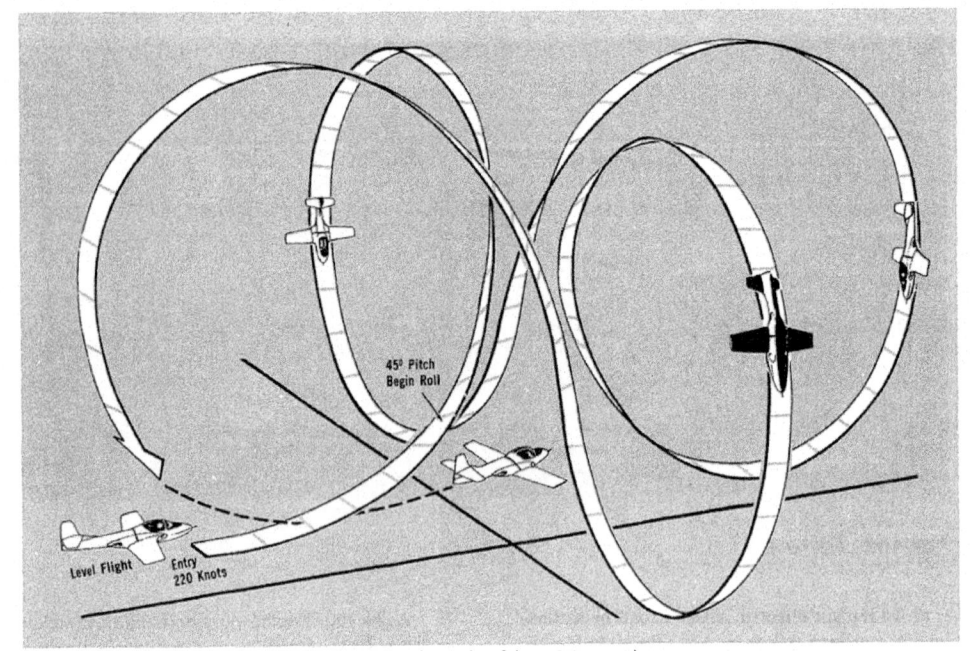

T-37 Cloverleaf (ATCR 51-4)

The first flight of the program has an official sounding name but everyone calls it the "Dollar Ride." Just like paying for a carnival ride, it can be a lazy day in the sun where the only thing out of the ordinary will be sucking on an oxygen hose while pulling 2 G's in the traffic pattern. Or it can be the most G-intensive, retina-detaching, lunch-propelling ride imaginable. It is up to the student, but everyone knew that any student not willing to try some aerobatics and at least one spin would be labeled a Whiskey Delta for the rest of the program. Ours was probably the last class the Air Force would ever send through without any females, so having the "weak dick" title would probably endure for the Whiskey Delta's entire Air Force career.

We showed up to the flight room at 0530, thirty-four mere mortals ready to take our first steps into the military jet brotherhood. The normal morning routine involved a weather report, "stand up," and preflight briefings. Stand up was just that: an instructor would talk about the topic du jour, point his finger at an unsuspecting student, and ask a question. The student stands at attention and spouts off the answer. For our first flight day, I feared the pigeon of choice would be student zero zero one.

Flight Lessons 1: Basic Flight

"Studs," the instructor began, "the final turn can be a vulnerable time in the mighty tee thirty seven bee and you are likely to have your hands full. You've got to get the bank just right, the pitch, the sink rate, and all the while you are trying to nail the throttle setting. Let's say you are doing a great job of that and then all hell breaks loose. You've got two fire lights, engines winding down to zero, and your airspeed falling fast." Ah, I thought, this will be easy. Now I wanted to be picked.

"Captain Wilson," the instructor turned to face our senior student, "what will you do?"

Ron Wilson stood at attention. "Sir, I will instruct the other pilot to exit the aircraft with the command 'eject, eject, eject.' Then I will follow using the emergency ejection procedure, hand grips – raise, triggers – squeeze." It was a textbook answer, the one I would have given.

"What is your minimum safe ejection altitude," the instructor asked, "in the configuration you would expect in the final turn?" One hundred feet, I thought to myself.

"One hundred feet, sir," Ron said. "That is with the D-ring lanyard connected for a zero delay. Of course that is in level flight. Since we will not be in level flight, I will pull the nose up with whatever smash I have left, and start the eject procedure once our vector is positive."

"Very good," the instructor said, "excellent." My mind raced with it all. Smash? Vector? It all made perfect sense, the ejection seat could only fire with a certain force and if the airplane was headed downhill the 100-foot minimum would be for naught. Why hadn't I thought of that?

"Lieutenant Haskel," the instructor said, "what would you do?"

What? I stood at attention. "Sir, please repeat the question."

There was a little laughter. "A little early for daydreaming. But okay. While taxiing for your very first takeoff today the left engine fire light illuminates but there are no other indications of fire. What do you do?"

"Sir," I said, "throttles – cut off, brakes – as needed, fuel shutoff T-handles – pull. If there are no other indications of a need to immediately egress, I will raise the canopy, turn the battery and generator switches off, and abandon the aircraft. Sir."

"Very good," the instructor said, "now pay attention in the future."

"Yes, sir."

Lieutenant Chesney, my instructor, shook his head from opposite our table. I lost style points before my first flight. He grinned. I guess it wasn't as bad as I thought. After stand up, Chesney departed with Marke Gibbs and eight other instructors with eight other studs. The rest of us were left to study, grab some breakfast, or wander the halls.

"Tough break," Kevin said, "getting called today."

"Yeah." As the first wave started to return, we heard stories of the glory of it all, despite the inability of most the studs to hold on to their breakfasts. Curiously, the rest of the class made a run on the snack bar for frozen breakfast burritos. Monkey see, stud do. I got mine with extra jalapeños.

"The spins are wild," Marke said, "the procedure definitely works, at least it did when Don did it."

"What about you?" Roger asked.

"I couldn't remember all the steps in the heat of the moment," Marke confessed. "It was hilarious watching the horizon gyrate while the altimeter was spinning like it was broken. It's hard not to panic!"

Marke relived the moments, including the queasy feeling in his stomach after the first loop. "I didn't toss," he said, "but man I was thinking about it the whole flight."

Roger looked at me, uneasily. "I bet Kevin loses it," he said.

Kevin came back and retold much of Marke's experience. But he held on to his burritos. Roger and I headed for the officer's club for lunch, both opting for something a bit less volatile than a microwaved burrito. I knew most studs lost it on the first flight, how could they not? You spend your life with two feet on the ground and even your airborne experiences are mostly right side up. It would only be natural to take a flight or two to get used to the strangeness of it all. Roger, however, was consumed with the thought.

"I hope I don't lose it," he said while munching on what looked to be a very bland tuna fish sandwich. "I lost it in glider school. The guys never let me forget it."

"Don't worry about it," I said, "this is just one flight of hundreds. Besides, most guys lose it. It isn't funny if it happens to just about everyone."

"It isn't funny unless it's cruel," he said.

Flight Lessons 1: Basic Flight

"What?"

"That's a motto at the Zoo," he said, "it isn't funny unless it's cruel." Roger was a Zoomie, as was most of the class. Marke and Kevin were both academy graduates too.

While Roger was flying I was doing a poor job of pretending to study. It was hard to concentrate as most of the class was reliving the thrill of slipping the surly bonds of earth, and here I was still a mere mortal. Finally, Roger and Don came back from the flight. Roger's flight suit was soaked in sweat but he looked none the worse for wear. He grinned his goofy grin, "It was a blast. I got sick three times, but still, it was fun." Three times? I started to worry.

I kept quiet as Don read from a notepad, giving Roger a few pointers on what to work on and even more encouragement that, yes, Roger had what it took to be a real jet pilot. I was hoping to hear the same thing in a few hours.

"Last but not least?" Don said, turning to me.

"Yes, sir!"

I followed Don to the flight operations desk where he filled out our flight plan and picked up our aircraft forms. "You will be doing this solo," he said, "soon enough." I followed him to the life support shack and found my personal peg with the sterile, white helmet I had fitted in the first week, and the heavy parachute I had fitted just a few days ago. Carrying the chute over my right shoulder, the forms and my helmet in my left hand, I started to sweat as soon as we walked outside onto the baking tarmac. This would be my life to come and it was great.

Don watched as I preflighted the airplane, only speaking up once after I missed a bolt just forward of the elevator. "Make 'em tight," he said as I cinched my parachute leg straps around each thigh. "The missus would hate it if you damaged those."

It was my first engine start with a crew chief giving me hand signals and another standing by with a fire extinguisher. Once everything was ready to go, Don and I placed both hands on the glare shield canopy rail while the crew chiefs gave the undercarriage one last look and pulled our chocks.

My first taxi. My first takeoff. My first slap of the gear handle. It was going by so fast. The T-37 is the butt of many jokes; it is the "Tweet," the "Five-thousand-pound dog whistle." But on this day in February, it was a smoking hot air machine.

"What d'ya wanna do?" Don asked as I got approval from center to enter our designated practice area.

"Everything," I said.

"You remember the procedures for a loop?" he asked. Without answering, I pushed the throttles to military, the full forward position, dropped a wing and allowed the nose to fall. Once we had 250 knots I pulled back until the G-meter read 3 and kept it there. "Grnnch!" I heard from the right seat. We were wired together and everything one pilot said the other could hear, even our breaths. The nose traced a line straight up. The attitude indicator tumbled well before then, as the book said it would, so I looked at the wing tips and corrected to keep them about even with the horizon. I felt the airplane mush a bit and before I could do anything else the nose was falling straight down.

"Now whatcha' gonna do?" Don said. A spin, I thought, we were entering a spin. Now we were a good sixty degrees of pitch up, now sixty degrees of pitch down. I pulled the throttles to idle, and centered the rudder and ailerons. I yanked the stick into my crotch and watched the world rotate beneath me. The turn needle was full scale right; we were spinning right. I stomped on the left rudder pedal. The rotation stopped immediately, the nose hung pointed straight to Arizona, the aircraft was at zero G and we hung there, weightless in our straps.

"One more step," Don said.

"Recover from dive," I said as I pulled the stick back.

"Well I've never seen that before," Don said, "but good job. Just because the manual says 3 G's doesn't mean you need all three instantly. You ran out of speed on top of the loop and you had a bit of yaw. We can fix all that."

Each properly executed maneuver was greeted with high praise and every blown maneuver with, "we can fix that." It was the best dollar ride ever. After an hour I didn't want it to end but it was time to go home. I flew the airplane over the runway at 200 knots, lining up behind another Tweet. After that Tweet hit the "break point" I counted to four and then did the same, rolling the airplane into 60 degrees of bank and pulling back to maintain altitude. "Two G's," I said to myself.

"What's that?" Don asked.

"Oh nothing, sir."

Flight Lessons 1: Basic Flight

Coming out of the bank, for the first time, my stomach complained. No matter, there was still work to do. I clicked the speed brake switch on the throttle and once the airspeed indicator reached 150 knots I pulled and lowered the gear handle to the down position. Looking over my left shoulder I could see the touchdown zone on about a 45-degree line, so I selected the flaps down and dropped a wing. The airspeed was supposed to be 120 but it was much higher. I pulled the throttle. The turn was looking pretty sloppy so I concentrated on the bank and backpressure.

"Speed," I heard from the right seat.

We were at 100, way too low. I shoved both throttles forward.

"Too much," from the right seat. I nudged them back. "Do you hear the thrust attenuators?"

"Yeah," I said, still concentrating on the runway. Each engine had a hunk of metal that threw itself into the turbine exhaust, canceling some of the thrust and requiring a higher throttle for the same power. It was Cessna's way of keeping the power at a higher setting so we wouldn't have sluggish response due to the engine's "spool up," or lag time, at low power settings. With the thrust attenuator out the engine made a high-pitched squeal.

"Just keep the throttles right into the attenuator and the speed takes care of itself."

Ah, a trick of the trade. It was too late now; it was time to land. We plopped onto the runway and sortie one as an Air Force pilot was done. I got the "you've got what it takes" debrief and some homework to study unusual attitude recoveries. I walked on air the rest of the day.

The next morning there was a stack of barf bags in front of Roger's seat. It was cruel and, well, maybe it was funny.

Aerodynamic Force

Potential and Kinetic Energy

Consider a metal ball traveling at a constant speed on a flat surface approaching a dip, as shown. We know the ball's speed will increase as it goes down the dip until it gets to the bottom where it will trade speed to climb the ramp. If we neglect the impact of friction, the ball returns to its original speed.

PE: High
KE: Low

PE: Low
KE: High

PE: High
KE: Low

Now consider air moving through a pipe with a narrowing in the center. If we consider the air incompressible, which is true for most subsonic velocities, then it too speeds up in the narrow passage and then returns to its original speed at the exit.

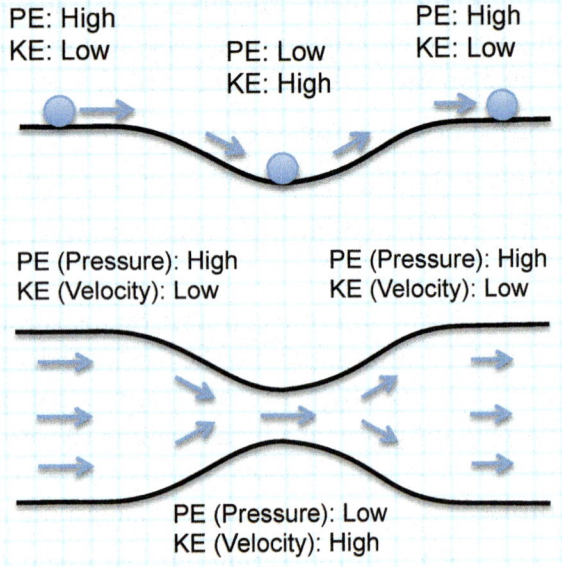

PE (Pressure): High
KE (Velocity): Low

PE (Pressure): High
KE (Velocity): Low

PE (Pressure): Low
KE (Velocity): High

The Bernoulli Equation for Incompressible Flow

[Hurt, pg. 9]

The kinetic energy of an object is found by K.E. = ½ MV². If the potential energy is represented by the static pressure, p, the sum of the potential and kinetic energy is the total pressure of the airstream:

$H = p + \frac{1}{2} \rho V^2$

where H = total pressure, p = static pressure, ρ = density, and V = velocity.

Dynamic Pressure = $\frac{1}{2} \rho V^2$

Velocity and Static Pressure Changes About an Airfoil

If you split the experimental venturi tube in half, you end up with what looks like the cross section of an airfoil which behaves like the tube. This can be verified in wind tunnel tests.

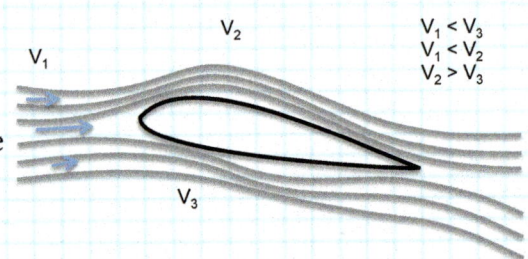

V_1
V_2
V_3

$V_1 < V_3$
$V_1 < V_2$
$V_2 > V_3$

Flight Lessons 1: Basic Flight

Airfoil Terminology

- The chord line is a straight line connecting the leading and trailing edges of the airfoil.
- The chord is the characteristic dimension of the airfoil.
- The mean-camber line is drawn halfway between the upper and lower surfaces.
- Maximum camber is the maximum distance between the mean camber line and the chord line. Maximum thickness is the maximum distance between the upper and lower surfaces.
- Leading edge radius is a measure of the sharpness of the leading edge.

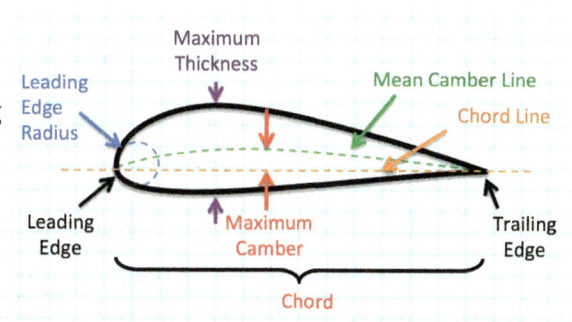

Wing Area

Looking at the wing from the top, the shape is called the planform of the wing. Because wings have become very complicated, it is helpful to simplify a drawing.

Aerodynamic Force

[Hurt pg. 23]

Aerodynamic Force $F = C_r q S$

C_r = coefficient of aerodynamic force

q = dynamic pressure

$= \frac{1}{2} \rho V^2$

S = surface area

Lift is the net force developed perpendicular to the relative wind:

$L = C_L q S$

Where C_L is the coefficient of lift. Most aero texts consider C_L to be the coefficient of lift for the entire wing, so we can remove S and get:

Lift $L = C_L \frac{1}{2} \rho V^2$

9: Recover!

T-37 Trail Formation (Bill Wilson - Creative Commons)

"I've got the jet," Chesney said, "close your eyes." I released the controls and closed my eyes while trying to follow the motion of the airplane with my inner senses. When I gave up control we were heading about 030 degrees, 300 knots, and straight and level at 12,000 feet. Five G's vertical, my gut told me. A rapid roll left, the vestibular canals of my ears reported. Unload, zero G, came next. It had to be a nose-high recovery.

"Recover," he said. I grabbed the controls and started to push the throttles. The ground below filled the windscreen, the speed was near the red line, and we were inverted. I pulled the throttles to idle and rolled towards the nearest horizon. As soon as the airplane was mostly right side up I pulled back on the stick until all was right with the world.

"Not bad," Chesney said, "but your first reaction on the throttles was wrong. That will earn you a bust on a check ride; better to wait a second before reacting on the power." So much for believing my inner ear, I thought. "Let's hit the pattern," he said, "get us out of here."

I called Albuquerque Center and got clearance for the normal exit back to the base. It was my eleventh ride in the airplane. Ron Williams was the

Flight Lessons 1: Basic Flight

first in our class to solo, the day before, and we had two more this morning. Our flight was down to an even thirty, having washed out another four once flying began. Now I was hoping to be the fourth to solo. Four out of thirty; that isn't the stuff aviation legends are made of, but it would do for me.

The overhead pattern is something uniquely military. It is a way of getting a lot of fast airplanes on the ground as soon as possible with the least amount of air traffic control. We fly right over the runway at 200 knots, about 1,000 feet. At the "break point" we roll crisply to 60° of bank and pull 2 G's. Once on downwind, we pop the speed brake, slow to 150 knots, then extend the landing gear and finally the flaps. And then the hard part: getting around the final turn without falling out of the sky.

"Eddie," I heard from the right seat, "I am due currency so I need to steal a landing from you. Do you mind if I take the first pattern?"

"Not at all," I said, "your jet."

In the civilian world the mantra was "I do, you watch, you do, I critique." So far I had never seen Chesney fly the airplane. He was perfectly comfortable talking me through each maneuver. This would be a treat. I tried to gently rest my left hand on the throttles and right on the stick, to see how a pro does it. There were no surprises until the break, we were right at 200 knots, right at 1,000 feet, and he gently rolled the airplane into 60° of bank. It was a quick roll, but the stick barely moved.

Rolling out on downwind he extended the speed brakes, the speed bled off nicely, and at 150 knots out came the gear. "Call the perch," he said. We were flying a left-hand pattern and we judged the perch, that point at which we begin the final turn, by looking over our left shoulder to imagine a 45° line to the touchdown point. He wouldn't be able to see that from the right seat.

"Perch," I said. He pushed the stick gently to the left and nudged the throttle back almost imperceptibly until we heard the familiar squeal of the thrust attenuators. The airplane smoothly rolled left to about 45° of bank and the airspeed settled nicely on 110 knots. The bank changed a little, here and there, but we seemed to be describing a perfect semicircle ending right on final. Once there he leveled the wings and nudged the throttles forward about the width of each knob. That's when it hit me. He hadn't touched the power at all since the perch.

The touch and go landing was perfect, and about a minute later we were on downwind again when I heard, "your jet."

The airplane was in perfect trim, 150 knots, right on altitude. I steeled myself against every urge to move the throttles until the perch and then only once to get the thrust attenuator squeal. It was the easiest final turn yet and that made for the best landing yet. "Do that again," he said as I slapped the gear handle up. So I did. "Make this a full stop," he said.

"Hook three one," I said rolling into the next final turn, "gear down, full stop."

This was it, I knew. We still had enough gas for thirty minutes. I landed the airplane and we taxied in. "Just shut down the right engine," he said, "I'm getting out and you are doing three more trips around the pattern."

Don hopped out of the jet and gave me a thumbs up. I gave the crew chief a "V" with my right hand and twirled the wrist, signaling I was about to start the right engine. Engine start and taxi out were surreal. It didn't hit me until I called tower, "Hook three one solo, ready for takeoff."

Flying on downwind I thought I heard the engine cough. Turning final it sounded like a generator was losing a bearing. "Hook three one solo, gear down, touch and go." No, it was nothing but nerves. Two more just like that and I was done, number four in the class to solo but number one of Chesney's studs. The beers were on me that night.

Marke soloed the next day and Kevin the day after that. We tried to contain our joy, as Roger was still a few sorties behind. It was easy to tell who in the class had soloed and who had not. We, the initiated, began to walk with swaggers, talk a little louder, and stand a little taller. "Nice talking with you girls," Marke said during a morning burrito run, "but I think I'll take the jet up for a while to see if I can perfect my chandelle." And off he went. About half our remaining flights in the airplane would be solo.

Solo means freedom. No instructor watching your every move, no long grade sheet to fill out, and no risk of busting a ride. We thought.

"Hooked," Kevin said, coming back from a solo ride.

"How?" we asked.

"I was in my final turn when an F-5 declared an emergency," he said, "and the RSU told everyone to bust out and reenter."

"So you went around," Marke said, "and flew to the extended downwind point?"

"Oh," Kevin said, "I guess that's what I should have done."

We pulled out our local procedures books and studied the pattern bust out procedures with renewed zeal. On my next solo I was ready for anything in the pattern, but first I needed to fly a few loops, a Cuban-8, and maybe a chandelle or two.

I was headed up hill, straight up hill. My entry speed was a little hot for the good old Cuban-8 but I could take care of that with a little extra G. My peripheral vision was starting to close in on me, limiting my field of view thirty degrees or so, forty degrees maybe. No matter, just squeeze down on the gut, force more blood into the upper body, grunt a bit. "Grnnch!"

There was utter silence. No engines, no rush of air. Nothing.

The engines were screaming, the air was screaming. My vision was full of the Arizona desert, just like a spin. No, there wasn't any rotation. Chesney's voice came to me out of nowhere, "Now what are you going to do?"

I rolled the airplane to the horizon, pulled the throttles, and loaded up the G's. Gently, I told myself, no sense passing out twice for one failed maneuver. We wouldn't see G-suits until the T-38, the next airplane in our future, so our only way of combatting the rush of blood to our feet was to squeeze down on our guts, forcing the blood back to the brain. The airplane could sustain a good 6 G's longer than you could if you weren't ready for it. I found early on that I could take only 3 without some grunting.

After about ten minutes of flying straight and level, turning only to stay within my assigned areas, I was ready for more. "Finesse," I told myself before each maneuver, "show some finesse."

James Albright

Unusual Attitude Recovery

Basic Procedures

[AFM 51-37, para. 2-8]

Verify that an unusual attitude exists by comparing control and performance instrument indications prior to initiating recovery on the attitude indicator.

The elimination of bank in a dive aids pitch control. The use of bank in a climb aids pitch control. The aircraft rolls better with no back pressure so you can get the airplane right-side up more quickly if you roll with no G and then push or pull on pitch.

Note: For attitude indicators with a single bank pointer and bank scale at the top, the bank pointer can be considered a sky pointer, it always points up and should be in the upper half of the case. Rolling towards the bank pointer to place it in the upper half of the case will correct an inverted altitude.

Power and drag devices used properly aid airspeed control.

Updated Procedures:

RECOGNIZE, UNLOAD, THRUST, AILERONS, PITCH

1. Confirm that an unusual attitude exists with backup control (ADI) and performance (altimeter, a/s, etc.) instruments.
2. Unload the aircraft. Reducing AOA keeps you out of a stall and allows the ailerons to roll the aircraft more responsively.
3. Leave most autothrottles engaged. They will automatically pull themselves if you are too fast and advance themselves if you are too slow. Otherwise, reduce thrust if nose low and accelerating, increase if nose high and decelerating. Leave the speed brakes alone on most airplanes. They might help in a dive but you have to time the retraction. They will hurt in a climb.
4. If nose low, roll wings level and upright with ailerons only. If nose high, use no more than 60° bank to help reduce pitch. In either case, leave the rudder alone, it can kill you. An autopilot can often be the cause of an unusual attitude, disengage it and hand fly the airplane.
5. If you know your V_A, getting closer to that helps. But finesse is more important.
6. If you are low to the ground, remember your CFIT recovery procedures.

Stalls and Spins

[ATCR 51-4, Para. 4-25a]

Two conditions are necessary for the aircraft to spin: (1) stall and (2) yaw; therefore anytime the aircraft is stalled, there exists one of the conditions necessary for a spin. If rudder is displaced from neutral during a stall, rotation will result.

[ATCM 51-3, pg. 291]

The most effective procedure for the conventional configuration is to use opposite rudder to stop the sideslip, then lower the angle of attack with the elevators. With sufficient rudder power this procedure will produce a positive recover with minimum loss of altitude.

Single Spin Recovery

"Should get any airplane in a recoverable spin out of the spin"

1. Throttles – Idle.
2. Rudder & ailerons – neutral.
3. Stick – abruptly full aft & hold.
4. Rudder – abruptly apply full rudder opposite spin direction (opposite turn needle) & hold.
5. Stick – abruptly full forward full rudder 1 turn after applying rudder.
6. Controls – neutral after spinning stops & recover from dive.

Spin Prevent

"If you aren't practicing or demonstrating spin recoveries, try this first."

1. Throttles to idle.
2. Release all back pressure to break the stall.
3. Apply rudder and aileron opposite the rotation.

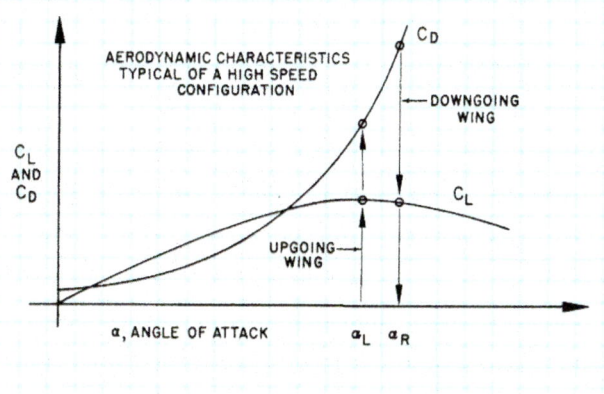

Smoothly advance the throttles after rolling movement has ceased.

10: Charlie Brown

T-37 Cockpit (J. Brew - Creative Commons)

"Ooompf!" I heard from the right seat. It was my mid-phase check ride, the first flight evaluation of many to come. The evaluator had been silent except for the occasional grunt. We were both strapped into our ejection seats and tethered together via our own oxygen masks and a common interphone system. I could hear his every breath, grunt, and sigh. He was grunting as I pulled into a loop. So far all the other maneuvers had been perfect.

The loop, too, I thought was pretty good. I hit the speeds exactly and the G-forces were right out of the textbook. So far the check ride was going quite well.

"Okay," he said, "let me have the airplane for a bit." I released the controls and he rolled and stood the airplane on its right wing and let the nose fall. As the nose reached its nadir he pulled out of the dive and pointed the nose to the sun, all in one continuous motion. I watched as the airspeed bled from over 250 to 200, to 150, to 100, to 50, to 0, to less than zero. The wings, with no airflow, failed to grab the molecules they needed for lift and the nose plunged unevenly into a yaw-contorted stall. The aircraft wrapped itself into a spin and after the first rotation, the nose tracing a spiral from way up to way down, the evaluator took his hands off the controls and said, simply, "recover."

I pulled the throttles to idle and centered the stick and rudder. I then pulled the stick sharply back to its aft stop, and watched the earth rotate below me. We were spinning left and a quick look at the turn needle confirmed that. Satisfied, I stomped on the right rudder and counted the rotation. After one complete turn I threw the stick full forward and watched as the spin suddenly stopped. At this point I recovered from the dive.

"Not Roger, not Sal," I heard from the right seat, perhaps sotto voce.

"What?" I asked.

"Nothing," he said in a normal volume, "that was excellent. Let me see another loop. But this time, show me some finesse. Just because the book says it takes three and one-half G's doesn't mean you need those G's instantaneously. Show me you can fly a loop with some style."

Finesse. That's the word that had bugged me early on in the program, became a goal, and then a forgotten goal. I noted the thought and pushed my mind forward, there was work to do. I flew another loop, trying to build the G forces more gradually. To my surprise, I ended up with more speed at the top of the loop and it worked out better than any before it.

"Very nice," he said, "let's head to the pattern."

We did so and in the end he passed me with a "Good" on the grade sheet. That was not as good as an "Excellent," but certainly better than a "Fair" or an "Unsatisfactory." There were congratulations all around the flight room and I pondered my promotion into the next phase while still wondering what "Not Roger, not Sal" meant.

Roger was obviously the smartest guy in the class. He got every test question right and he grasped every classroom lesson before anyone else. Before we hit the flight line I was betting he would be leading the pack. That wasn't how it all turned out, however. He was the last in the class to solo and was also last in the sortie count. But still, he was smart.

Salvatore, on the other hand, did not exude intelligence. He barely passed every test. "If the minimum wasn't good enough," he would say not caring a whit, "it wouldn't be the minimum." If the instructor leading the morning "stand up" wanted to be entertained, he would call on Sal. Invariably, predictably, Sal would give the wrong answer but it would be hilarious. Everybody liked Sal. He was funny and you couldn't help hoping he would join your table at the bar.

When he came back from a flight after a botched maneuver, he would give everyone the play-by-play.

"I was watching the spin, counting the rotations," he said with his loud, booming voice, "but the instructor didn't say recover. Are we playing chicken here? I started to wonder about that and by the time he said recover, I forgot which way we were spinning." We howled as one, knowing we had all feared that very situation. Perhaps some had been there. "So I pushed the wrong rudder! Next thing you know, we are spinning upside-down!"

Sal had gotten himself into the dreaded inverted spin and was bragging about it. You had to love Sal.

"Not Roger, not Sal." There is a Yin and Yang about military flying, no doubt about it. You had to have intelligence, discipline, and stick-and-rudder skills. But you needed something else too. You need a balls-to-the-wall, devil may care, blood-thirsty aggressiveness. You had to have a confidence that made up for all shortcomings. Your Sal had to overpower your Roger. I liked Sal, I idolized Roger.

Passing my mid-phase check ride early meant I could concentrate more on the afternoons in class. On Monday we were greeted with yet another pilot training memory aid that served more to confuse than to explain.

Charlie Brown + 30

Tom Collins + 45

"Okay boys and girls," the instructor said, "write this down and commit it to memory." I scribbled dutifully.

He explained that when intercepting a course inbound to a radio station, you turned to a heading that put the Course on the further side of the Bearing Pointer and the aircraft heading 30 degrees further still. When intercepting a course outbound, you turned to a heading that put the Tail of the bearing pointer on the further side of the desired Course and the aircraft heading 45 degrees further still.

To a fledgling pilot with zero instrument time, the idea of a course intercept

Flight Lessons 1: Basic Flight

is daunting. It is a vital skill basic to all instrument flight, however, and must be mastered. I wasn't mastering anything until Roger drew a few pictures. As it turns out, they were worth a thousand words.

If flying a 360° heading south of a 090° course, you would obviously want to turn right. But how far right? The rule said turn right until you have the Course further away from you than the Bearing pointer and settle on 30 degrees. In this case the course is already on the correct side of the bearing pointer, so you need only turn right until you have 30 degrees offset from the bearing pointer.

From this point you wait until the bearing pointer falls to the desired course and turn to join. Simple.

"The head always falls," Roger said, waiting for me to laugh. "Get it?"

I finally got it. "I guess when you're locked up in a mostly boys school for four years," I said, "this kind of stuff is hilarious." Roger nodded, thinking that too was hilarious.

"How about the Tom Collins thing," I asked, "and who is Tom Collins?"

"You Purdue boys are pretty dull," he said, "I guess I wasn't missing as much as I thought I was in the zoo."

Roger drew some more. "If you are due west of a 360 degree course flying a parallel heading, you need to turn right. But how far right?"

The rule says to place the Tail

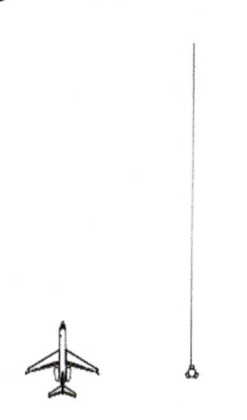

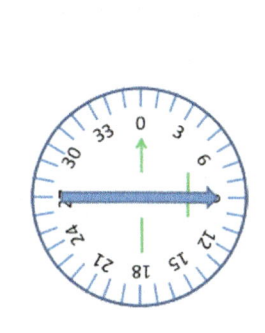

of the bearing pointer on the far side of the desired Course and fly a 045° offset.

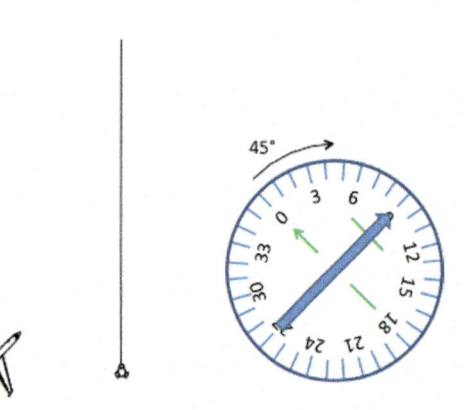

From this point the tail will eventually rise to the 360° course and you can turn left to join.

"The tail always rises," Roger said, waiting.

"Got it."

Before the week was out I had the concepts down and headed for the simulator where everything was set in stone. Since I was done with the mid-phase check ride, I spent most of the week in the simulator, which made class easier which then made the simulator easy. Another Yin and Yang kind of thing, not Roger not Sal. It seemed half our flight was in the simulator, the other half catching up with the flying. We had four or five guys who busted their mid-phase checks, got another practice ride, and then a recheck. If they busted that, they would be gone forever. I heard rumors of the busts, rechecks, and eventual passes, but only rumors.

Sal passed his recheck on Thursday and on Friday I saw him at the simulator. "How's it going?" I asked.

"I could use a Tom Collins," he said, "see you at the bar?"

"Sure," I said, "I was going to see if I could drag Roger over for a change. He should have passed his recheck today."

"Oh," Sal said, "okay."

I couldn't find Roger but showed up where a good portion of the flight was already celebrating. The mood was light and we wore the added confidence of meeting another milestone on our way to our wings. As usual, the party didn't really start until Sal showed up. You couldn't help feeling good just talking to him. There was joy in his every syllable and even bad news prompted a grin. The mood of any room improved when Sal showed up. I started wanting to be like Sal.

Not Roger, Sal.

Monday morning I walked into the flight room and was greeted with a little

Flight Lessons 1: Basic Flight

less clutter, the room looked bigger for some reason. I walked over to our table opposite Chesney's desk and discovered the reason. We had one less chair. There were several chairs missing, as if their owners ceased to exist.

"And then there were twenty-five," I heard from behind me. "It was a blood bath," Marke said.

"I guess they want the deceased out as soon as possible," I said, "to keep the living uninfected."

As the room filled with studs and instructors alike the mood lifted, and soon it was as if nothing was wrong. After the formal stand up Chesney looked somberly at his three remaining studs, obviously with a prepared speech.

"Roger's doing fine," he began, "better than I've ever seen him. I don't think he was cut out to be a pilot, to be honest. And I think he knows that. He told me that he already got an assignment to Wright-Patterson Air Force Base as a civil engineer."

We let that sink in. We three also had engineering degrees, but that was the last thing we wanted to be doing.

"I usually have a prepared pep talk when a stud washes out," Chesney continued, "but I didn't need it for Roger. In fact, it was like he already heard it. He told me that the only thing he wants out of his professional career is to use his intelligence to make things better for the country. Mom, apple pie, that sort of thing."

"Yeah," Kevin said, "that's Roger. We were roommates as duelies at the zoo. He always had that Uncle Sam thing going on."

"So that got me thinking," Chesney said, "you three should think about what you want out of all this. What do you want out of life? So that's your homework for the day. We got morning sims, but before we fly this afternoon I want you to write a single sentence on what you want out of life. We'll put them all on one sheet of paper and when you three get your wings, we can have a good laugh.

I didn't need to think about it, in fact I didn't until Marke reminded me after lunch. I ducked into the flight room and spotted a yellow steno pad on Chesney's desk. There were three lines, each with a name, two already filled in. I added mine:

> **"What I want"**
>
> Davies: To be a professional aviator.
>
> Gibbs: To kill people and break things for God and country.
>
> Haskel: The meaning of it all.

As I put the pen down Chesney walked in. "Gibbs," he said, "I can't tell when he's joking or not."

"Yeah," I agreed, "somewhere there is a cockpit with a trigger in it made just for him." It seemed like a good time to leave, but I didn't. "Can I ask you a question, sir?"

"Shoot."

"What does it mean when someone says 'not Roger, not Sal?' I mean when an instructor says that."

"You heard that?"

"Yeah," I said, "during my mid-phase."

"Oh," he said and then fell silent. I waited. "I guess I can tell you now, just don't repeat this. Especially to Sal. Roger had brains but no hands, no feel for flying. Sal has natural flying skill but is too lazy to study. Your examiner was saying you aren't either of those. It was a compliment."

I thought about that for quite a while. I liked to think I had the brains and certainly wasn't lazy. But I also had to admit I certainly wasn't a natural pilot, like Sal. "Play the hand you are dealt," I added to my notebook.

Flight Lessons 1: Basic Flight

Course Intercepts

Inbound: Course to Bearing ("Charlie Brown Plus 30, the Head Falls")

Set desired course under CDI (example: 090°).

Turn in a direction that places head of the course arrow above the CDI (example: the aircraft is south of the course and the bearing pointer is already above the CDI).

Continue the turn so the aircraft heading is 30° further than the Bearing Pointer ("B").

"30"

"Brown"

"Charlie"

The bearing pointer should fall to the course (no wind).

When the CDI centers, turn inbound.

Outbound: Tail to Course ("Tom Collins Plus 45, the Tail Rises")

Set desired course under CDI (example: 360°).

Turn toward the CDI in the outbound direction (example: the CDI is to our right, we turn right.)

Continue the turn so the aircraft heading is 45° further than the course ("C").

The tail of the bearing pointer should rise to the course (no wind).

When the CDI centers, turn outbound.

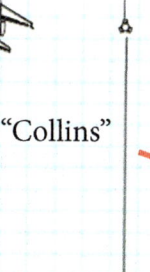

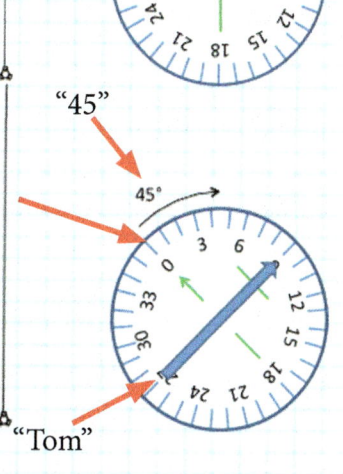

"Collins"

"45"

"Tom"

73

11: Getting Cross

Haskel on the Wing (Eddie's collection)

The last month in Tweets was the best, and not because there was no classroom learning going on. It was the solo formation flying. We got our own jet and flew in fingertip formation from another jet from takeoff to landing and all the aerobatics in between. It was the first truly military flying of the program and it was intoxicating.

The routine, in fact, was about as much fun I'd ever have as a human being. Classroom learning was over. In the morning we would have simulators that now were concentrating exclusively on flying instrument approaches. In the afternoon there was "form," half of which was solo. We'd takeoff as a flight, head to the practice area, fly a series of loops, barrel rolls, or whatever struck our fancy, and head back to the pattern. Typically we would break up after the first approach and then it was touch and go landings until the gas said the sortie was over. That's where I found myself on the first day I ever got in trouble as an Air Force officer.

It was a windy day but I had lots of gas and wanted to get every ounce of fun from the petroleum. My formation partner called it quits after two.

Flight Lessons 1: Basic Flight

"Whiskey Delta," I thought to myself. One more touch and go and I had the pattern to myself. A quick look at the gas and I knew I could do one more. "Hook four two solo," I said while keying the mike, "gear down, touch and go."

"Hook four two solo," the runway supervisor replied, "cleared touch and go."

As I scanned the final turn I saw the RSU, the Runway Supervisory Unit, where I knew two instructor pilots were watching over everyone in the pattern. And today that was just me. I had to make it a good final turn, landing, and takeoff. The airplane was crabbing pretty well, angled into the wind, as I lined up on final. No matter, "aileron into the wind, rudder to align," I said to myself. Perfection. One more and the day was done.

I was walking on air after the flight until I walked into the flight room where I was greeted with an inquisition from my instructor, the flight commander, and the squadron commander.

"Lieutenant," First Lieutenant Chesney began, "what is the dry runway crosswind limitation of the T-37B?"

"Seventeen point five knots," I spat out while assuming the position of attention, "sir."

"Why does that limit exist," Major Delehunt asked.

"The aircraft cannot maintain adequate ground control," I answered, "after aerodynamic effectiveness is lost on the rudder with a crosswind above that speed, sir."

"And what was the crosswind," the lieutenant colonel standing on everyone's right asked, "when you landed thirty minutes ago?"

"Seventeen knots," I ad-libbed, "sir."

"Did you look that up?" Chesney asked.

"Ah," I stammered, "no sir."

I was given the next few days off the flying schedule to consider my sins. I was just one flight away from completing the T-37 program and was set to be the first stud in the class to finish Tweets. Now I was relegated to permanent snack bar officer duty. I was the "food dude" charged with selling breakfast burritos, candy bars, and sodas to my fellow studs. Between sales I reflected on the flight that ruined my chance at superstar status in the flight.

The tower called the winds 260 at 25 when our flight of two first showed up in the pattern and there were three other Tweets doing the same thing I had planned, touch-and-go after touch-and-go until time or fuel was up. By the time I had three touch-and-go's under my belt the pattern was empty but I didn't have the gas for another, so I called one last time, "Gear down, full stop."

"Cleared to land," the tower said, "winds are 240 at 25."

I landed.

Looking at the chart I should have looked at the day prior, my transgressions became clear. Runway 30 has a magnetic heading of 300 degrees. When the winds were called 260 at 25, there was a forty-degree difference and according to the chart I had a 16-knot crosswind, perfectly okay. When the winds changed to 240 degrees, the crosswind became 22 knots. Not good. I placed a large tape marker on the crosswind chart in my checklist and moved on. There had to be an easier way, I knew. It was, after all, simple trigonometry.

After a week in food dude purgatory I had my crosswind rules of thumb down and was released to fly. Sortie last would be dual with Major Henry Delehunt, the flight commander and senior instructor pilot. I had never flown with him, though he was supposed to fly with every student at one point or another. Our flight was now down to 24; he could have made the time. No matter, from what I heard he wasn't a lot of fun in the cockpit and he stole a lot of stick time from students who had their requirements met. Like me.

We were number two in the formation and I dutifully lined up left and just behind lead as we were cleared for takeoff. It was fellow stud Lieutenant Groves at lead with his instructor in the right seat. I didn't know Groves' first name; everybody called him Grover. He was a real goof ball and I really didn't know him at all. This wasn't sortie last for him so we organized the trip from start to finish to check off the remaining items he had to complete his formation requirements.

Grover raised his left hand and twirled his wrist. I nodded and pushed both throttles full forward and stood on the brakes. Grover tilted his head aft and then forward and as he did so we both released our brakes. Rotate, gear up, flaps up, and slide into position, nestled just a few feet from his wing tip. I was getting ready for the "Mind if I fly" routine, but it never came. After a while I was having fun.

Grover wasn't the smoothest pilot out there and I had some difficulty keeping

Flight Lessons 1: Basic Flight

on his wing, but Delehunt kept quiet. The signal to move from one wing to the other was a barely perceptible wiggle of the wing tip. Grover practically turned into me with his signal but the message was understood. I dipped the airplane down a few feet and slid to the right. With a little backpressure I was nestled again, this time on the right. After a few lazy barrel rolls the nose came down and then, a bit abruptly, straight up. We were halfway through a loop and I could feel the aircraft mushing for lack of speed and I could see Grover's instructor pounding the glare shield. Screamer, I thought. It was the worst insult we studs had for an instructor.

"Look at this," I heard from the right seat. It was the first thing he said to me in the airplane.

"What?"

"Look at this," he repeated.

We were now fully inverted and the nose was coming down rapidly. My head was turned to the left as I was concentrating on keeping my T-37 a few feet away from Grover's without hitting it. "I'm busy."

"Just turn your head for a second," he said, "look at this."

We were now about 45 degrees nose low, inverted, but pulling less than two G's. We needed more G's to make this work. I turned my head and saw Delehunt with both hands sitting on his lap. "Pretty neat, huh?"

I jerked my head back just in time to see Grover reverse his roll, I guess he was abandoning the backside of the loop. I pushed hard to stay in position. "What are you talking about, sir?"

"You see how Grover's IP is banging on the glare shield?"

"Yes, sir."

"Well that's usually me," he said, "I fly with Groves a lot. This is the most relaxed I've been in months." In four months flying that Tweet, it was the best compliment I ever got, it was quite a graduation present. I got the next week off as all but one more of our flight finished. We were down to 23. Thirteen didn't make it, but those of us that did were headed to the fast mover.

Crosswinds

The Regulation...

[14 CFR 25.237 (a)]

For land planes and amphibians, the following applies: (1) A 90-degree cross component of wind velocity, demonstrated to be safe for takeoff and landing, must be established for dry runways and must be at least 20 knots or 0.2 V_{SRO}, whichever is greater, except that it need not exceed 25 knots.

The Math...

An isosceles triangle has three equal sides and three 60 angles, therefore ..

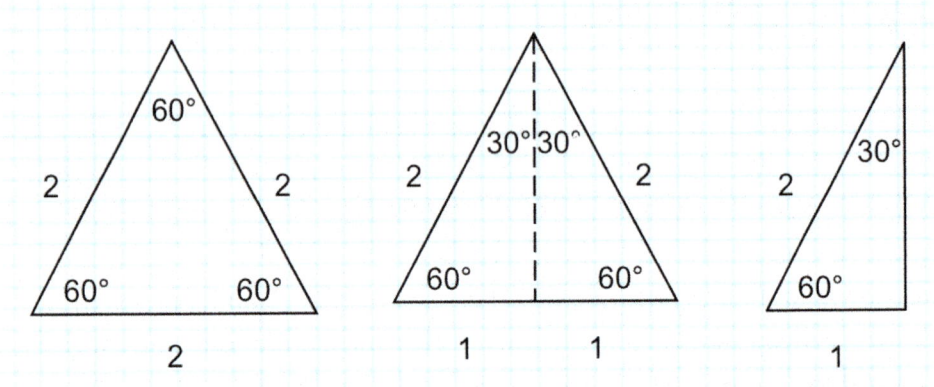

Using Pythagoras, $a^2 + b^2 = c^2$, we can find the value of the leg opposite the angle ...

A 30° Crosswind is equal to one-half the full wind factor.

A 60° Crosswind is equal to 90% of the full wind factor.

A 45° triangle can be constructed by splitting a square in half, diagonally. The legs will be equal to 1 and the hypotenuse can be found using Pythagoras.

A 45° Crosswind is equal to three-fourths the full wind factor.

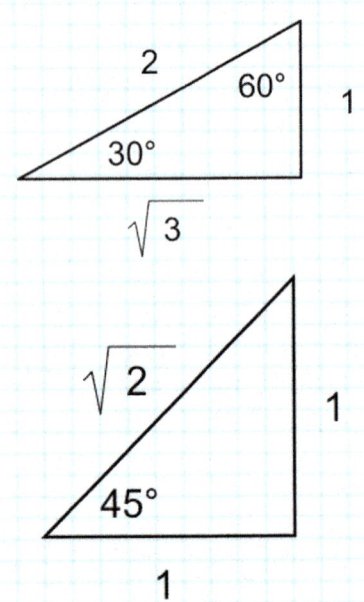

12: Everybody has an Angle

Haskel's Ladder Shot (Eddie's Collection)

Everything about the Northrop T-38 commanded respect. It was everything the T-37 was not. The T-37 was slow; the T-38 was supersonic. The T-37 was unpressurized, ugly, and took forever to climb; the T-38 was pressurized, sexy, and still held many world time-to-climb records. Even the names spoke volumes: the T-37 was a "Tweet," the T-38 was the "Talon." In 1979 the world's premier aerial demonstration team, the United States Thunderbirds, flew the T-38. And starting on June 19th of that year so did I.

We began the journey as 77 studs divided into two flights: "No Loss" and "Warlock." All the T-37 flight names were chosen from Las Vegas or Hollywood. None of that in the world of the T-38, where the names all came from Korean War fighter squadrons. The 23 studs in my flight removed our "No Loss" patches and sewed on the historic "Gombey" insignia. Our sister flight became "Boysan." Their attrition rate was almost as bad, they were now 28 studs strong, our class went from 77 to 51.

Day One with Gombey began in our new flight room with our new flight commander, Major Steve "Slam" Curtis. He was a short and stocky man with a flat top haircut and a wide grin slightly askew to a face that wasn't completely parallel to the rest of his body. "Studs," he said while standing perfectly erect with legs spread a bit and arms akimbo, "welcome to Gombey where we are in the business of producing fighter pilots. No flight in the squadron has a higher F-A-R rate and with you wonderful men that record is going to continue. Anyone not fit enough to fly a fighter might as well be an airline pilot. You got that?"

"Sir," we all said as one, "yes, sir."

"Good." The wide grin grew wider. "Now I see you all found your new desks okay which puts you a cut above your average killer so that's good. Your instructors will be in shortly so let's get to it. Remember, the pointy end goes forward."

And with that he marched out. I looked to Kevin Davies, seated with me at our new desk opposite our new instructor's seat, "F-A-R?"

"Fighter, attack, reconnaissance," he said. "What's he mean about the pointy end?"

"Subsonic airplanes usually have a blunt front end to improve airflow over the fuselage and a pointy end in back to reduce drag," I said. Then I pointed to the picture on the cover of our new flight manuals. "The white rocket is pointy in front to break through the supersonic shock wave and the blunt end of the afterburners in back."

Marke Gibbs, our T-37 tablemate, was farmed out to another instructor with another stud. Kevin and I were treated to First Lieutenant Harvey Gray.

Gray appeared from nowhere and plopped into his seat, facing us. Kevin and I stood at attention.

"So," he began his relationship with us, "you two are the talentless blobs of clay for me to mold into fire breathing baby killers."

"Yes, sir," we both said.

"Well be seated," he continued, "let's begin."

Harvey Gray was Dave Chesney's evil twin. Where Dave always had a smile and talked to us as equals, Harvey scowled and every word was dripping with condescension. He spoke for an hour on how he expected to be greeted every morning (Studs at attention), the decorum of his desk and our table (spotless), and when we were allowed to ask questions (only when he was done speaking). While most our fellow studs left the morning session with

Flight Lessons 1: Basic Flight

springs in their steps, Kevin and I plodded out to lunch.

"What did we do to deserve this?" Kevin asked.

"I think I once hit a cat with a stick," I said, "other than that I've led a spotless life."

"I wish you had left that cat alone," Kevin said.

"Me too."

We wouldn't be seeing Harvey for another week, however. Our next five days were devoted to the classroom. Six months ago it was all strange and intimidating. Now, with half a year of flying in our log books and after having seen almost a third of our class washed out, this was going to be a new world. Even our now familiar chalkboard had a new seriousness to it.

"Everybody knows this," the instructor began, "you wouldn't be here if you didn't. The T-38 is a new breed for all of you. You haven't flown anything like it and there is a mistake on this diagram when it comes to the thirty-eight."

We studied the diagram intently. It looked textbook perfect to me. Our textbook, and probably every aero textbook ever written on the subject, defines angle of attack as the acute angle between the relative wind and the chord line of the airfoil. The relative wind was simply the speed and direction of the air impinging on a body passing through it — the opposite of the aircraft's flight path. The Greek symbol alpha — α — was the engineer's nomenclature for angle of attack.

"The wing," our new instructor said after the prolonged silence, "is wrong. This wing has a camber to it, the top is curved and the bottom isn't. Your mere mortal pilot thinks that's what creates lift. That pilot is only half right. What would that pilot say about this wing?" He flipped the chalkboard over, end-for-end.

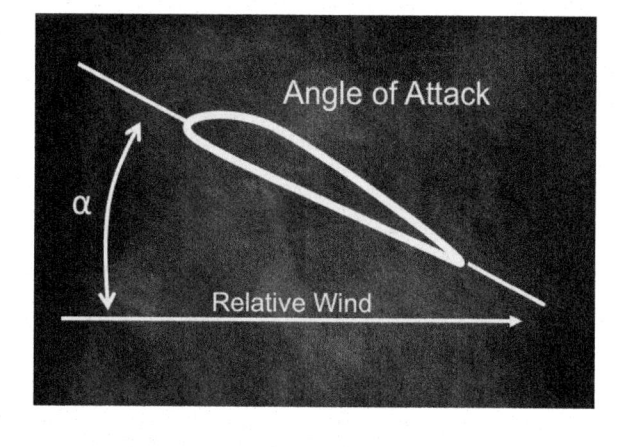

"This wing is symmetrical, it is the same on top as it is on the bottom. It produces zero lift at zero angle of attack." We sat back to the let the beauty of the airfoil sink in. "The skinny wing on the T-38 means you can go fast, but you need a helluva lot of AOA to produce any kind of lift at all. If you don't understand that, you will become a smoking hole."

"No angle of attack, no lift," the instructor said. "The wing is so thin you are going to spend most of your time in the traffic pattern feeling the buffet in the stick, that's normal. You are going to have to get very familiar with the angle of attack indicator. It will save your life in this airplane and just about every fighter you touch from here on out.

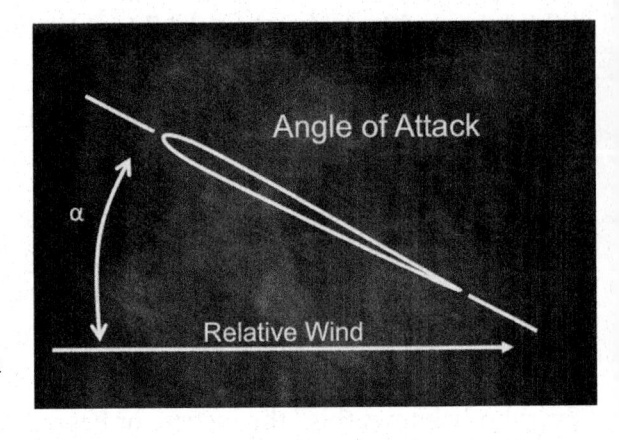

Willy was in the business of producing fighter pilots and anyone daring to voice a desire to something that didn't drop bombs or shoot bullets was a heretic. I was starting to think my path would lead me elsewhere, but AOA would forever be in my future.

Flight Lessons 1: Basic Flight

Angle of Attack

Aerodynamic Force

[Hurt, pg. 23]

The lift force is described by the following: $L = C_L qS$

Where L = Lift, C_L = lift coefficient

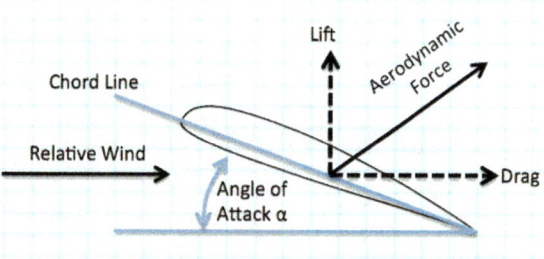

Boundary Layer

[ATCM 51-3] Because air has viscosity, air encounters resistance over a surface. This reduces the local velocities on a surface (drag of skin friction), relative velocity at the surface is near zero; at some distance above that velocity reaches full value of airstream. This layer of air is the "boundary layer." A cambered wing generates an aerodynamic force at an earlier angle of attack but suffers boundary layer separation earlier and with a more rapid reduction of its coefficient of lift.

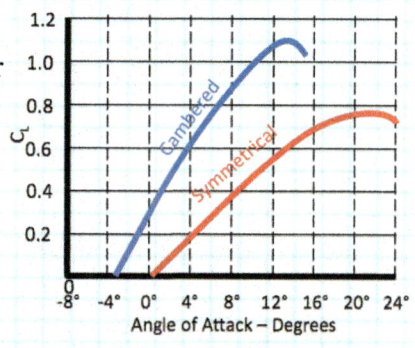

The pressure over and under the wing decreases as the velocity of the air increases. The point of minimum pressure divides the airfoil into two. Forward of that point the pressure gradient helps to produce lift and a pulling force forward. Aft of that point we have what is called the adverse pressure gradient. The pressure here contributes to drag and a separation of the air flowing over the wing. As the angle of attack is increased, the point of minimum pressure moves forward and the size of the adverse pressure gradient increases. Three things happen as a result: The lift component of aerodynamic force increases, up to a point. The drag component of aerodynamic force increases. The turbulent flow area increases, encouraging separation of the boundary layer.

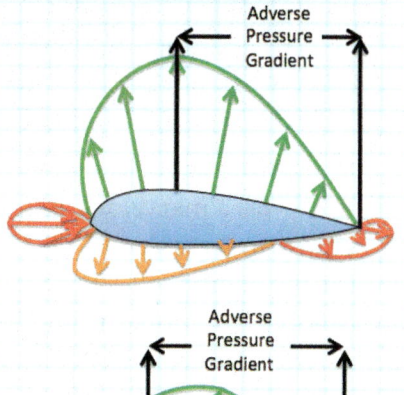

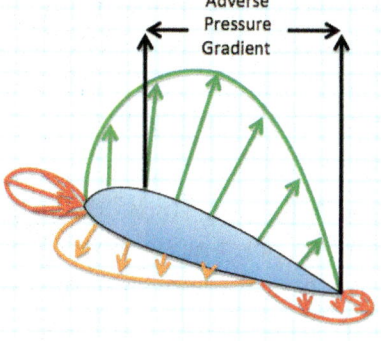

13: In a Fix

T-38A Cockpit (USAF Photo)

The T-38 was a marvelous aircraft and had two things going for it when flying instruments that the T-37 did not: a flight director and DME, distance measuring equipment. Now by just looking at a gage, we knew our distance to a station. No more timing the RMI needle. What we still didn't have was an electronic method of determining our course from one point to another. Even though our first week was confined to the simulator, we instantly appreciated the beauty of it all. But, as with all things aviation, understanding began in class.

"Good morning studs," the instructor began, "today you learn the secret of point-to-point navigation." He pulled the inner chalkboard hidden behind two others at the front of the class. "You are on the 270° radial of this TACAN, heading 360°, and have been cleared direct waypoint STUDD. What will you do?"

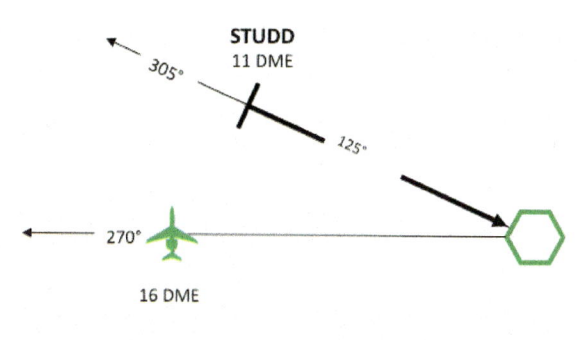

Flight Lessons 1: Basic Flight

"Time to get out your crayons boys and girls," he said while turning to a large, wooden HSI at the front of the class. The horizontal situation indicator was a new instrument for us, it combined our old RMI, radio magnetic indicator, with our old CI, course indicator, into a single, easy to read, gizmo.

"You are the tail, the target is the radial, the higher DME is the edge of the card, the lower DME is inside by whatever ratio that comes to, draw a line, move the line, make the line vertical. Easy!"

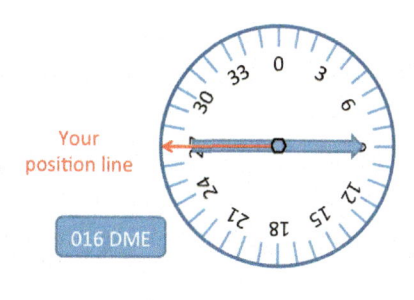

By now we knew the routine. The instructor would rattle off the procedure to make it all seem impossible, then break it down into steps. But this really did seem impossible. We all started missing good old Charlie Brown Plus Thirty. The bearing pointer is pointing to the radio station so "you are the tail." The instructor pointed to the tail of the bearing pointer. You had to visualize the TACAN station at the pointer and your airplane at the tail.

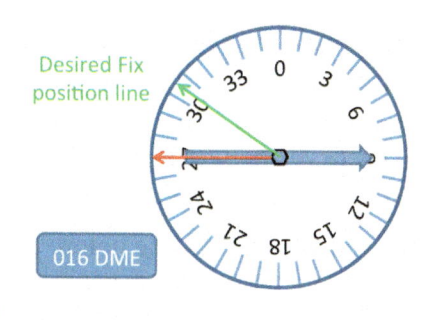

"Your desired fix is on the 305° radial, so just visualize a line heading in that direction." He made a slashing motion with his hand toward 305°, this was starting to tax the neurons.

A lot of formation flying involves thinking about airplanes in space over a 2-dimensional map, so this was just doing that with a waypoint instead. In theory. This shouldn't be so bad after all.

"If we are at 16 DME and the fix is at 11 DME, we are further from the station, right"? The instructor asked but did not wait for a reply. "So we are at the edge of the card, the fix is somewhere inside the card, say about here." He pointed to what could have been a third of the way in, but we engineers realized it was an 11/16th proportion.

"Draw a line in your head," the instructor continued.

"Too hard!" Salvatore cried. The instructor ignored him. "The line connected your position to the fix position, this is your 'fix-to-fix' line." It made sense looking at a large HSI mockup in the classroom. But what about at 300 knots on an instrument about five-inches in diameter?

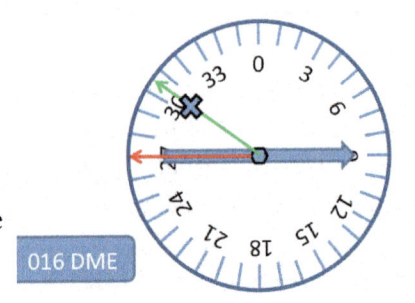

"Now it is just a matter of turning the airplane to make the line vertical," the instructor said. He spun the compass card on the mockup while holding two fingers along the imaginary line. The line became vertical on about a 050° heading.

I looked at the mess of my notes, the sterility of the classroom mockup, and the smug look on Marke Gibbs' face. "Not so bad," he said.

"From here," the instructor said, "we wait for the tail of the bearing point to . . ."

"Rise," we answered as one.

"Yes boys and girls," he said, "it really is just that easy. Now practice that in the sim and you won't have any problems for the rest of your flying careers."

Most of the first few sim sessions were devoted to switchology, cockpit flows, and basic procedures. We got in a few instrument approaches and a fix-to-fix or two. The visualization wasn't so hard after all, but keeping that imaginary fix-to-fix line in your head while turning the airplane was not easy. I decided some high school geometry was in order for the last step.

By transposing the line before turning the airplane you would have a heading to turn to. Now it was easy.

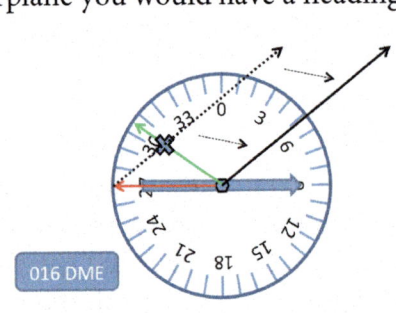

Flight Lessons 1: Basic Flight

Fix-to-Fix

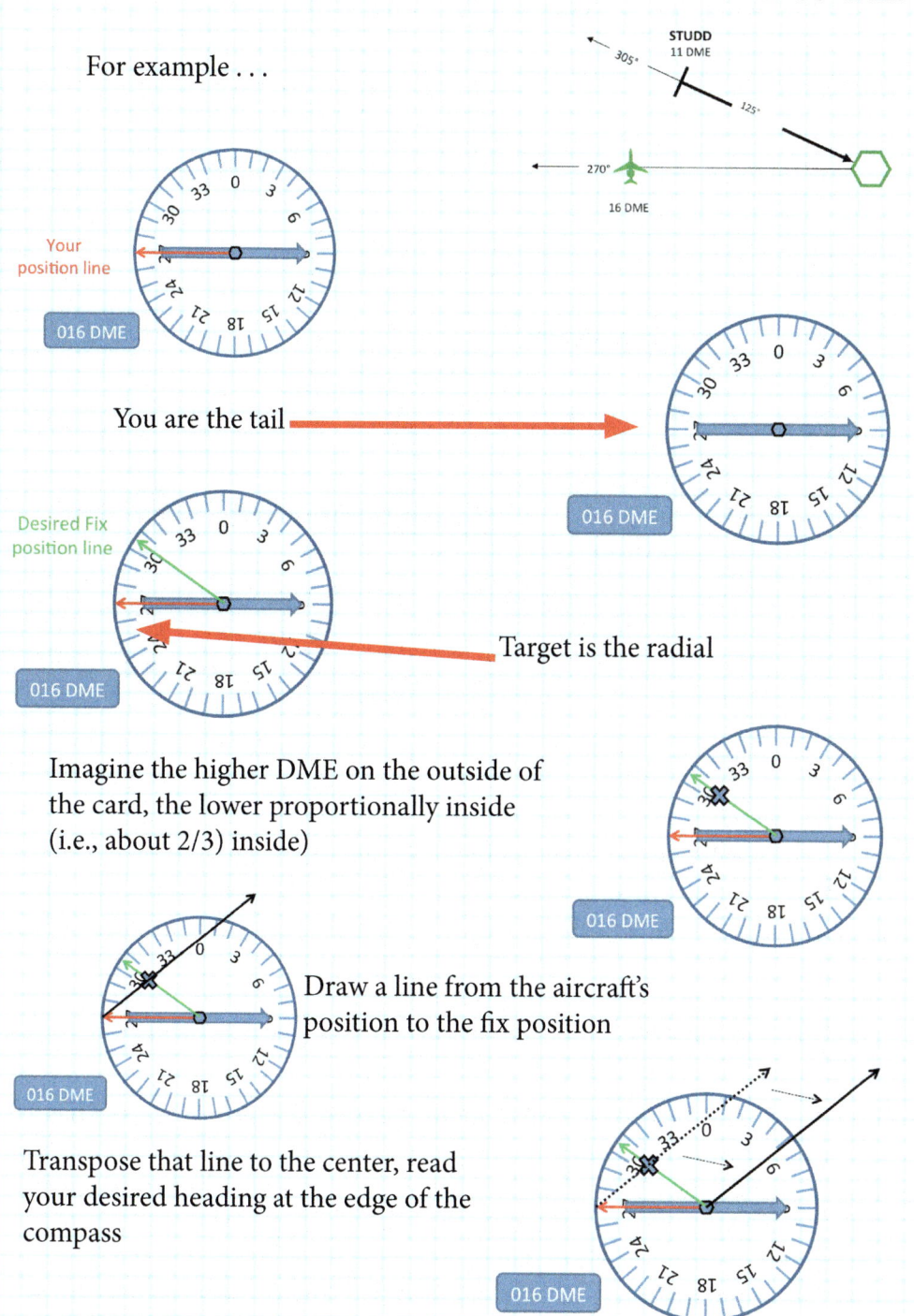

For example . . .

Your position line

016 DME

You are the tail

016 DME

Desired Fix position line

Target is the radial

016 DME

Imagine the higher DME on the outside of the card, the lower proportionally inside (i.e., about 2/3) inside)

016 DME

Draw a line from the aircraft's position to the fix position

016 DME

Transpose that line to the center, read your desired heading at the edge of the compass

016 DME

14: Cooking With Gas

T-38 (USAF Museum)

The first time a pair of afterburners kicks you in the pants it surprises you. One second you are on the ground, the next you are passing a couple of thousand feet with Harvey yelling at you. "Don't over-speed the gear!" A few seconds later you are passing flight level one eight zero and there is more yelling, "Nine, nine, two! What's wrong with you?" Despite all the screaming, what little instruction Harvey was doing was somehow working. Kevin Davies and I traded notes on when the screams come and how to avoid them. "The screamer" is the worst insult we studs had for an instructor, and in our flight of ten instructors Harvey earned the honors as having the top set of lungs.

He seemed to be worried the most about the traffic pattern. The T-38 has a razor thin, symmetrical wing that produced zero lift unless fed a steady diet of AOA. So critical was angle of attack, in fact, that it was the primary instrument sitting on our glare shields. You flew the airplane over the runway at 300 knots, rolled into 60° of bank and pulled the nose around the turn with 2 G's of pulling force. That is the so-called "break." You roll out, throw

Flight Lessons 1: Basic Flight

out the gear and flaps, and then comes the "perch" and the final turn.

"Red and green," Harvey would say, "red and green."

The easiest way to visualize the T-38's final turn is a falling version of the break. You roll the airplane into 45° of bank with no backpressure which causes the nose to fall. Once it is about 15° below the horizon, you pull the airplane's nose around the pattern. How hard do you pull?

"Red and green," Harvey kept saying. We were doing the program backwards. Most studs thoroughly embraced and enjoyed the aerobatics and struggled in the pattern. We were both failing miserably in the practice area. "Recover!" Harvey would let us fail at a maneuver, yell "Recover!" and demo how it should be done.

"Now is this so hard?" He would say as the nose traced a perfect loop. "Entry is easy, 450 knots, 550 EGT, 5 G's, and show some finesse. Now you try it." And we would fail. "You ever notice," I said to Kevin at the officer's club bar one night, "that most of the fighter pilot instructors are jerks and most of heavy pilots are more laid back?"

"Yeah," he said, "and the FAIPS are worse than the fighter pilots." I hadn't thought of that but it was true. The First Assignment Instructor Pilots, like Harvey, were usually pretty bad. "I guess they are trying to prove something to the fighter pilot mafia around here."

"Kind of strange that two closet heavy studs get a FAIP," Kevin said, "and a confirmed baby killer like Marke gets a heavy pilot IP." I let that go uncommented. I was wrestling with the thought of not actually volunteering for a fighter, but had kept that to myself. Kevin would joke about it now and then. "Wanna be a FART?" he would ask. The qualification for a fighter, attack, reconnaissance aircraft was known as F-A-R but the instructor pilots assigned to the T-37 and T-38 imagined themselves in the same club. Trainers were deemed a part of the F-A-R mafia. "Speak of the devil."

"Ladies," Marke said while pulling up a bar stool. "What's the word?"

"450, 550, 5," I said, "we are licking our wounds because we can't fly a loop at 450 knots, 550 EGT, and 5 G's."

"What in the hell are you talking about?" He said, "Entry is 500 knots and military power. If I started a loop at 450 knots and 550 EGT, I'd fall out of the top. What are you guys doing?"

"Falling out of the top," we both admitted.

The T-38's engines have afterburners that dump raw fuel into the tail section of the engine and nozzles that focus the resulting fury. Maximum power is known as maximum afterburner or "Max AB." The next step down is 100% rpm, known as "Military Power." Setting the thrust to 550 degrees exhaust gas temperature, or EGT, is several percent lower. We learned in academics that going from 100 percent to 97 percent didn't cost you 3 percent of your power, it cost you more like 10 percent.

"My instructor gave us a cheat sheet from their manual," Marke said, "I'll get you a copy. The next morning we both saw that students were responsible for mastering the loop with an entry speed of 500 knots and military power. The lower numbers came later in the program, after we managed to fly solo. "Oh yeah," Marke added, "my IP is going to have a word with your IP."

I feared the worst. What kind of retribution did we face on our next flights? Apparently none. Harvey was a changed instructor the next day. He didn't mention the issue and said nothing when I accelerated to 500 knots with the throttles pushed to full military power. I managed my best loop and followed that with a pretty good chandelle. Day after day Kevin and I competed to get signed off on every maneuver and even thought we might be the first in class to hear, "make this a full stop so I can step out of the jet while you show me three touch and goes by yourself." Of course that honor belonged to senior stud Ron Wilson. But who would be next?

We both showed up one morning for our daily flight assignment and noticed there was no instructor listed on the scheduling board next to either of our names.

"Who's my IP today, sir?" Kevin asked the scheduler.

"You ain't got no stinking IP today," the scheduler said without looking up, "you lieutenants got an objection to flying solo today?"

"No sir!" we both answered. There was no ceremony, no final dance around the pattern. Just two 22-year old second lieutenants headed out to their jets for a one-point-three of white rocket aerobatics and a few trips around the traffic pattern. We both got back about the same time and the smile on Kevin's face said it all.

Flight Lessons 1: Basic Flight

Thrust and Drag

It is extraordinarily difficult to measure thrust from a jet engine in flight, but you can measure drag in a wind tunnel and thrust = drag in steady flight.

Induced Drag

[Hurt, pg. 66]

The lift on the wing has a component of force parallel to the remote free stream. This component of lift in the drag direction is the undesirable – but unavoidable – consequence of developing lift with a finite wing and is termed induced drag.

Parasite Drag

[Hurt, pg. 87]

A wing surface will have "profile" drag due to skin friction and form. Other parts of the airplane contribute to drag because of their own form and skin friction.

Thrust Required Thrust required is equal to total drag in steady flight conditions. When in unaccelerated flight, the sum of all forces must be equal after all.

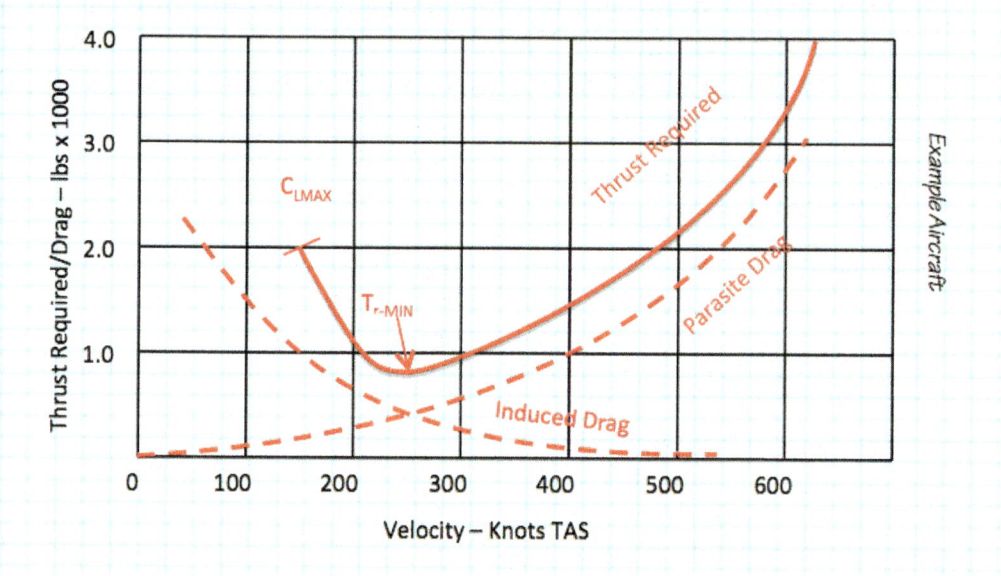

Example Aircraft

Thrust Required/Drag – lbs x 1000 vs Velocity – Knots TAS. Curves shown: Thrust Required, Parasite Drag, Induced Drag. Labels: C_{LMAX}, T_{r-MIN}.

Thrust Available vs. RPM   [Hurt, pg. 116]

The variation of thrust output with engine speed is a factor of great importance in the operation of a turbojet engine. By reasoning that static pressure changes depend on the square of the flow velocity, the changes of pressure throughout the turbojet engine would be expected to vary as the square of the rotative speed, N. However, since a variation in rotative speed will alter airflow, fuel flow, compressor and turbine efficiency, etc., the thrust variation will be much greater than just the second power of rotative speed. Instead of thrust being proportional to N^2, the typical fixed geometry engine develops thrust approximately proportional to $N^{3.5}$. The turbojet engine usually has a strong preference for high RPM to produce low specific fuel consumption.

Thrust Available and Required vs. Altitude   [Hurt, pg. 119]

Altitude strongly effects the performance of a turbojet engine. An increase in altitude produces a decrease in density and pressure and, if below the tropopause, a decrease in temperature. Above the tropopause, no further favorable decrease in temperature takes place so a more rapid variation of thrust will take place. Above the tropopause the temperature is constant and altitudes slightly above the tropopause cause no further decrease in specific fuel consumption. Actually, altitudes much above the tropopause bring about a general deterioration of overall engine efficiency and specific fuel consumption begins an increase with altitude. Note: This general rule must be tempered in the case of a turbo fan jet, especially one controlled by a Fully Automatic Digital Electronic Control (FADEC), which can extract more efficiencies above these altitudes.

Thrust Required vs. Weight

Recall that an increase in weight requires an increase in lift to maintain steady, unaccelerated flight, so the Aerodynamic Force must increase.

As Aerodynamic Force is increased, so to is induced drag.

This moves the thrust required curve up and to the left. That also means the buffet limit speed increases and the airspeed for L/D_{MAX} increases.

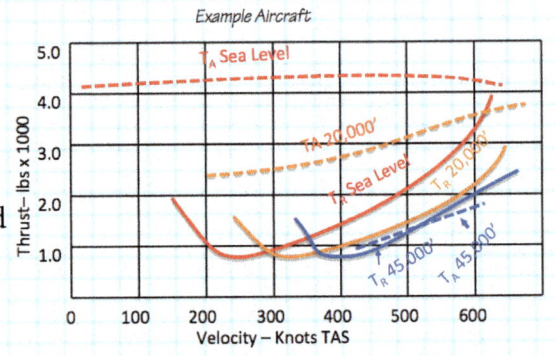

Flight Lessons 1: Basic Flight

15: Go Around Burners!

T-38 Formation (USAF Photo)

"The T-38 has a published maximum roll rate of 720° per second," the instructor said to our flight of twenty-two studs while starting the morning stand up. We nodded knowingly, a full stick aileron roll was an early maneuver. By now half of us had all soloed and we were all feeling pretty comfortable in the jet. Still, we didn't have a clue why this could be a topic for stand up.

"Lieutenant Haskel," he said and I popped to attention. "You are flying along solo, lightly cradling the stick with your right hand. All is right with the world when all of a sudden the world is spinning at 720° per second, a perfect aileron roll. What will you do?"

"Sir," I said, "opposite aileron."

"This isn't your day, Eddie, no change in the roll rate." I knew that was going to be his answer. "How about some rudder?"

"No sir," I said, "I think my next step would be hand grips raise, triggers squeeze."

"Excellent," the instructor said, "be seated." I exhaled and sat down. Harvey sat emotionless in his seat but I got a thumbs up from Kevin. This problem wasn't in any of our books. The instructor handed a stack of stapled technical order supplements to the nearest stud who then passed a copy to each student and instructor.

"Here's the latest addition for your flight manuals," the instructor continued. "Two guys just bought the farm at another base last week. A pin holding the right aileron actuator fell out and the aileron deflected full down, turning that T-38 into a corkscrew. Read this, post this, and know this. But let me cut to the chase for you. If you are flying along and your white rocket turns into a corkscrew, eject. After more than one or two seconds you won't be able to get to those handgrips. That's it for stand up, first sorties launch in half an hour." We silently unwrapped our supplements and read. So far in 1979 we had lost three T-38's and it was all treated casually. It was a cost of doing business.

"Okay studs," Harvey said, "I guess you are both solo today and they've got me flying with some of the stragglers. See you later." I followed Kevin out the door and as soon as we were out of earshot I said, "and fly safe, Kevin." It was our private joke that Harvey hated seeing us fly solo and never said what the rest of the instructors said to their chicks leaving the nest. "Fly safe," poor grammar or not, was what an instructor was supposed to say.

The stragglers were all working on the final turn, something Kevin and I had mastered early. They wouldn't give you the keys to the jet solo until you had mastered the final turn. It was perfectly normal to hear "final turn, go around" from the runway supervisor, but you had to get that out of your system early. The worst thing you could hear was "go around burners!" That meant you were thirty seconds from killing yourself.

So there I was, flying the final turn like I owned the pattern when I got the call, "go around, burners!"

I lit the burners and was back on downwind seconds later. I got the airplane on the ground the second time around and was greeted by an instructor I had never met before. "You and me," he said, "let's get you sorted out." After an hour in the pattern he said he was satisfied and signed me off. "No problem here," he said, "every now and then it happens to the best of us. Just make sure you never find yourself on the back side of the power curve."

"Yes, sir."

He was satisfied but I wasn't. Nobody in the flight seemed to know of my sins and my name appeared on the next day's schedule to fly the next train-

Flight Lessons 1: Basic Flight

ing sortie with Harvey, a navigation leg. Marke Gibbs was sitting alone at his table, posting his flight manual supplement. He knew more about this stuff than most.

"You ever heard of the back side of the power curve, Marke?"

"No," he said, "but the answer to all questions is in that blue book right over there." He pointed to a bookshelf behind his instructor's desk. I looked around. There were no instructors present.

"Mind if I borrow it," I said.

"Borrow what?" he said, turning his back to me.

I reached for the volume when Marke's instructor tapped me on the shoulder. "Help you, Eddie?"

"Ah," I stammered, "I want to learn about the back side of the power curve."

"Yeah," he said, "I heard." He took the book from me, flipped a few pages and handed it back. "Right here," he said. "I want this back when you're done with it.

So my sins weren't private after all. The book, NAVWEPS 00-80T-80, "Aerodynamics for Naval Aviators," gave several pages to what it called the "Region of Reversed Command." It was a newer version of the one I got from an instructor at Purdue.

It seems that a swept wing jet aircraft can find itself in the awkward position where it takes more and more power to fly slower and slower speeds. If you find yourself on the "back side" of this curve, the only solution is to grab a lot more power and reduce the angle of attack to get onto the other side of the power curve. "Go around, burners." The two afterburners on my jet saved my hide. But the burners have been known to sputter and fail. Then what?

The sink rate was a symptom, not the cause. The cause was too little airspeed. I felt confident again that I was the master of the aircraft and the next day it was as if nothing had happened. I was a sinner no more.

The Region of Reversed Command

Region of Normal Command [Hurt pg. 354]

At Point 2 the airplane is in what an aeronautical engineer calls the region of normal command and at the "available power setting." If you were operating at any point between the bottom of the curve and this point, you would notice:

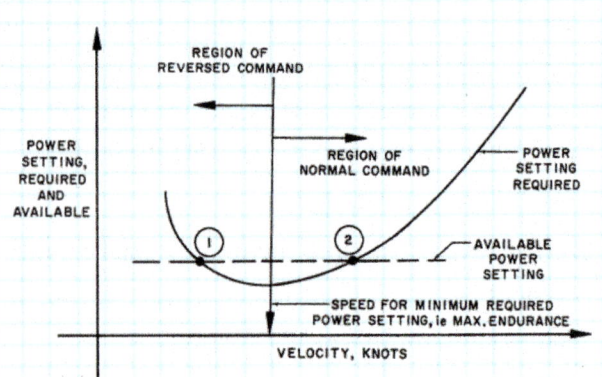

Reducing power allows you to reduce velocity and then maintain that velocity by increasing the power setting to some point less than the original power setting. This holds true for any point between the bottom of the curve and the available power setting.

Adding power allows you to increase velocity and then maintain that velocity by reducing the power setting to some point more than the original power setting. This relationship holds true for any point between the bottom of the curve and the available power setting.

In other words, the thrust relationship to velocity is as you would expect it to be. It should be intuitively obvious that pilots should always want the airplane in this region.

Region of Reversed Command

You could find yourself at Point B in the diagram and the airplane will fly just fine. But if the airplane is momentarily disturbed and the AOA favors a lower airspeed, you could find yourself at Point C. It will take more power to hold this speed and if you don't have that amount of power, you could stall. The only way to increase speed is to decrease the angle of attack.

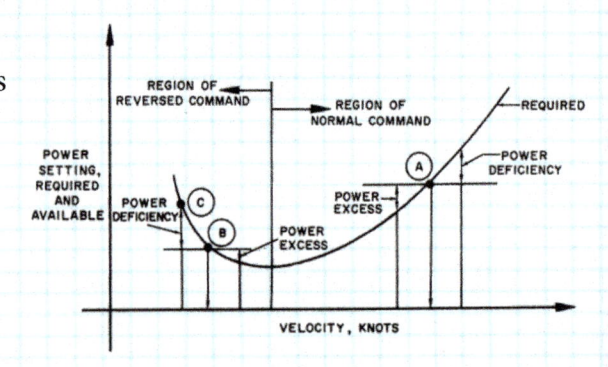

16: Too Hot!

"Hey Eddie," Willie said while overtaking me in the hallway, "You got signed off for solo last week?"

"Yeah," I answered, "even a blind dog finds a bone now and then."

"Can you talk me through the final turn?"

Willie was a natural pilot, something I am not. I wasn't sure I could speak his language, but we were all in this year of pilot training together. We had already lost three studs to the final turn. They couldn't solo so they were gone.

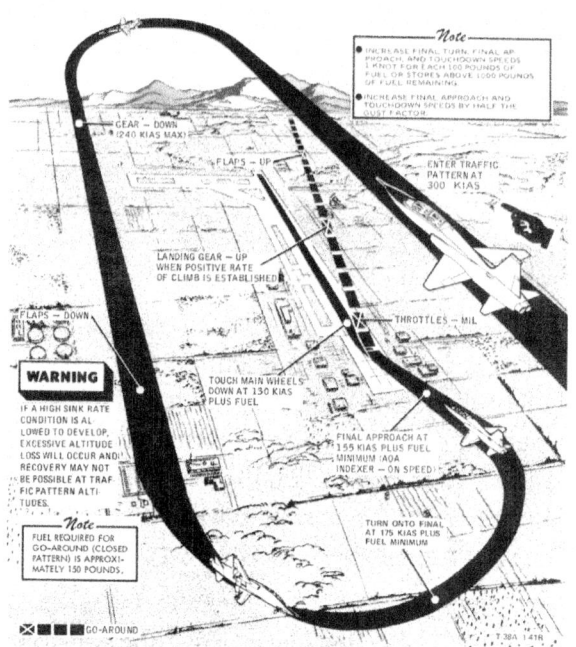

T-38 Pattern (TO 1T-38A-1)

"Sure," I said, "let's sit down and hash it out." For me the final turn was just a matter of following procedure and flying with a light hand. You roll the aircraft crisply to forty-five degrees of bank and absolutely no backpressure. The nose falls of its own accord and when you get to about twenty degrees of pitch you pull until the wings start to buffet. "The key," I told Willie, "is you are pulling the nose around the turn, you pull hard enough to buffet the wing into a moderate stall. You aren't banking around the turn, you are pulling the nose around the turn."

"Oh, I see." The next day, it seems he did indeed. I was riding the flight line trolley back from our airplane with Harvey when it stopped next to another T-38. Willie and his instructor boarded.

"You got the final turn down solid," Willie's instructor said with a smile, "next we are going to work on the roll out. Then, when you've mastered that, we'll nail those landings. One step at a time, Willie, that's how we do it!" As we hung our parachutes and made our way to the flight room, Willie slapped me on the back, "thanks for the lesson, Eddie!"

I smiled at him and turned to face Harvey who sounded like a new instructor. "Good job today," he said, the first compliment I'd ever heard from him. "I am going to sign you off on navigation." This was great! Most the class was still working on getting signed off solo and here I was finished with the next block of training.

"Tomorrow we are going to fine tune the landing pattern," Harvey announced, "starting with the final turn."

"What?" I said in a bit of a shock, "why are we doing that?"

"Because that's how we do it."

The next day I flew the final turn just like I always did and Harvey said nothing. I rolled out and landed the airplane just like I always did and all hell broke loose. "Too hot!" yelled Harvey, "we're going to try that again." I pushed both throttles to full military power, rotated the nose, raised the landing gear, and pulled up to another closed traffic pattern. I replayed the landing in my head and realized that I touched down about 700 feet down the runway. The book said we were shooting for 500 feet. I vowed to do better.

"Too hot!" he yelled again, this time even angrier. Landing after landing I got the same result and Harvey's voice grew hoarse with exasperation. "I don't understand what your problem is," he yelled, "this should be easy!" For the first time in pilot training, I was unsure of what I was doing. Harvey gave me a failing grade, writing into my permanent record: "Landings too hot." It was my first ever "hook" on a grade sheet and it stung. I went home and memorized the aircraft technical order landing procedures anew. I would do better. I did not: Harvey gave me a second failing grade. Now I would have to fly with another instructor and risk washout. How the mighty had fallen, I thought. A week earlier one of the best pilots in the flight was asking for my advice on how to land the aircraft, and now I was about to wash out for landings.

On my next flight I made sure the wheels touched brick number one on every single landing. No more hot landings! The new instructor said nothing and simply handed me my grade report: "Landings too hot, recommend final evaluation."

Now I was not only afraid of washing out, I was confused on every aspect of the landing. What was I doing wrong? I was forced to sit for a few days as more members of the class were signed off for landing. I was getting advice

Flight Lessons 1: Basic Flight

from all quarters but none of it made any sense. The techniques they were offering wouldn't help.

The day came for my "final evaluation," potentially my last flight piloting an Air Force aircraft. The instructor told me to relax and just fly the airplane the way my grade book said I had done just a week prior. "Piece of cake," he said.

I put the wheels down on the very first millimeter of that runway and smiled internally, knowing I had nailed it.

"Why did you do that?" he asked from the rear cockpit. "You fly such a good airplane and everything was perfect until you got over the end of the runway and you just forced the airplane down. Why?"

"I don't want to land hot," I explained as I pulled the nose around for the second pattern, "Captain Gray says I land too hot."

"You don't know what 'landing hot' means," he asked, "do you? Try it again."

I pulled the aircraft around the final turn again and aimed for the threshold, flaring for the landing as usual.

"Hold it off," the instructor yelled, "not yet." I did as instructed. "Now." I put the aircraft down and he whooped in glee, "perfect."

"A hot landing," he explained as I pulled it around again, "means you have too much speed when you touch down. By shooting for brick one, the way you did on the first pattern, you only make matters worse. Remember you are going to gain a few knots when the airplane enters ground effect if you force it down."

Ah, ground effect. We didn't have much of a wing, but at one-half our wingspan we would lose a lot of induced drag and that made me even hotter.

The "final evaluator" signed me off and wrote a note on my copy of the grade report that didn't appear on the original. "Remember, if you don't know what something means, ask. You can't do anything in life well if you don't master the fundamentals first. You can't master the fundamentals until you define the terms."

Wise words.

Ground Effect

[Hurt, pg. 380]

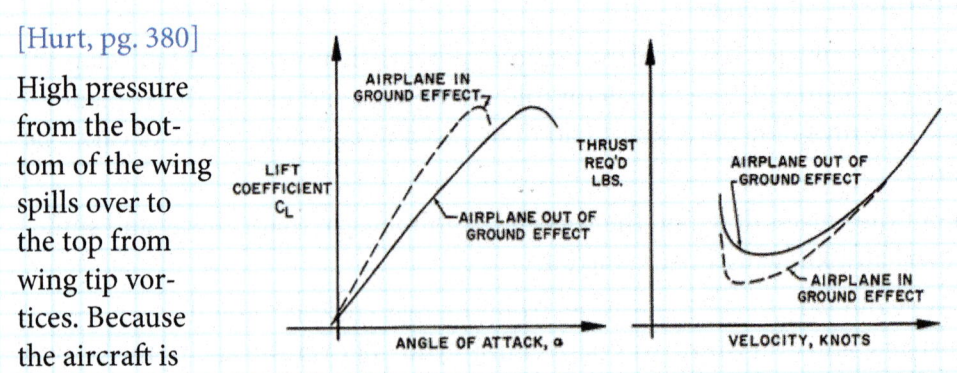

High pressure from the bottom of the wing spills over to the top from wing tip vortices. Because the aircraft is moving forward, this air spirals downward to depress the down wash of the wing and pulls the aerodynamic force of the wing aft. The aft component of aerodynamic force is induced drag.

The vortices spiral into a growing circle until they hit the fuselage, at which point they end. That is one-half of the wing span.

When the aircraft enters ground effect during landing, the decrease in induced drag means less of the aerodynamic force is directed parallel to the relative wind. The wing becomes more efficient and the aircraft may have a tendency to float. This effect can be so pronounced that some aircraft must be flown onto the runway, they cannot be flared to "zero sink."

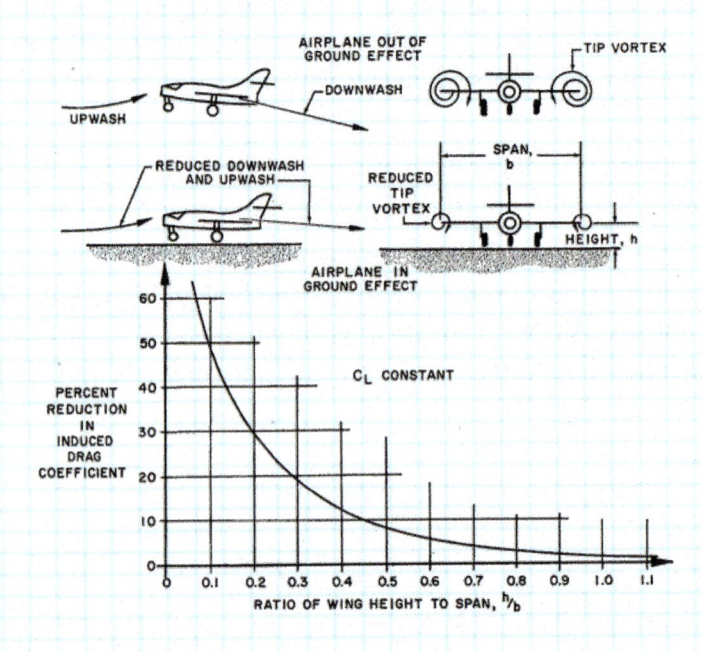

17: Hold

T-38 Formation (NASA Photo)

In 1979 the United States Air Force Thunderbirds were flying the T-38. They changed to the jet from the F-4 Phantom in a move to cut costs and to put a cleaner look to a country growing an environmental conscience. Gone was the long plume of black smoke and loud, thunderous noise. The T-38 was virtually smokeless and relatively quiet. Once you got cleared for formation, in theory, the airplane had become an extension of yourself. You stopped manipulating the aircraft with stick and rudder; you started to will the airplane via an unseen mind-machine interface. Formation, then, is where the magic act is revealed. You start to understand those death-defying maneuvers by the pretty red, white, and blue airplanes are really no big deal. "Keep your eye on air show center, ladies and gentlemen, as the aircraft fly by at over five hundred miles an hour with just inches of wing tip spacing!"

This was our second formation airplane and in many respects it was easier than the first. The T-38's controls are very crisp and maneuvering the airplane with only "inches of wing tip spacing" is not so difficult.

"Where do you want to be?" Harvey asked on "Form 1," the first instructional ride in T-38 formation.

"Wing tip on the star," I said. Exactly where I am, I thought to myself.

"How close should you be?" he asked. I flicked my eyes left to see both nozzles of lead's engines. By keeping on the diagonal line formed by lead's wingtip and the star, I could judge distance by checking how much of the tail I could see.

"Closer," I said as I nudged the throttles forward. Keeping the airplane in fingertip formation was the easiest part. As long as lead knew what he was doing, flying loops, weaves, even a chandelle was child's play. But if lead screwed up, you were both screwed. You had to have your act together as lead.

The hardest part of T-38 formation was keeping your interest level up for the rest of the program. Once formation training started you were knee-deep into instrument flying and low-level navigation. Most of the washouts at this point came from an inability to get the airplane down to instrument minimums while flying an approach speed of over 155 knots and circling at over 175 knots.

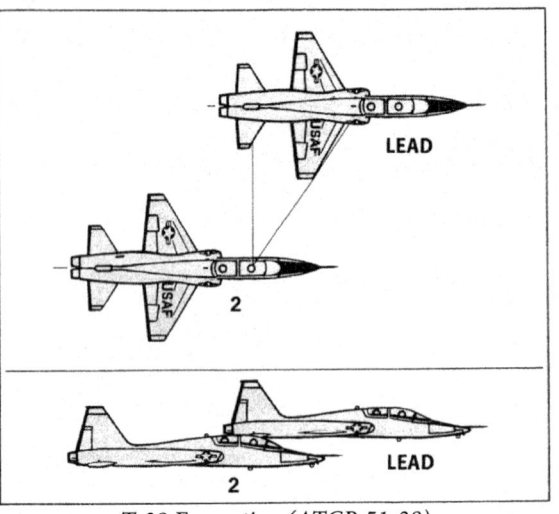

T-38 Formation (ATCR 51-38)

Williams Air Force Base was in the business of producing fighter pilots. You had to get the formation down to get your wings. But don't ignore the instruments! The Air Force wasn't going to let you graduate unless you could pass an instrument check ride. We did all of our formation flying from the front seat of the airplane and most of the instrument work from the back, where there was a curtain to keep us from looking outside. We would fly the airplane down to minimums and the instructor would land it.

"I've got it," Harvey would say, "I think I can land out of this." Or if things didn't go so well, "we aren't even in the ball park, go around."

There were several rites of passage along the way to our instrument ratings. The first was passing the simulator check, then a solo cross-country, and then

Flight Lessons 1: Basic Flight

the airplane instrument check. The simulator check had over a fifty-percent bust rate but all of Harvey's screaming somehow served us well so Kevin and I both passed, finishing first and second in the class. Once the entire class got by the sim check it was time for the solo cross-country. Kevin led the first flight, and I got lead of the second. We both reported to the flight commander's office the morning of the big day. It was the first time I had ever met him face-to-face.

"Kevin, you got the morning flight. Eddie, you take the afternoon. You will each have nine other studs following you at ten-minute intervals with an instructor in the last airplane. Fly the flight plan to Hill Air Force Base, request vectors to the ILS, fly the ILS and land. Once everyone is refueled, come on home. Everything by the book."

"Yes, sir," we said together.

"Now I probably shouldn't be saying this," Major Curtis continued, "but I'm going to anyway. I've got my two strongest instrument studs in front, and the only instructor will be in tail end Charlie. Between you and the IP we've got some guys who I think are going to be doing nothing but following your contrails. You gotta do things by the book because you are each going to have nine other studs following you. By the book, you got that?"

"Yes, sir." We saluted and marched out of his office.

I was in the weather office as Kevin's flight was returning. Weather was clear between Williams and Hill, just outside of Salt Lake City. There was some cloud cover north of the city, but nothing to worry about. I hopped in the jet, followed by nine classmates and one instructor. At the appointed hour I lit the fires and took off; Willie Five One Solo was heading north. With each passing air traffic control sector I was hearing more and more of my flight-mates. "Willie Five Two Solo, level four one zero." A few of the studs dropped the "Solo" part, thinking it unmanly. But I had to be "by the book."

Checking in with Salt Lake City Center I got a bit of news, but nothing to worry about. "Willie Five One Solo, good afternoon. Hill is closed at the moment, they have a disabled airplane on the runway. Proceed direct the Hill Tacan and hold, expect further clearance at 2135, time now 2110."

I repeated the clearance, tuned in the Tacan, and turned to the KHIF HI-TACAN/ILS Rwy 14 approach. It looked like a perfect opportunity for a left turn into a teardrop entry followed by right turns until my time was up. Time was up? Oh yes, time to worry about fuel. I had the fuel to hold for almost thirty minutes, so the next fifteen were nothing to worry about. What then? Worry about that then, I told myself. I have a holding pattern to fly.

When I got to the Tacan I turned left a few degrees for the teardrop, hit the clock, waited a minute, and turned right. I was holding. At each turn I tried to look for the airport, but I was in the middle of a cloud so that wasn't going to happen. I was wondering what the next airplanes were going to do. Would air traffic control stack them up above or below me? Since I got here first, shouldn't I get the first approach clearance?

It was a moot point. "Willie Five One Solo, the runway is clear. You are cleared the approach on your next turn inbound."

I accepted the clearance, shot the approach, and landed. Sitting at the Hill Air Force Base snack bar, every ten minutes another stud would show up and we would relive our journeys. Nobody else had to hold and everyone was impressed that I handled the situation so well. "Wow," a few said, "I'm glad it was you and not me." A few even admitted to following contrails. But we had all done it. It was another notch on our belts along the way to our wings. When the last airplane showed up the instructor headed straight for me, probably to congratulate me on a job well done.

"Lieutenant Haskel," he said, "I heard you had to hold in the weather."

"Yes, sir, I did."

"Are you allowed to fly in instrument conditions solo?" he asked.

"Ah," I realized the answer but couldn't verbalize it.

He pointed to his wings, the ones I didn't have yet. "Don't ever do that again until you get a set of these. Got that?"

"Yes, sir." I went from hero to goat in nothing flat.

Flight Lessons 1: Basic Flight

FAA Holding

Standard Holding Pattern [FAA-H-8083-15]

The standard pattern is a racetrack pattern with 180° turns to the right and one minute legs. Pilots are expected to compensate for the effect of a known wind except when turning and to adjust outbound timing so as to achieve a 1-minute (1-1/2 minutes above 14,000 feet) inbound leg.

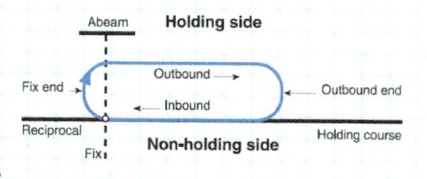

Maximum Speed [FAA-H-8083-15, page 10-11]

Reduce to holding speed when within 3 minutes of the holding fix. Maximum permitted speed is:

200 KIAS (when below 6,000 feet), 230 KIAS (when 6,001 - 14,000 feet), 265 KIAS (when 14,001 feet and above).

USAF Turns and Winds [AFM 51-37 §5-6]

If not compensating for winds, fly turns at standard rate (3° per second) or 30° of bank whichever requires the lesser angle of bank. If correcting for wind, do not exceed 30° of bank, nor shallow to less than 15° of bank, or one-half standard rate (1-1/2° per second), whichever is the lesser.

A technique which may be used to adjust bank angles is to shallow turns into the wind and steepen turns downwind 1° for each degree of drift correction necessary to maintain inbound course. If a wind correction is applied on only one turn, double the drift correction on the outbound leg. If you do not apply bank correction to either of the turns, triple the drift correction on the outbound leg.

No Holding Instructions Given [FAA-H-8083-15, page 10-11]

If you arrive at your clearance limit before receiving clearance beyond the fix, ATC expects you to maintain the last assigned altitude and begin holding in accordance with the depicted holding pattern. If no holding pattern is depicted, you are expected to begin holding in a standard holding pattern on the course upon which you approached the fix.

[Aeronautical Information Manual §5-3-8.b.]

If the holding pattern is charted and the controller doesn't issue complete holding instructions, the pilot is expected to hold as depicted on the appropriate chart.

Holding Instructions Given, Fix Undepicted

[Aeronautical Information Manual §5-3-8.i.] Where a holding pattern is not depicted, the ATC clearance will specify the following: Direction of holding from the fix in terms of the eight cardinal compass points (i.e., N, NE, E, SE, etc.). Holding fix (the fix may be omitted if included as the clearance limit). Radial, course, bearing, airway, or route on which the aircraft is to hold. Leg length in miles if DME or RNAV is to be used (leg length will be specified in minutes on pilot request or if the controller considers it necessary). Direction of turn if left turns are to be made, the pilot requests or the controller considers it necessary. Time to expect-further-clearance (EFC) and any pertinent delay information.

Wind Arrow Technique

You can copy uncharted holding instructions while drawing the pattern if you think of the initial instruction as a wind arrow.

For example: "Hold northwest"

Remember to draw the arrow FROM the stated direction.

"of the 30 DME fix, Austin VORTAC,"

If you are given a fix, draw it at the head.

"130 radial"

You will be typically given a radial, in which case the Navaid goes at the tail of the arrow. While not common, you might also be given a course, in which case the Navaid goes at the head of the arrow.

"10-mile legs, left turns."

When given the length of the pattern you must still wait to hear if "left turns" is given. If it isn't then the turns will be to the right. In any case, you have to wait until the end of the instruction to make this determination. In this case, we draw the pattern to the left.

Once we've drawn the pattern on the correct side, adding the leg distance comes next.

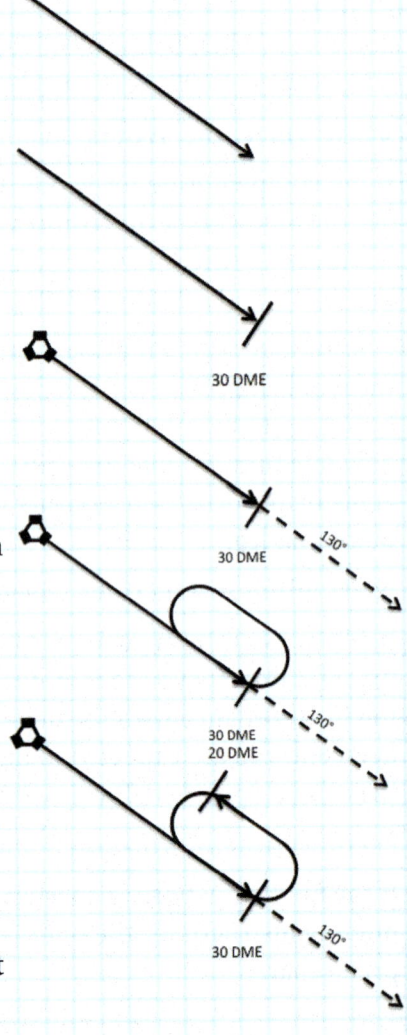

Flight Lessons 1: Basic Flight

Entry Procedures

[Aeronautical Information Manual §5-3-8 ¶3.]

Parallel – When approaching the holding fix from anywhere in the parallel sector, turn to a heading to parallel the holding course outbound on the non holding side for approximately 1 minute, turn in the direction of the holding pattern through more than 180°, and return to the holding fix or intercept the holding course inbound.

Teardrop – When approaching the holding fix from anywhere in the teardrop sector, fly to the fix, turn outbound using course guidance when available, or to a heading for a 30° teardrop entry within the pattern (on the holding side) for approximately 1 minute, then turn in the direction of the holding pattern to intercept the inbound holding course.

Direct – When approaching the holding fix from anywhere in the direct entry sector, fly directly to the fix and turn to follow the holding pattern.

USAF Technique [AFM 51-37 §5-6]

If the holding course is located within 70° of the aircraft heading, enter the holding pattern by turning in the direction of holding (right for standard holding, left for non-standard).

If the holding course is not within 70° of the aircraft heading, turn outbound in the shorter direction to parallel or attempt to intercept the holding course.

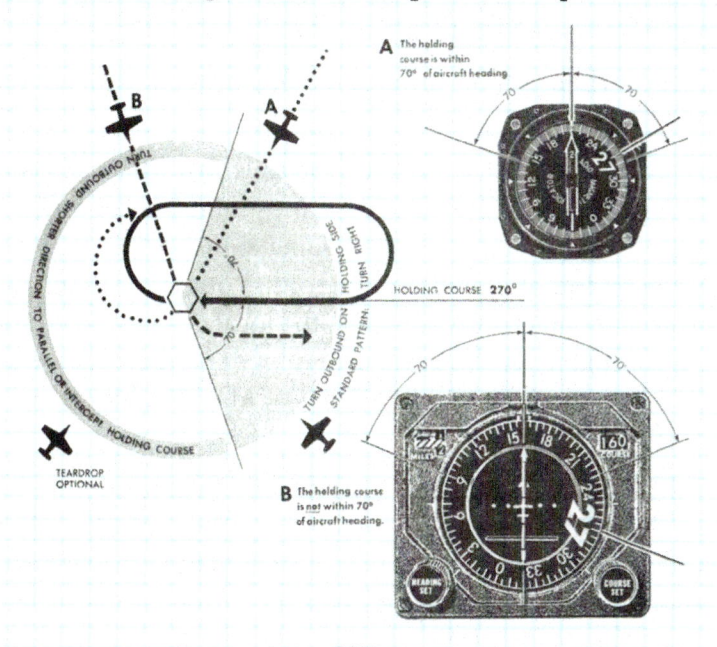

18: Critical

Haskel's Lead (Eddie's Collection)

As the year of Undergraduate Pilot Training was coming to an end, studs were either finishing their requirements or washing out. With a month to go I had only one item left: my cross-country check ride. I rushed in each morning to see if it was on the board, only to be disappointed by a scheduling board without my name. The evaluators were busy giving formation and instrument checks; I would have to wait.

"Haskel," I heard while moping around the flight room, "how about a boom ride?"

"Beats staring at the walls," I said. The T-38 sails past what early movies called the "sound barrier" because of its skinny wings, clean skin, and elegant fuselage design. Most aircraft cannot fly supersonic because their wings are too thick in the middle and blunt in the front. Both of these encourage the speed of the air in contact with the wing, the local velocity, to go supersonic well before the airplane. A shock wave develops and destroys the aerodynamic force. These airplanes with low "critical Mach" numbers were doomed to be subsonic.

Flying over the high deserts of Arizona I nudged the throttles to full military and watched the Mach meter creep forward. At about Mach 0.92 the meter stopped its steady move around the dial. I pushed both throttles into afterburner, dumping fuel into the engine aft of the turbine blades where it exploded in orange fury. The nozzles at the tail of each engine clamped down to focus the thrust straight aft.

It was the anti-climatic version of any movie made on the subject: "point nine seven, point nine eight, she's buffeting, point nine nine!" And then the radio would go dead. There was none of that for us in the white rocket. After point nine nine the altimeter jumped along with the airspeed indicator as the shock wave in front of the aircraft went past the pitot tube and we were supersonic. The airplane settled on Mach 1.15. I looked at the fuel flows and estimated we would be a glider in about fifteen minutes so I pulled both throttles out of afterburner. "Back to the patch?" I asked the guy in the back seat.

"Sure." It was quiet for a while. I had spent so much time flying with Harvey I had gotten used to a steady stream of abuse; this was more like flying solo. I vowed to keep my mouth shut until the engines wound down in the chocks but the instructor had other plans. "What do you want out of life, Eddie?"

"The meaning of it all," I said.

"Okay," he said, "let's try this. What do you think of the F-4?"

"Not much," I said. "They seem to crash two or three a year."

"Yeah," he said, "but it is the definition of a fighter pilot's fighter. You should think about it. Your class is getting one F-15, one F-16, and the rest of you guys are getting the Phantom or trainers."

It was assumed we wanted fighters. The class would be racked and stacked so that anyone they thought could handle it, would get a fighter, attack, or reconnaissance aircraft, known as the "F-A-R" qualification. Left out of the acronym was those guys could also get a trainer. "You gonna be a FART?" Kevin and I would ask each other in private. But we had to be quiet about it. You couldn't show your hand until the formal requests were filled out. One of the clauses of the newly unveiled F-A-R system was any stud could opt out of a fighter simply by not listing any on the "dream sheet." Asking for a trainer was certainly an honorable option, but after spending six months with Harvey Gray I decided instructors needed to have experience in something other than a trainer to have any self-respect. I was headed for a fighter or a heavy.

Critical Mach

Critical Mach Defined [Hurt, pg. 223]

Critical Mach number has been defined as the flight Mach number which produces first evidence of local sonic flow.

When below critical Mach number, all of the local air flow is subsonic and the lift and drag are "conventional"

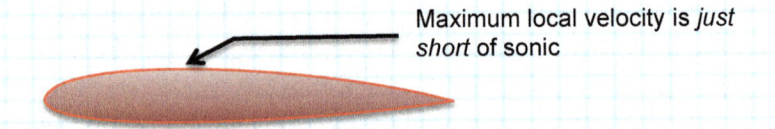

Maximum local velocity is *just short* of sonic

At the point where the first hint of supersonic air flow occurs above the wing, the air foil is said to be at its critical Mach number. This is the last point at which air can be considered incompressible and there is no shock wave to disturb the local air flow.

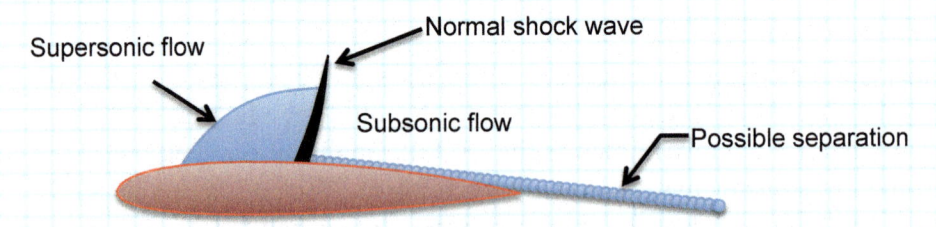

Supersonic flow
Normal shock wave
Subsonic flow
Possible separation

As critical Mach number is exceeded a normal shockwave forms between the boundary of supersonic and subsonic airflow. The area in front of this shockwave tends to be smooth, as the airflow has a gradual transition over the leading edge of the airfoil. Behind the shockwave is a greatly increased static pressure, fighting to pull up the boundary layer. There is a tug of war between the kinetic energy of the air holding it to the airfoil, and the static pressure pulling it away. As the speed of the airfoil is further increased, the static pressure begins to win out and airflow separation occurs. As a result, induced drag increases, lift decreases, and the wing may experience stability and control issues.

19: Decision

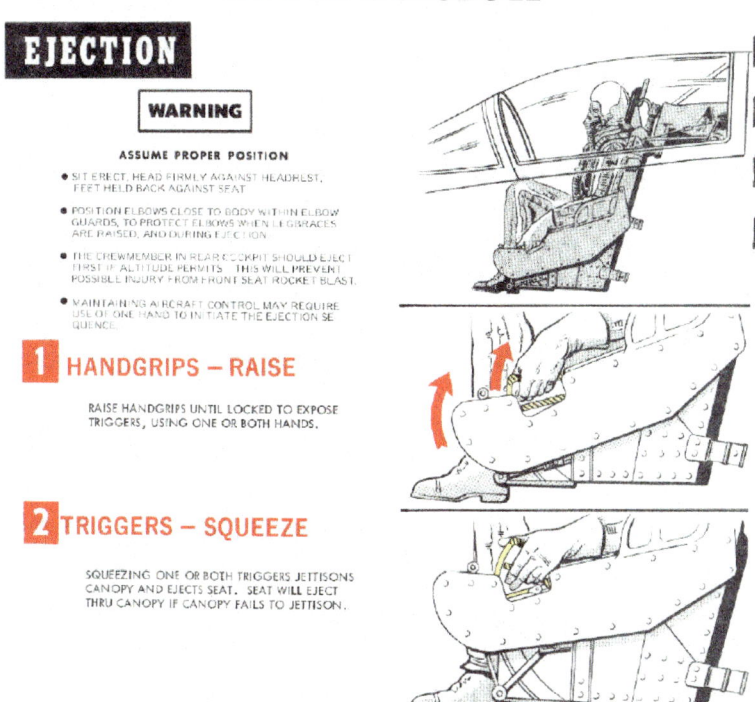

T-38 Ejection Procedure (TO 1T38A-1)

"What would you do?" the instructor asked at our morning stand up.

"Handgrips raise, triggers squeeze." Kevin's answer was textbook, just like the one I had given a month earlier to the exact same question.

"You wouldn't try to counter the rapid roll with opposite aileron first?" the instructor asked.

"The roll will be so rapid," Kevin answered, "I need to exit the aircraft as soon as possible."

"Be seated," the instructor said. "That was true a month ago but we've just had two needless ejections because of this. Yesterday Lieutenant Gibbs was flying his cross-country check when he or the evaluator hit the stick and the other pilot countered with opposite stick. They both thought they had a hard over aileron. They did not. They punched out of a perfectly good airplane." It was a common problem in a tandem seat airplane: you don't know what the other guy is doing. That also explained the empty seats that morning. We thought Marke just got stuck out overnight.

"Both guys are okay," the instructor said, "of course the airplane is in a smoking hole someplace in New Mexico. Nobody was hurt on the ground either. But it drives home a fundamental rule: make sure you know who is flying the airplane at all times!"

The instructor sat down and Major Curtis stood in his place. "Gents, it is that time you've all been waiting for. Here are your dream sheets. Those of you who are F-A-R will be getting a form with two sections, one for fighter, attack, reconnaissance, and trainer aircraft. The rest of you will get the same form with the F-A-R section crossed out. Remember, you still have to graduate so don't lose focus. I want these filled out and on my desk no later than tomorrow morning." Kevin and I stared at our forms, both blank. "You first," he said.

"I'm thinking about it," I said. I got up to see my name in grease pencil on the scheduling board for the next day: "XC Check: Haskel / Wortham" and there was an asterisk denoting I had a message in the scheduler's inbox.

"Plan XC CHD-NTD-RTB 14 NOV 0700." I was to plan my cross-country check ride from Williams, CHD, to Point Mugu Naval Air Station, NTD, and "Return to Base" leaving at 0700. Point Mugu is near Ventura, California. I had never been there, but it would be easy enough.

"Duck soup," I said to myself as I finished the fuel log and flight plan. Of course I never cooked duck soup, in fact I probably never had duck soup. But in Hawaii if something was easy it was duck soup. This was duck soup. I left the mission paperwork and my grade folder on Lieutenant Wortham's desk. It was nearly bare, with only a family photo on one side of the desk and his uniform hat on the other. His hat looked just like mine, but where I had a single gold bar his was silver, and where the braid on mine was chewed up from the zipper in my flight suit pocket, his was good as new. Lieutenant Wortham, it would seem, is one of those clean as a whistle guys.

That night, when I should have been studying for the last check ride of the program, I was staring at a blank dream sheet. I filled in the non-F-A-R section: C-9, C-141, and EC-135. The C-9 was the hospital aircraft, the C-141 was a transport, and the EC-135 was an airborne command post. I left the F-A-R section blank. I'd get back to it.

I showed up one hour prior to scheduled takeoff the next morning, as was expected, and Lieutenant Wortham greeted me coldly and assured me that the check ride should be easy for me, given my record and the quality of my flight planning. "Just don't have any mental flatus and you will do fine." I was trying to connect that word with the sentence.

"Brain fart," he said, "Don't have a brain fart." He went on to confide that almost half the students he gave these cross country evaluations actually passed, so I had nothing to worry about.

We would graduate in about a month, I realized, and this would be my last day of flying the beautiful T-38. One flight out to California, another back, and the program was over. I would never again have the experience of flying an airplane several times a day for months on end, never again have that blissful union of neurons to jet fuel. But on that day in 1979, I willed myself and the guy in the back seat from Phoenix, Arizona to Ventura, California at nearly six hundred miles an hour, and so it was.

Lieutenant Wortham and I sat at the base operations snack bar at Point Mugu Naval Air Station, eating greasy chilidogs and sipping cokes. The Navy line guys were refueling our T-38, parked next to two Navy jets, both ugly monstrosities made more so by their proximity to our sleek, white, rocket.

"What's the lowest weather minimum authorized for a precision approach?" he asked. "What about the ceiling?" he followed. "What if you don't have that?" And so it went. The oral evaluation was where most of the check ride busts happened at this stage of the game.

As the questions continued he became more and more relaxed. I think that as it became apparent I would be one of those almost half who actually passed, he started to lower the evaluator-to-evaluatee barrier. Lieutenant Wortham became Skip. How can any adult go by Skip? He was still Lieutenant Wortham to me.

The aircraft was finally fueled and I did a quick exterior preflight inspection and hopped into the front seat. As Wortham plugged his helmet into the aircraft interphone system I could hear he was humming to himself. I clenched my right fist above my head and moved it toward my open left palm. The navy linesman nodded and connected the external air cart to the aircraft. A few button presses later both engines were cooking with gas. I held both hands above me, resting on the metal bar lining the front of the canopy windshield. From the two mirrors I could see Wortham was doing the same in the back seat. With this precaution taken, the linesman scurried underneath the aircraft to disconnect the external air cart and remove the wheel chocks.

After a short taxi, Mugu Tower cleared us for takeoff and we both lowered our canopies. Although we sat in tandem, one pilot in front and the other in back, we had separate canopies which were hinged behind our heads and pivoted forward, to the closed position. The canopy unsafe light extinguished and my master caution panel was blank, no red or amber lights. I pushed both throttles to their first forward stop and watched the gauges for both spin clockwise to 100% rpm and 600°C exhaust gas temperature. Satisfied, I released the wheel brakes and pushed the throttles all the way forward to light the afterburners. With a kick in the rear we leapt forward.

Decision speed, the speed before which we would abort and after which we would continue the takeoff, was around 115 knots, depending on the conditions. The airplane could lose an engine at that speed and still accelerate to around 160 knots to allow rotation and climb out. I suffered hundreds of engine failures in the simulator but the nearest thing in an airplane I had seen was an afterburner nozzle failing full open, reducing the engine to zero thrust. We didn't practice engine failures on takeoff in the airplane; that would be very risky sitting in front of two afterburners. But I digress.

That's where we were that day: half the runway behind us, half in front; the AB shooting two orange flames of thrust behind us; 100 knots of speed with the indicator winding itself higher nicely, and a black dart heading right at us. The shadowy blur shot by on my left, just missing the canopy. The next thing I saw was a huge ball of fire shooting in front of the aircraft and then the instrument panel lit up like a Christmas tree. The loud explosion was replaced by an urgent "beep, beep, beep" in my headphones, which was the aircraft's way of telling me it was very unhappy.

"What was that?" Wortham asked from the back seat.

"I think it was a duck," I said. I pulled back on the stick and pointed the nose skyward. I slapped the landing gear handle and was happy to see the three green lights extinguish and the red light in the gear handle go out; our gear was safely retracted. With the reduced drag the airplane climbed nicely.

"Are you sure it was a duck?"

"No, sir. But it looked like a duck."

"Well," he said, "keep flying." We had 190 knots in no time; I moved the flap handle up.

"Willy Two One," I pressed the switch on the right throttle while trying to keep my steeley aviator's voice calm and, well, steeley. "Declaring an emergency, one engine shut down, request wide right downwind pattern for immediate landing. Roll the trucks."

"Approved as requested," the tower answered, "you can pull up closed if you want." A closed traffic pattern would get us on the ground sooner, I knew, but did I really want to subject the airplane to that with one engine turning and the other on fire? Or was it?

"Left engine is seized," I heard from the back seat. Sure enough, it was at zero percent and the left system hydraulics were at zero as well. We were lucky we got the landing gear retracted.

"No thanks," I answered. "We need the pattern for the landing gear." It probably took about ten minutes to fly that wide pattern. We extended the landing gear using the emergency system and talked about ejection. With one engine left the procedure would be to eject if that one failed. The airplane could not be landed without engine power; it could not be "dead sticked." The flight controls were hydraulically powered and with both engines shutdown the aircraft could not be controlled. Even if both engines were windmilling, spinning in the wind, once decelerated below 190 knots the aircraft could not be controlled.

As I banked right and looked up to see the runway, my gaze took in the sparsely populated farm lands and more developed towns. Ejection would not be a problem. But where would the aircraft end up? Strawberry field or shopping mall? I was determined to land.

Lined up on final everything was pretty calm and quiet. I looked at the three landing gear lights and the flap indicator over and over, they were okay. Airspeed? Okay. Engines, well, engine. Okay as well. "Maybe we lost a bearing," I heard from the back seat.

"It was a duck," I said.

"It wasn't a duck."

The landing was uneventful, just like every single-engine landing in the simulator. Two months previous, when I had the AB nozzle failure, the other three airplanes gave me priority and I led the group back. That time, the six other pilots watching my every move was more stressful than this landing. This time, it was, well, duck soup.

I considered holding the nose up for some steeley-eyed fighter pilot aero braking, but then thought better of it. "Get the airplane stopped," I said to myself. The fire trucks were waiting at the end of the runway. I pulled off and came to a stop. We both popped our canopies and dropped our oxygen masks. The smell was overpowering.

"Roast duck," I heard from the back seat.

"Yeah." They towed us back to base operations, us two pilots sitting in a Navy jeep behind the broken bird and a procession of fire vehicles. Of course we had collected a crowd by this time; if the entire base didn't see the fireball on takeoff, they were sure to have seen the black plume of smoke as we limped back to land.

A gaggle of Naval aviators — Air Force pilots congregate in "flights" while the swabbies collect in gaggles — waited for us just to talk and second-guess. "Why didn't you pull up to a tight pattern to get the thing back on the ground as soon as possible?"

"I only had one engine left," I said confidently, "I wasn't about to subject it to any G-forces. Besides, I needed the time to emergency extend the gear."

They were not impressed. "That's not how we do it in the Navy."

Lieutenant Wortham called back to the base and was told two solo birds were headed our way so we could take one back. We had a few hours to hang out at the Officer's Club. Wortham was worried about walking around base hatless, his pristine flight cap was sitting on his desk back in Arizona. I took my hat off and tucked it into my pants pocket.

"Maybe we can fool these Navy toads into thinking we Air Force guys are too cool for hats."

Wortham smiled for the first time that day. "Naval aviators," I continued, "they would be dumb enough to pull up closed with an engine on fire and about to seize."

He slapped me on the back. "Damned straight," he said, "fly the airplane first."

"Yes, sir." I said.

"Call me Skip." We got our rescue bird, flew home, and I walked into the traditional Gombey post incident greeting. All twenty of them were standing at attention with marshmallows on sticks, waiting to be roasted over an open fire. "Oh," they said as one, "he survived," and walked away as if disappointed.

"Haskel!" I heard from the flight commander's office.

Flight Lessons 1: Basic Flight

"Sir?" I said after marching in and saluting.

"Everybody's dream sheet has been sent except yours. I need it now."

I returned to my desk, took the dream sheet and crossed the F-A-R section out with a big "X" – I wasn't going to fly a fighter. I returned to Major Curtis' office and handed him the form.

"Your engine failure got anything to do with this, Eddie?"

It didn't, but maybe that was a graceful way out of the situation. "Maybe," I said.

"Okay," he said. "But you know this puts you at the mercy of the personnel weenies."

"Yes, sir" I said. "I'll take my chances."

V_1 (Decision Speed)

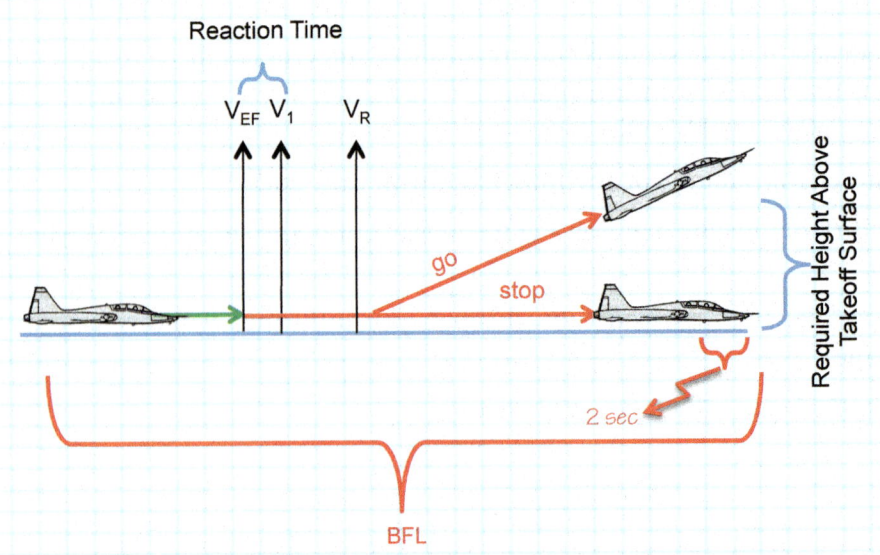

Takeoff is continuing on all engines or one engine failed

At V_1 — Abort is in progress (idle, speed brakes, wheel brakes)

[14 CFR 1.1] V_1 means the maximum speed in the takeoff at which the pilot must take the first action (e.g., apply brakes, reduce thrust, deploy speed brakes) to stop the airplane within the accelerate-stop distance. V_1 also means the minimum speed in the takeoff, following a failure of the critical engine at V_{EF}, at which point the pilot can continue the takeoff and achieve the required height above the takeoff surface within the takeoff distance.

[14 CFR 25.107] a) V_1 must be established in relation to V_{EF} as follows:

(1) V_{EF} is the calibrated airspeed at which the critical engine is assumed to fail. V_{EF} must be selected by the applicant, but may not be less than V_{MCG} determined under § 25.149(e).

(2) V_1, in terms of calibrated airspeed, is selected by the applicant; however, V_1 may not be less than V_{EF} plus the speed gained with critical engine inoperative during the time interval between the instant at which the critical engine is failed, and the instant at which the pilot recognizes and reacts to the engine failure, as indicated by the pilot's initiation of the first action.

[14 CFR 25.109] (a) A distance equivalent to 2 seconds at V_1 [will be added to distances needed to continue or reject the takeoff to determine accelerate-stop distance].

Flight Lessons 1: Basic Flight

Going Forward

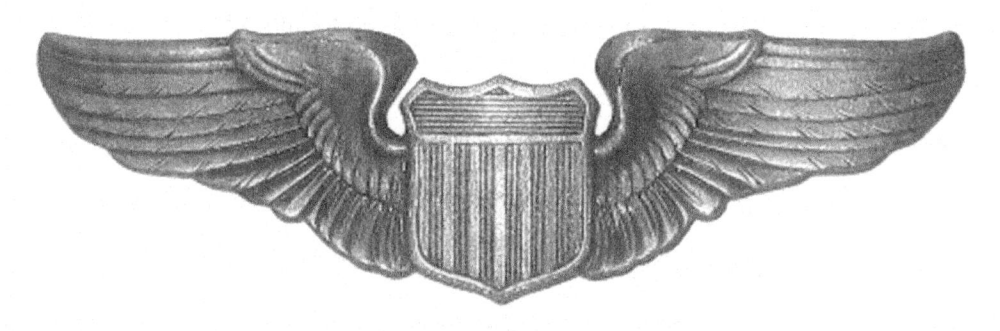

USAF Pilot's Wings (Eddie's Collection)

Gombey lost another stud to an instrument check ride, our sister flight lost two. As we became the senior class on base the wing commander notified us that any studs with mustaches would not get their graduation pictures in the base paper. The entire class grew mustaches as a result. Only Kevin Davies appeared to be clean-shaven, though it wasn't for a lack of trying. Williams Air Force Base Undergraduate Pilot Training Class 80-02 started with 77 studs and ended up with 44 brand new Air Force pilots. That was on November 28th, 1979. Marke Gibbs walked away from destroying a perfectly good T-38 with only injured pride and a blemish in his otherwise perfect grade book. He was assigned to fly the A-10 Warthog, the only one awarded to our class. Kevin Davies struggled with his formation check and had his F-A-R status reduced and was given a C-141. He was ecstatic. I thought he purposefully blew the form check; he denied that. Me? That's a bit more complicated.

Three weeks prior to graduation our next-door neighbor, a T-38 instructor, was killed. "Gravity always wins," I told the lovely Mrs. Haskel, trying to make light of it. Four pilots died in the T-38 that year. As many died in the F-4 Phantom. By then I had already had my last flight of pilot training and it seemed to be someone else's problem, depending on the assignment process roll of the dice.

Two weeks prior to graduation a brand new security police officer discovered seven aircraft guards huddled around a B-52 bomber in northern Maine smoking marijuana. In the investigation that followed, half the base's security guards were thrown out as were about a third of the pilots and navigators. One week prior to graduation, every pilot training stud without an assignment got orders to report to Loring Air Force Base to fly either the

B-52 bomber or the KC-135A tanker. It seemed I was destined to be a tanker pilot.

On graduation night Kevin, Marke, and I managed to avoid Harvey and got a table with Don Chesney, our T-37 IP. He gave us each something we had written six months ago.

"What I want"

Davies: To be a professional aviator.

Gibbs: To kill people and break things for God and country.

Haskel: The meaning of it all.

"I think at least two of you are probably going to get what you want," he said after our first beer. "Kevin, I had you spotted as a future airline pilot on day one. Marke, I didn't guess the A-10, but it wasn't a surprise. Eddie, I thought for sure you were coming back as an IP. But I guess that wasn't what you wanted."

Of the twenty-one Gombey graduates I think the only guys who were really unhappy were those going to the B-52 and C-130. I really didn't know what to expect with the tanker.

"At least its safer than an F-4," I said to the lovely Mrs. Haskel.

"This is as far as we can get from Hawaii and still be in the country," she said. "But maybe you will find your answer there."

Could the meaning of it all be found in the northern forests of Maine?

20: SERE
Fairchild Air Force Base, Spokane, Washington
1980

"Cool School" (USAF Photo)

"Lieutenants Haskel and Honable," the gruff sergeant bellowed from the front of the bus, "you're next."

Mark and I shuffled forward, our self-made snowshoes in one arm and survival kits in the other. Second lieutenant Mark Honable was a few months senior to me and had already graduated KC-135 Combat Crew Training School (CCTS), so in many ways he was senior to me. But as a navigator he automatically deferred to me, a brand new pilot. CCTS was still a month in my future and I had never flown the KC-135 tanker, but he had his second-class status beaten in to him. I took the lead at the front of the bus.

"You got ten minutes," the sergeant said, "the time starts the second your foot hits the ground and if you get caught before sunup it is an automatic fail. You two got that?"

"Yes, sergeant."

It was 3 a.m. in January on a mountain just northwest of Spokane. I made a note of the minute hand on my watch and as soon as Mark's feet hit the ground we ran across the road. The bus pulled away; when its taillights disappeared the world turned black. We sat in our ditch and waited for the pupils in our eyes to dilate. As the starlight began to illuminate the trees and general silhouette of the mountain, we gave each other a nod and were off.

Along that highway another fifty sets of pilots, navigators, flight engineers, loadmasters, and all manner of Air Force flight crewmembers were scattered, like pumpkin seeds in a neatly manicured garden row. Unlike those fruits to be, we seeds scattered like the wind, knowing the bad guys would soon be in hot pursuit. We made it about two minutes before it became obvious we needed our snowshoes. They were the survival school's only concession to the conditions. They normally dropped you in the middle of nowhere with your survival kit and parachute. It had snowed, non-stop, for a week and they gave us a day in class to turn our parachutes and a collections of branches and twigs into snowshoes. To my surprise, they worked. We slogged our way to a ravine of some sort, the better to remain unseen, and tied our oversized galoshes onto our feet. It was cold, in the low twenties. But sitting in our hole in the ground it was actually comfortable and for a moment I considered taking a nap.

"Ten minutes," Mark said. I looked down on my government-issued watch.

"You think they are really going to chase us in the dark?" I asked.

"No," he said, "but I think most predators aim for the weakest of the herd so we are better off being in front. You got the chart?"

I handed our shared chart over and watched him as he studied the contour of the mountain and a guessed drop off point. I thanked the Gods of the alphabet that placed a navigator with an H-name next to a pilot with the same. I didn't think he was thanking any deities when he found he was paired with me. "What, a stinking copilot?"

I hadn't yet accepted the fact I was no longer a pilot, after only recently earning my military pilot's wings. I knew that was my fate: KC-135A tanker copilot. But it hadn't sunk in yet. But Mark, the first real navigator I was ever to know, didn't hold me in high regard.

"There," he said, pointing to a gully in the map. "We've got a long way to go, ten miles at least."

It was probably half that as the crow flies, but there was a steep hill devoid of vegetation just prior to the rescue point. The bad guys were sure to be on the

Flight Lessons 1: Basic Flight

ridges looking for us and we would have to go the long way around. I pulled out the compass the school had issued us when we started training.

"Put that thing away," Mark said, "unless you want to get us lost."

"A navigator who doesn't like compasses," I said, "that can't be right."

"Trust me, I was an Eagle Scout," he said. Mark oriented the chart with the ground around us and drew a line with his hand towards a mountain peak. "See that peak?" he asked. I nodded. "We need to head in that direction, I'll do point. You follow and look at that Cracker Jack toy and let me know what our heading is along the way."

Mark set out and I followed. While we couldn't walk a perfectly straight line, it was close. The compass started out at north-north-east, 030 degrees. The next time I looked it was 090. And then 330. By the time we got to the peak, the compass was reading full south, 180.

"What a piece of junk," I said.

"What did you expect?" Mark said, "you are on a mountain made of ferrous rock."

"Why did we spend two weeks learning to use it and that chart?"

"The chart," Mark said, "the chart is worth its weight in gold. The compass is useless. It's no wonder you pilots can't fly without navigators."

"What have you got against pilots?"

"Nothing," he said. "It's copilots I got a problem with."

"What have you got against copilots?"

"You flown the tanker yet?"

"No."

"Then you will find out." Mark started off in a direction of his choosing. I was obviously no longer the lead dog in our twosome. "All the copilots in school couldn't keep the airplane right side up. The instructors called it Dutch Roll. I called it a death wish."

I put the compass away and let the subject drop. Dutch roll was a chapter in an aero textbook to me, nothing more. We navigated point-to-point, trying to keep in the wooded areas to avoid detection as well as the deepest snow cover. Mark led the way for the first two hours and appeared ready to keep on going.

"Wait," I whispered, pulling his shoulder back. We knelt into the snow. The only sound was a rustle of the branches overhead and a faint caw of a bird in the distance. I pointed back to ground we had already covered.

"See um," he said. "they are headed away from us." The bad guys were dressed in white snow fatigues and black berets. It was the line of three berets against the snow that caught my attention. Mark and I were in our green flight suits, easy targets. We removed all external insignia except our rank, which the school insisted we keep.

"I think we outpaced them," I said. "How about we roll the dice and get even further ahead?"

SERE School Student (Defense.gov Photo)

"What are you thinking?"

I pointed down a steep slope that was free of the deep snow and was in the direction we were headed. If we didn't kill ourselves barreling down it, we could save three or four hours plodding around it. "We are all ending up in POW camp no matter what we do," I said. "Nobody is going to follow us down this slope. Besides, we were probably the only ones who didn't get suckered into going in circles following their compasses so all the bad guys are behind us. You just run down the mountain as fast as you can, if you trip just roll sideways and the snow eventually brakes you to a stop. We end up at the rendezvous point first, get a gold star for effort and a cup of hot coffee while the rest of the chumps try not to twist their ankles in snowshoes."

Mark thought for a bit, looking once behind us to the bad guys and twice

Flight Lessons 1: Basic Flight

down the incline. "About twenty, thirty degrees," he said.

"At the most," I said.

The circling bird flew on and the only sound left was the wind in the trees. The bad guys were gone from sight. "Race you down," he said. Before I could respond he was off, straight down the mountain in the middle of a clearing, violating every rule in the escape and evasion handbook.

Mark is five-seven at the most and his backpack was almost longer than his torso. With the limbs attached to my six-foot frame I was past him in a second and kept the lead until I tripped. I rolled with the hill and seemed to accelerate, listening to the thump-a, thump-a of my backpack alternating with my face pounding into the snow, accentuated by his laughter. It would have made a good study in the Doppler effect, that laughter. I could almost track his overtake by sound alone. By the time I came to a stop we were both at the bottom of the hill, not a soul in sight.

I brushed the snow off my flight suit, out of my hair, and spat what I hoped was snow from my mouth. I walked the few yards to Mark, not a scratch on him, where his cheek-to-cheek grin revealed all before I caught sight of the map he was holding. "We are here," he said, pointing. "We'll be at the rendezvous point in an hour." He looked up to the sun. "It's not even noon yet."

I looked at my watch, it was 11:15. "How'd you get that from the sun, it isn't even close to the top of its arc yet."

"It won't get much higher at this latitude in winter," he said. We walked on, forgetting to stick to the tree line. I thought about the latitude, maybe forty-six or forty-seven degrees north. Yes, I knew the sun doesn't get as high in the sky in the wintertime and I reasoned the further north you were the further south that arc would be. As an engineer I should have a pretty good understanding of the geometry involved and as a pilot I could benefit from it. But it was knowledge I was lacking.

"You know how early deep water sailors could judge latitude?" Mark asked, as if reading my mind. "What was the first piece of machinery that made that possible?"

"The sextant," I answered, knowing I was right.

"Before that," he said.

I looked up at the sun and the shadows the trees were casting. I rechecked my watch and noted it was noon, straight-up. Shadows at noon. I knew that ancient Egyptians figured the circumference of the earth within a few percent by placing a stick vertical to the ground at noon on the equator and another five-hundred miles away. The stick further north cast a shadow. But it only worked at noon.

"A clock," I guessed.

Mark smiled. "I guess not all copilots are dumb after all."

He explained that sea going captains measured the length of each day from the sun's highest point in the sky from one day to the next. With an accurate clock they could determine their latitude since the day's length varied with the distance from the equator. "They needed a good clock to do that," Mark explained, "it wasn't possible until the British made the first accurate clock."

"What about longitude," I asked.

"You needed a second clock to do that," he said. "You kept one clock set to your departure port and updated the second every local noon. The time difference gave you your longitude. If you lost an hour that would be one-twenty-fourth of the globe, so . . ."

"Fifteen degrees of longitude," I said.

"You are too smart to be a copilot," Mark said, "you should have been a nav."

"I'll take that as a compliment."

"It was."

We talked easily and almost forgot the first "E" in our school's name: Survival, Evasion, Resistance & Escape, or SERE.

We walked into the rescue point where the bad guys sat around a fire, drinking coffee and chatting over a 30-pack of donuts. They looked up at us, dirty, disheveled, but both beaming with our accomplishment.

"What in the hell," one of them said.

"Well that's a school record," another said. There were handshakes all around and we each got our own cups of coffee and share of the donuts. I had three.

"You two sirs relax," the top sergeant said, "you've got nothing to do for another six hours I bet. But you know you are both headed to POW camp. Part of the program."

We suspended our talk of navigation theory and found a comfortable corner of the tent for naps. At one point I heard an instructor ask if that was allowed under our training rules. "Relax," another said, "there's gotta be some

Flight Lessons 1: Basic Flight

kind of reward for being first. Besides, they aren't going to get much sleep in the next two days."

I slept soundly until I felt my arms tugged upwards and then a quick kick in the pants. "On your feet, animal."

I was blindfolded and tossed into a truck with forty other animals. The next two days were a nightmare. I spent most of my time in solitary for some reason and I earned more than my share of beatings. I think that may have been due to my particular fondness for the "R" in SERE, resistance. The worst of the bunch came when an interrogator asked me what I was doing deep inside his country, "Perhaps you are planning a little espionage. What is it you American pig are trying to learn here?"

"The meaning of it all," I said with a grin. I think the grin is what did it. After that beating I told the senior POW that the accommodations no longer suited me and I thought it would be best if I left. He nodded and wished me luck. I managed to escape, got recaptured an hour later, shackled, beaten some more, and dragged back to the prison camp and made a demoralizing spectacle in front of my fellow POWs, ah, animals.

I won't go into any more detail. Not because it was traumatic, it really wasn't. Not because it was classified, the security clearances needed were minimal. But because keeping it a secret will save lives. Those who follow should get the benefit of the full experience.

They say the experience toughens you as a person and I suppose that is true. But it definitely leaves you a changed person. The day after the prison camp was liberated Mark and I got an award for setting the land speed record during the evasion and I got another one for the escape. He left for his base in North Dakota and I went to California for training and to confront the dreaded Dutch Roll.

Basic Navigation

Great Circle

[AFM 51-40, pg. 2-1]

For most navigational purposes, the earth is assumed to be a perfect sphere, although it is not. (There is a height variation of about 12 miles from the top of the tallest mountain to the bottom of the deepest point in the ocean.)

Measured at the equator, the earth is 6,887.91 nautical miles in diameter, while the polar diameter is 6,864.57 nautical miles.

A great circle is defined as a circle on the surface of a sphere whose center and radius are those of the sphere itself. From a pilot's perspective, a great circle is simply the shortest route between two points on the globe.

Latitude

The zero degree parallel of latitude is fixed by the laws of nature, it is the middle parallel. Sailors from the earliest days of navigation could gauge latitude by the length of the day or the height of the sun.

Longitude

The zero degree meridian of longitude is arbitrary and has moved several times in history until now.

[AFM 51-40, pg. 2-3]

There is not, as with latitude, a natural starting point for numbering, such as the equator. English speaking people chose the meridian through their principal observatory in Greenwich, England. Longitude is counted east and west from this meridian, through 180 degrees.

[AFM 51-40, pg. 2-3]

A system of coordinates has been developed to locate positions on the earth by means of imaginary reference lines. These lines are known as parallels of latitude and meridians of longitude. Once a day, the earth rotates on its north-south axis which is terminated by the two poles.

The equator is constructed at the midpoint of this axis at right angles to it. A great circle drawn through the poles is called a meridian, and an infinite number of great circles may be constructed in this manner.

Each meridian is divided into four quadrants by the equator and the poles. Since a circle is arbitrarily divided into 360 degrees, each of those quadrants therefore contains 90 degrees.

Flight Lessons 1: Basic Flight

Coordinates

Latitude is expressed in degrees up to 90, and longitude is expressed in degrees up to 180. The total number of degrees in any one circle cannot exceed 360. A degree (°) of arc may be subdivided into smaller units by dividing each degree into 60 minutes (') of arc. Each minute may be further subdivided into 60 seconds (") of arc. Measure may also be made, if desired, in degrees, minutes, and tenths of minutes. A position on the surface of the earth is expressed in terms of latitude and longitude. Latitude is expressed as being either north or south of the equator, and longitude as either east or west of the prime meridian.

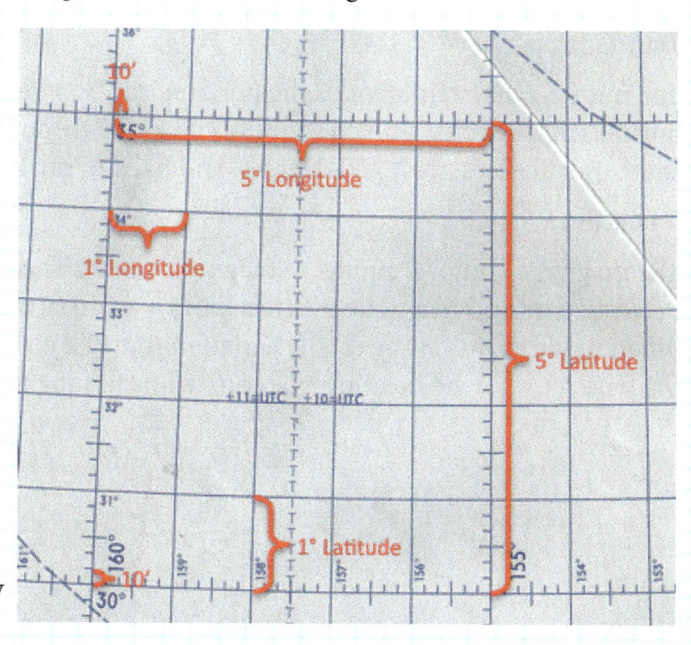

Direction [AFM 51-40, pg. 2-8]

The numerical system, divides the horizon into 360 degrees starting with north 000 degrees, south 180 degrees, west 270 degrees, and back to north.

The circle, called a compass rose, represents the horizon divided into 360 degrees. The nearly vertical lines in the illustration are meridians of position A passing through 000 degrees and 180 degrees of the compass rose.

Course is the intended horizontal direction of travel.

Heading is the horizontal direction in which an aircraft is pointed. Heading the actual orientation of the longitudinal axis of the aircraft at any instant, while course is the direction intended to be made good.

Track is the actual horizontal direction made by the aircraft over the earth.

Bearing is the horizontal direction of one terrestrial point from another.

True Course [AFM 51-40, pg. 2-5]

The numerical system divides the horizon into 360 degrees starting with north as 000 degrees, and continuing clockwise through east 090 degrees, south 180 degrees, west 270 degrees, and back to north.

Variation [AFM 51-37, pg. 1-13]

The magnetic compass points to magnetic north. The angular difference between true and magnetic north is known as variation and it changes for different locations on the earth. Variation must be considered when converting true course, true headings, or true winds to magnetic direction.

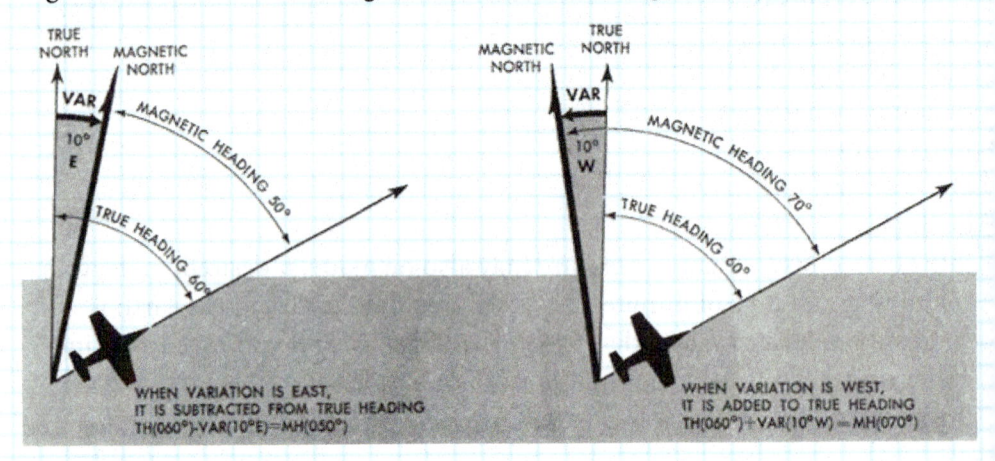

Conversion

Magnetic variation changes over time and can lead to great differences in true and magnetic courses throughout the world.

To convert: True + Variation = Magnetic

Where westerly variation is positive and easterly variation is negative.

Deviation [AFM 51-37, pg. 1-12]

Deviation [is] an error in compass indications caused by magnetic disturbances originating within the aircraft. The magnitude of deviation varies with operation of different electrical equipment. Periodically, the compass is checked and compensations are made to reduce the amount of deviation. Deviation errors remaining after the compass has been checked are recorded on a compass correction card in the cockpit. The STEER column on the compass correction card is the compass heading you should indicate to maintain the TO FLY magnetic heading.

21: Unstable Aircraft
Castle Air Force Base, Merced, California
1980

KC-135 with B-52 (USAF Photo)

After drinking from a fire hose for 48 weeks during undergraduate pilot training I was expecting more of the same at the Strategic Air Command's premier teaching facility at Castle Air Force Base in Merced, California. This was, after all, where nuclear deterrence starts, the home of Curtis LeMay and Slim Pickens' "noo-clee-ar combat, toe-to-toe with the Rooskies." Any thought of that disappeared on day one. It was to be a month of self-paced academics, a month of simulators, followed by a month of flying. As soon as you satisfied a specified minimum, you were free to go. But you couldn't start the next phase until everyone else was ready.

Before the week was out I had finished all the academics. Something wasn't right but nobody seemed to care that I had nothing to do, so the Lovely Mrs. Haskel and I hopped in the Camaro and spent two weeks in Napa Valley. Upon our return I discovered I was the "Academic Ace," having managed to pass every test without missing a question. As a reward, the school paired me with another copilot, the guy who finished last in academics, second lieutenant Laddy Olsen. Laddy was a charismatic sort, words came easily to him. He was destined to be a lifer on the Air Force weight control program, probably right at the limit for his six-foot-three frame, but he carried the pounds well.

Our instructor, Captain Walter Dillingham, introduced himself and insisted we call him Wally. He unveiled the plan for us, his first two-copilot set of students. Loring Air Force Base was short thirty copilots because of a drug bust. The system was surging to produce nothing but copilots for the foreseeable future. Laddy and I would trade seats in the simulator but take turns in the right seat in the airplane. The simulator would focus on basic procedures and instrument flying. After ten sorties in the sim, we would be turned loose on the airplane.

In many ways the simulator was easier to fly than the T-38. The tanker had an autopilot, a very good flight director, and redundant systems. I was pleased to get the thing on the ground on my first try and blurted out, "so what's the deal with Dutch roll?"

"The sim is nothing like the airplane," Wally answered. "Don't worry about it, everybody struggles with it until the light clicks."

"How do we get to that light?" I asked.

"You just have to struggle with it," he answered. "There's no other way."

"How long does it take?" Laddy asked.

"Don't know," Wally said. "Some guys get it after four or five flights, some take a year or two, some guys never get it."

For the first time in the KC-135 training program I was worried. What if I was one of those guys who never got it? The flight manual had a couple of paragraphs that didn't make any sense. The training guide made note of the KC-135's negative lateral stability, but offered little advice.

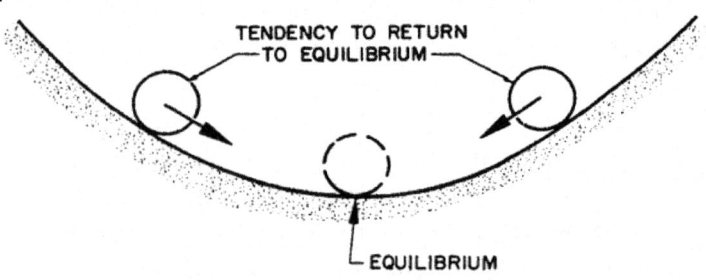

Most airplanes, the guide said, exhibit a positive lateral stability. Imagine a marble sitting in the bottom of a bowl that is pushed to one side. It will eventually settle down back in the bottom of the bowl. So too with an airplane; if a gust of wind or some other external force were to upset the bank angle, the airplane naturally seeks to level the wings. As Wilbur and Orville had intended. The KC-135A, however, had a negative lateral stability.

Back to the marble and the bowl, according to the guide. You flip the bowl upside-down and carefully place the marble right on top. If something were to upset the marble, it would fall to one side and keep going. That's what the KC-135A wing is like. "That's as clear as mud," I said to myself.

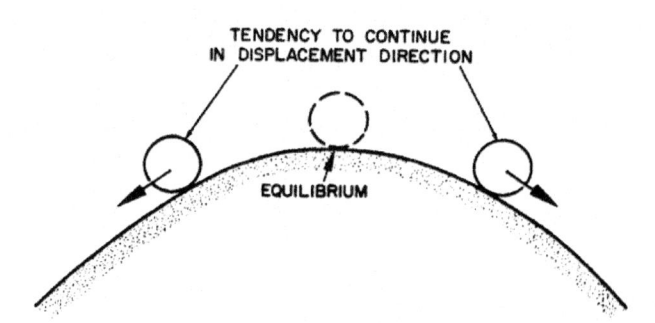

After a month of academics and three weeks of simulators, I longed for the flight line. While loitering around the squadron scheduling office I noticed each initial training sortie, marked "S-01," was circled in orange grease pencil. While considering that I tried to stay in the woodwork, not to draw attention to myself. The phone rang and the guy behind the desk picked it up.

"Yeah," he said, "tomorrow with a 0700 go. They should be in the pattern by noon." I scanned the sorties for the next day and spotted the 0700 go, it was another S-01.

"Lots of interest in an S-01," I said.

"Yeah," the captain said, "the alert facility is right off the end of the runway and the guys like to watch the Dutch Rolls. It's pretty entertaining."

The next day, about 1100, I was in the alert facility parking lot watching landings. The B-52's were what struck me at first. They landed in a crab, just like a T-38, but because of their extraordinary length and wingspan, they looked quite unnatural in the landing flare. The few KC-135s that landed seemed tame by comparison.

As I was watching I noticed a line of lawn chairs inside the barbed wire fence and a collection of bomber and tanker crews out for some sun and fun. Just as the crowd reached twenty or thirty all eyes were on final approach. In the distance I spotted a tanker rocking back and forth, a good thirty degrees of bank, left and right. As the airplane got closer to the ground the oscillations got worse and, from the perspective of a pilot who had never flown the airplane but was going to, it was terrifying.

The airplane descended lower and lower and the lawn chair crowd grew louder and louder. Finally, at not more than 50 feet, the engines roared and the airplane pulled up. The crowd cheered. It was madness.

"Hey," I heard from behind me. "What are you doing here?" It was a captain I had never met. He had pilot's wings and the patch of the local tanker squadron.

"Just watching S-01, sir."

"Oh," he said, "you in copilot school?"

"Yes, sir."

"Had your first flight yet?"

"No, sir."

"Don't let any of this freak you out," he said, "everyone who's flown the tanker has gone through this. Just hope your instructor let's you take it to the last second, like that last guy did. It's the only way to learn. I'm sure you will do fine."

I thanked the captain and got back into the Camaro, not reassured at all. Once back at the hotel I dug through my books in search of an answer. Only "Aerodynamics for Naval Aviators" was of any help.

"The static lateral stability of an airplane involves consideration of rolling moments due to sideslip. If an airplane has favorable rolling moment due to sideslip, a lateral displacement from wing level flight produces sideslip and the sideslip creates rolling moments tending to return the airplane to wing level flight. By this action, static lateral stability will be evident."

Left unsaid, of course, is what if an airplane does not have static lateral stability? With each passing simulator ride my apprehension increased. I found myself hanging around the squadron, hoping the aura of the more experienced pilots would instill in my hands the ability to conquer Dutch roll without "four or five flights" or even "a few years" of experience.

I found myself sitting at someone's desk with a pile of unread books sitting underneath. The title "Handling the Big Jets," caught my eye. It was written by D.P. Davies and seemed to focus on the difference between flying props and very large jets. On a page opposite the heading "Dutch roll" I found a diagram that explained the "why" behind a lack of static stability.

When a swept wing airplane yaws away from the relative wind, the effective aspect ratio of the wing away from the yaw increases. It becomes a more effective wing because the angle of the relative wind to the leading edge increases. That wing produces more lift, tending to roll the airplane into the yaw. The opposite wing's effective aspect ratio decreases because the angle of the relative wind to the leading edge is less. Less lift means that wing helps the roll into the yaw. So the airplane wants to roll in the direction of the yaw. But as soon as the vertical fin catches the relative wind the yawing motion reverses, which eventually reverses the rolling motion. If the airplane is well designed, all this dampens itself out.

"Positive Dutch roll is basically safe because the aeroplane, left alone, will either quickly or more slowly, finally bring itself under control." It seems airplanes either had positive Dutch roll stability by design or were equipped with yaw dampers to provide it electronically. Unsaid in "Handing the Big Jets," however, was the fact some Air Force airplanes had neither. The author did provide some advice for pilots saddled with a laterally unstable airplane:

"The control of a divergent dutch roll is not difficult so long as it is handled properly. Let us assume that your aeroplane develops a diverging dutch roll. The first thing to do is nothing — repeat nothing. Too many pilots have grabbed the aeroplane in a rush, done the wrong thing and made matters a lot worse. Don't worry about a few seconds delay because it won't get much worse in this time. Just watch the rolling motion and get the pattern fixed in your mind. Then, when you are good and ready, give one firm but gentle correction on the aileron control against the upcoming wing. Don't hold it on too long — just in and out — or you will spoil the effect. You have then, in one smooth controlled action, killed the biggest part of the roll. You will be left with a residual wriggle, which you can take out, still on ailerons alone, in your own time."

"Patience is the key," I said to myself.

S-01 began with Laddy Olsen in the right seat and Captain Dillingham in the left. The takeoff, climb, and rendezvous with the bomber were unspectacular. I wandered back to the boom pod to watch the student boom operator plug the bomber. After that the student navigator worried over his charts and sextant to fly us around the western half of the United States. We had been airborne for nearly four hours. Still not having actually flown the airplane, I came to the conclusion the tanker was going to be a boring airplane. All that changed when the student copilot flew our first approach.

Laddy had struggled with instrument approaches in the simulator but was doing a fine job in the airplane until he caught his first glimpse of the runway. At that point, the bank oscillations began and only got worse. Wally let him take it to about 200 hundred feet before saying, "Go around."

"As a wing comes up," Wally said, "bring it down with aileron only, but take out your correction immediately." That was no help. After three tries Wally tried something new. "Keep your hands on the yoke, I'll take care of the Dutch roll and you complete the landing."

Right around 100 feet Wally's hands were on the yoke from the left seat and with an imperceptible flick of his wrists the Dutch roll was gone. "See?"

"I think so," Laddy said. On the next approach it was obvious he did not.

"Okay Laddy," Wally said, "great job today. Don't be frustrated, you are well ahead of the curve. Good job, really. Now let's get Eddie in here." Laddy unstrapped from the right seat as I unstrapped from the jump seat. I lowered myself into the now vacant copilot's seat and was repulsed by the wetness of it. Laddy must have lost a gallon of sweat in the seat. I suppressed any urge to flee and strapped in. The instrument approach really was easier than the simulator and I was happy to see the needles centered when Wally said, "okay, let's go visual."

I looked up to see the runway, right where it was supposed to be. I felt the airplane yaw to the right and the right wing dip. I countered it with left aileron and was greeted with a new yaw to the left. For someone used to the nimble controls of a T-38 it was stomach churning. I dampened the oscillation slowly, just like D. P. Davies suggested. My bank never got out of control, but it still wasn't good enough to land.

"Go around," Wally said at about 50 feet. As I pushed all four throttles forward and raised the landing gear, Wally's critique began. "Very nice, Eddie. Laddy was a bit too quick with the corrections, you were a bit slow. Let's do that again." On the next approach Wally gave me the "keep your hands on the controls" routine. As the Dutch roll established itself and was a good fifteen degrees of right bank, Wally snapped the left aileron very quickly and the yoke ended up perfectly centered and all the Dutch roll was gone. "See?" he asked.

"Yes," I said. "I do see."

Flight Lessons 1: Basic Flight

"One firm, but gentle correction," I remembered from D. P. Davies. On the next approach, just as the Dutch roll started, I flicked the aileron and the Dutch roll was gone. I landed the airplane.

"Remarkable," Wally said. "Some guys are naturals. You are a natural. I think you were born to fly the tanker." That night, at the bar, Laddy was surrounded by five or six other S-01 victims describing my performance. As I joined the table all six looked at me. "What's the secret?"

"It's just like shifting gears on a motorcycle," I said. "You know your right hand is going to have to flick forward on the throttle and then back again as you release the clutch. After a while you realize all you have to do is flick your wrist in time with your left foot on the gearshift and left hand on the clutch. Easy."

"This isn't a motorcycle, Eddie."

"You just time the wing coming up," I said. "Just as it reaches the maximum bank, you quickly put in a little opposite aileron but take it out just as fast as you put it in."

"Okay," one of them said, "don't tell us."

Laddy figured it out on S-05 and I heard all but two of us copilots had it figured out by the end of the program. The slow learners got released to their bases with notes saying they needed more work. That would be a terrible way to get introduced into your first operational squadron: "Training wheels required."

The day before we graduated Wally handed me a phone directory with a paperclip on one page and the "Director, Tanker Assignments" number circled.

"I just got my next job," he said, "I will be in charge of tanker assignments. As soon as you get 1,000 hours, you give me a call. I'll make sure you get out of the tanker as soon as possible."

"The director of tanker assignments wants to get people out of the tanker?" I asked.

"No, not at all," he said. "Just you. You can do a lot more in another career track. You call me in two or three years."

The Lovely Mrs. Haskel and I stuffed everything we owned into our Camaro and set off for the northern tip of Maine. It was a drive of 3,376 miles to the east, and about thirty years backwards in time.

Stability

Static Stability [Hurt, pg. 244]

The static stability of a system is defined by the initial tendency to return to equilibrium conditions following some disturbance from equilibrium. Only its initial tendency is considered.

Imagine a marble in a bowl which is perfectly rounded, inside and out. The marble tends to gravitate to the bottom and stay there. If the marble is pushed to one side, it will roll back to the center. The marble is said to have positive static stability. Now consider the same marble atop the same bowl inverted. Even the slightest force will cause it to move away from the center. The marble is said to have negative static stability. A final case of static stability places our marble on a perfectly flat, frictionless surface in a vacuum. If you push the marble in any direction, it will move and continue to move.

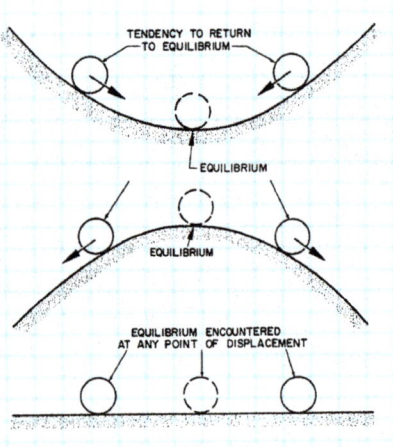

Directional Stability [Hurt, pg. 284]

The directional stability of an airplane involves moments about the vertical axis and their relationship with yaw or sideslip angle. The vertical tail is the primary source of directional stability for the airplane. When all other possibilities are exhausted, the required directional stability may be obtained by increases in tail area. The contribution of the wing to static stability is usually small. The swept wing provides a stable contribution depending on the amount of sweepback but the contribution is relatively small. The contribution of the fuselage and nacelles is of primary importance since these components furnish the greatest destabilizing influence.

Dynamic Stability [Hurt, pg. 246]

Dynamic stability concerns the resulting motion over a span of time. If the initial tendencies tend to decrease, the object is said to have positive dynamic stability. If they increase, it is negative dynamic stability. If they stay the same, of course, that is neutral dynamic stability.

Flight Lessons 1: Basic Flight

Dutch Roll

A Dutch roll is a combination of yawing and rolling motions where the rolling motion continuously reverses itself with less noticeable yaw moments unless the rolling is significant. It is better called "oscillatory stability." A straight winged airplane tends to roll as it is yawed because the inside wing has a lower effective aspect ratio and loses lift. The effect is made worse with a swept wing aircraft. The faster (outside) wing becomes less swept and generates increased lift at a constant incidence because of the increase in effective aspect ratio. (The projected span of that wing is increased.) The slower (inside) wing becomes even more swept and loses lift at a constant incidence for. This further unbalances the lift and the rolling tendency increased.

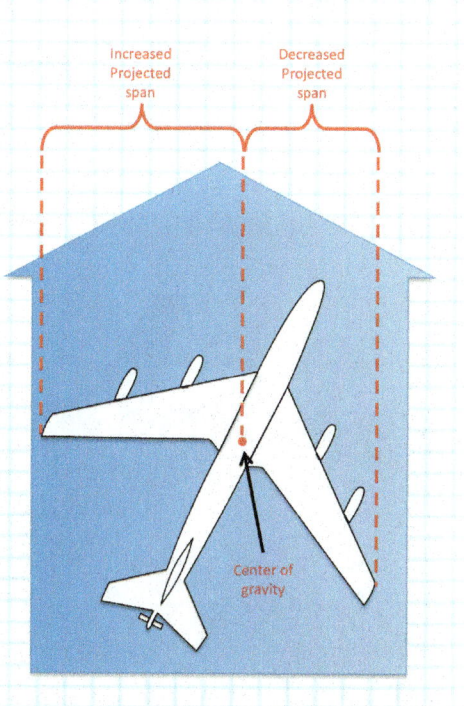

Manually Damping Dutch Roll [Davies, pg. 102]

The control of a divergent Dutch roll is not difficult so long as it is handled properly. Let us assume that your aeroplane develops a diverging Dutch roll. The first thing to do is nothing — repeat nothing. Too many pilots have grabbed the aeroplane in a rush, done the wrong thing and made matters a lot worse. Don't worry about a few seconds delay because it won't get much worse in this time. Just watch the rolling motion and get the pattern fixed in your mind. Then, when you are good and ready, give one firm but gentle correction on the aileron control against the upcoming wing. Don't hold it on too long — just in and out — or you will spoil the effect. You have then, in one smooth controlled action, killed the biggest part of the roll. You will be left with a residual wriggle, which you can take out, still on ailerons alone, in your own time.

Time the rise of a wing and estimate the amount of down force needed to arrest it. Then apply that amount of force quickly and remove the correction just as quickly, returning the yoke to its previous position.

22: Unstable Pilots
Loring Air Force Base, Limestone, Maine
1980

KC-135 Preflight (USAF Photo)

Loring sat at the northern tip of Maine, just three miles south of the Canadian border. It was a relic of the Cold War, built in a hurry when it was considered of vital national importance to have as many bombers stationed as close to Russia as possible. Most of the bomber bases in the Midwest are further north than Loring, but the Maine Congressional delegation made certain that fact remained a secret.

Loring was, however, closer to the Atlantic Ocean where a Russian submarine with submarine launched ballistic missiles was parked. None of our bombers were going to make it off the ground. The base was made irrelevant in the early seventies by those SLBM's and the Air Force tried unsuccessfully every year to close it. But Congress would not permit it. As a result, it was next to impossible to get orders out of Loring and only the dregs of each career field got sent there. The Lovely Mrs. Haskel and I arrived in May of 1980.

Flight Lessons 1: Basic Flight

Every Air Force officer has a boss and when arriving at a new base must report to that boss in an expeditious manner. I showed up at 0700 on a Monday morning, wearing my blue uniform, two gold bars, and shiny pilot's wings. The 407th Air Refueling Squadron sat in an abandoned hospital building parked in a corner of the heavily wooded base. It was a disheveled, bleak, gray building. Up three flights of stairs I found myself in the mission planning room, where sat a solitary captain. He was dressed in a flight suit, the "green bag," and wore navigator's wings with a star on top. That meant he had been a navigator for at least seven years. I greeted him with a smile and he returned a scowl that stopped me in my tracks. I managed to start moving again and couldn't help but notice his eyes following my every step. I bumped into another navigator, this one a first lieutenant wearing a smile. "Don't let him bother you," the newer nav said, "that's just T.C. He's that way. I'm Ben."

Lieutenant Ben Neavis explained that Captain T. C. Blow was non compos mentis and to ignore him. Many of the captains were prone to these kinds of quirks and it would be best if a new second lieutenant not engage others without some kind of sign it was safe to do so. He also explained that the squadron commander would seek me out when he was ready, he didn't react favorably to uninvited guests.

"This place is nuts," I said.

"See," he said, "you are getting the hang of it!"

My first flight was already on the boards, a week away. "Word to the wise," Ben said as he steered me out of the squadron. "Don't show up around here unless you need to. No sense providing the wolves any raw meat." I did as I was told and spent the next week getting settled and avoiding the squadron at all cost. I showed up at 0730 for the standard day-before-mission-planning-session to an empty mission planning room. Another copilot recognized my second lieutenant blank stare and guided me to the mail cabinet where I had my very own manila folder. "The navs usually do their flight log the day prior," he said, "they usually put it in the copilot's folder."

Sure enough, there it was. It was to be a standard training mission: we were to take off with our bomber, air refuel, and come home. I spent the next hour adding fuel computations to the navigator's work and completing a set of takeoff data. By 0930 the navigator and boom operator showed up and we three sat quietly. I didn't know Captain Fred Block or Sergeant Tom Parrish, but as a new guy that was expected. We were just missing our aircraft commander. "What's the AC like?" I asked.

"Major Harry S. Butters," Fred said. "Harry is a large man."

"A very large man," Sergeant Parrish said.

"With a large handle bar mustache and a large personality," Fred continued. "At any other base he would have been dismissed as a Vietnam War leftover with some kind of defect leaving him unsuitable for the airlines. At Loring, Major Harry S. Butters is allowed to live in his own world because he is at Loring and therefore irreplaceable."

"I see," I said. I didn't know if they were making sport of Harry or me.

Harry didn't enter the room, he made an entrance. Harry greeted everyone in sight with his deep, booming, baritone. "How's Crew S-105 this gorgeous summer day?"

"Okay," the other two said.

"Okay, sir," I said.

"A butter bar!" Harry was beside himself with joy. "A fresh block of clay ready for molding, welcome aboard!" Major Butters conducted a very thorough mission briefing and never failed to elaborate on any line in his mission planning checklist. The navigator and boom operator were resigned to the routine, it would seem this was the normal Major Butters show, not a matinée put on for my benefit. Finally, it came time to review the paperwork.

Harry breezed through the boom operator's weight and balance and the navigator's log. He looked at my fuel log with suspicion, running down the column of pencil numbers with the end of his silver Cross pen. Finally he pulled out a small electronic calculator. Not many people owned these gizmos. They were expensive and all they could do was add, subtract, multiply, and divide. A really good one might have a memory key. He sat back in his chair and punched in a few numbers. He looked at my log and punched in a few more. "Your log is off by a hundred pounds of fuel," he said, "not bad for a brown bar."

"How did you do that," I asked, "with just a few button pushes?"

"Ah," he said, "tricks of the trade, tricks of the trade. And I see here a complete set of takeoff data!" The other two snickered. Most copilots, I knew, left the climb gradient section blank when it didn't apply but I was still practicing each section and included it. Our takeoff path was divided into four segments, each with its own minimum. I thought we might have an issue like we

Flight Lessons 1: Basic Flight

did back in California but didn't anticipate below freezing temperatures in May. "You didn't reduce our weight, did you?" Harry asked.

"No sir, it is going to be pretty cold tomorrow."

"Repeat after me, boy," he said. "Climb gradient at Loring is not a problem."

"Climb gradient at Loring," I said, "is not a problem."

With that he got up, "that'll do it boys. See you at oh dark thirty."

The next morning, at 0430, we met in the squadron parking lot where a blue Air Force bus picked us up with our bomber crew. We made stops at the command post for our secrets, at the life support shop for our parachutes and helmets, at the weather shop for our weather, and finally to our aircraft. I sat in my seat and ran updated numbers for my takeoff data. The forecast was for 35 degrees Fahrenheit. It was actually in the twenties. The takeoff data form had about twenty entries, each from a chart or table in a book of aircraft performance. Some of the numbers came from one-page tables and were no-brainers. Some of the numbers required chasing through multiple pages of graphs, each line introducing a chance for error. The end result would tell us how to set our power and what speeds to fly for takeoff. The most important number was critical engine failure speed, the speed at which we could lose an engine and still make it off the ground. An error on that number could kill us. My first set of takeoff data took me an hour to produce. I was down to about fifteen minutes. A seasoned copilot could do a set in five.

The Strategic Air Command didn't trust copilots with the external preflight so I had the cockpit to myself until Harry was done outside. At last he lowered himself into the left seat and surveyed the realm of his kingdom. I offered my clipboard. "Here's your data, sir." Harry took the page and scanned the entries. He pulled out his trusty calculator, tapped a few keys, and smiled. "Looks good," he said, "I guess you are going to be okay after all."

The temperature was right at 25 degrees Fahrenheit, a cold day in May, even by Loring standards. The aircraft wasn't heated and wouldn't have any heat until we started the engines. I sat in the right seat with my parka, winter gloves, and wool hat. Harry was just in his flight suit and Nomex flight gloves. I read the checklist and he flipped the switches.

"No good," I heard from behind me. It was our crew chief standing at the crew entry ladder, just behind the pilot's seat. "Major we've got two heat carts on number three and she ain't budging."

"Well you got ten minutes my boy," Harry said, "you keep on her and we'll start the other three."

"We got a problem, sir?" I asked.

"Yeah," he answered, "the number three engine is frozen solid, won't spin at all. Must have got some water in the turbine. I had them put a heated air cart to her. Sometimes that works, sometimes it doesn't."

Soon we had engines one, two, and four running. On our aircraft interphone I heard the click-click of the crew chief plugging in with his headset. "She's frozen solid, sir. We are going to have to pull the airplane into a hangar."

"Don't bother," Harry said, "just disconnect all the ground gear, we are going with three."

"You got it, sir."

"What?" I couldn't believe it. "We can't do that."

"Sure we can," he said with a grin, "we always plan on losing an engine. That's why you spend all that time doing three-engine data."

"No sir," I said, "we plan on four engines for every takeoff until critical engine failure speed. The distance is based on accelerating to that point with four engines."

"We're going," Harry said with finality. 'Boomer, close the door."

"You're not going with me," I said, unstrapping my lap belt.

"Navigator," Harry said sternly over the interphone, "unholster your weapon. If the copilot leaves the aircraft, shoot him."

I looked at Captain Block as he looked at me, speechless. "You do what you have to do," I said, "I'm leaving."

Just then the crew chief shot up the crew entry ladder. "We got her, we got her! Give number three a try."

I heard the engine wind up. What could I do? I returned to my seat and we flew the mission. As I left the squadron that day, Fred saw me in the parking lot. "Welcome to Loring," he said, "there's no other place like it.

Flight Lessons 1: Basic Flight

Climb Performance

Force Analysis [ATCM 51-3, pg. 152]

If it is assumed that the aircraft is in a steady climb with essentially small inclination of the flight path, the summation of forces along the flight path resolves to the following: (Forces forward = Forces aft)

$T = D + W \sin \gamma$

Where:

T = thrust available, lbs.

D = drag, lbs.

W = weight, lbs.

γ ("gamma") = flight path inclination or angle of climb

This basic relationship neglects the inclination of thrust from the flight path, lift not equal to weight, subsequent change of induced drag, etc. However, this relationship defines the principal factors affecting climb performance.

$\sin \gamma = T - DW$

This relationship simply states that, for a given weight airplane, the angle of climb (γ) depends on the difference between thrust and drag (T - D), or excess thrust.

Best Angle of Climb Speed (V_x) [ATCM 51-3, pg. 152]

The maximum angle of climb occurs where (T-D) is at a maximum. For propeller powered airplanes, this occurs just above stall speed. The thrust curves for most jet aircraft show thrust is very nearly constant with speed. If the thrust available is essentially constant with speed, the maximum excess thrust and angle of climb will occur where the thrust required is at a minimum, $(L/D)_{MAX}$. Thus, for maximum steady-state angle of climb, the turbojet aircraft would be operated at the speed for $(L/D)_{MAX}$.

V_X Trade-off in a Jet

But there is a trade-off for a jet – you have to accelerate to L/D_{MAX} which gets you closer to the obstacle. The best speed in a jet turns out to be V_2.

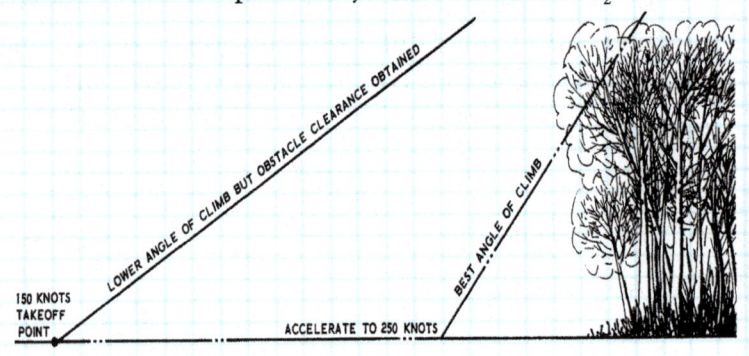

Best Rate of Climb Speed (V_Y)

[ATCM 51-3, pg. 152]

The vertical velocity of an airplane depends on the flight speed and the inclination of the flight path. In fact, the rate of climb is the vertical component of the flight path velocity. By [the diagram], the following relationship is developed:

$RC_{fpm} = 33000 (P_a - P_r) / W$

Where:

RC = rate of climb, fpm

P_a = power available, h.p.

P_r = power required, h.p.

W = weight, lbs.

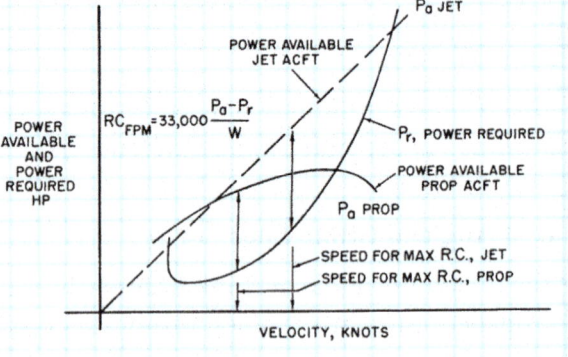

33000 is the factor converting horsepower to ft-lbs/min. The above relationship states that, for a given weight airplane, the rate of climb (RC) depends on the difference between the power available and the power required ($P_a - P_r$). The maximum rate of climb. By the previous equation for rate of climb, maximum rate would occur where there exists the greatest difference between power available and power required, i.e., maximum ($P_a - P_r$).

Unlike Best Angle of Climb Speed (V_X), there is no cut and dried way to find the best Rate of Climb Speed (V_Y) for a jet aircraft other than to flight test it.

TERPS

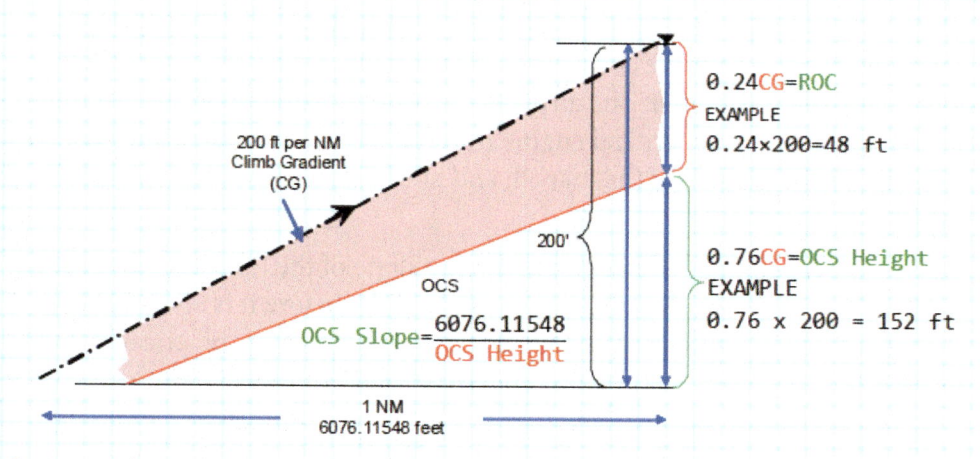

Figure: TERPS climb gradient diagram showing 200 ft per NM Climb Gradient (CG), OCS, with 0.24CG=ROC (example: 0.24×200=48 ft), 0.76CG=OCS Height (example: 0.76 × 200 = 152 ft), and OCS Slope = 6076.11548 / OCS Height over 1 NM (6076.11548 feet).

[FAA Order 8260.3B United States Standard for Terminal Instrument Procedures, paragraph 203.b]

The obstacle evaluation method for a climb segment is the application of a rising obstacle clearance surface (OCS) below the minimum climbing flight path. Whether the climb is for departure or missed approach is immaterial.

The vertical distance between the climbing flight path and the OCS is required obstacle clearance (ROC). ROC for a climbing segment is defined as ROC = 0.24 CG .

This concept is often called the 24% rule. Altitude gained is dependent on climb gradient (CG) expressed in feet per NM. The minimum ROC supplied by the 200 ft/NM CG is 48 ft/NM

(0.24 X 200 = 48). Since 48 of the 200 feet gained in 1 NM is ROC, the OCS height at that point must be 152 feet (200 − 48 = 152), or 76% of the CG (152 / 200 = 0.76).

The slope of a surface that rises 152 over 1 NM is 40 (6076.11548 / 152 = 39.97 = 40).

TERPS covers instrument procedures under normal conditions, that is without engine failures or other abnormalities.

Certification Climb Performance [14 CFR 25.111]

The takeoff path extends from a standing start to a point at which the airplane is 1,500' above the takeoff surface, or at which the transition from the takeoff to the en route configuration is completed and V_{FTO} is reached, whichever point is higher. The airplane must be accelerated on the ground to V_{EF}, at which point the critical engine must be made inoperative and remain inoperative for the rest of the takeoff; and after reaching V_{EF}, the airplane must be accelerated to V_2.

During the takeoff path determination: The slope of the takeoff path must be positive at each point; The airplane must reach V_2 before it is 35 feet above the takeoff surface and must continue at a speed as close as practical to, but not less than V_2, until it is 400 feet above the takeoff surface;

At each point along the takeoff path, starting at the point the airplane is 400' above the takeoff surface, the available gradient of climb may not be less than:

(i) 1.2 percent for two-engine airplanes;

(ii) 1.5 percent for three-engine airplanes;

(iii) 1.7 percent for four-engine airplanes.

The airplane configuration may not be changed, except for gear retraction and automatic propeller feathering, and no change in power or thrust that requires action by the pilot may be made until the airplane is 400' above the takeoff surface.

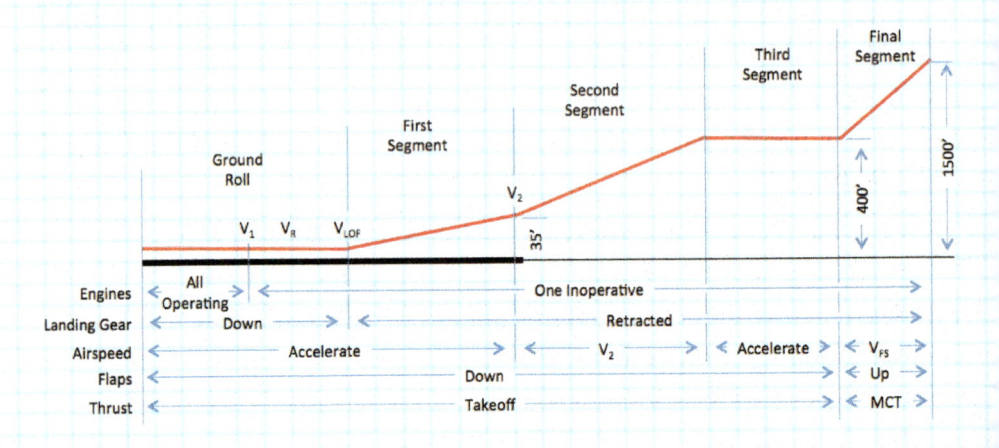

23: Lost

Air Refueling View of B-52 (USAF Photo)

After the first flight the squadron scheduled one more training sortie for a final evaluation prior to assigning me to a crew and certification as a bona fide SAC-trained killer. I heard the instructor, Captain Paul Craft, was one of the good ones. The day before the mission planning routine went well except for three math errors in navigator T. C. Blow's flight plan. I made the corrections without fuss, thinking that would be best.

Captain Blow stared at the log, expressionless and without complaint. As soon as Captain Craft walked into the room, Captain Blow erupted. "Who the hell are you," he said, "to change my flight log? You, a fucking brown bar! If you ever erase so much as a comma on any of my paperwork, I will rip your head off and shit down your lungs!" I stared at him for a second and shifted my gaze to the AC. Nothing in my 23 years of existence had prepared me to react intelligently to that.

"So I see we've all met," Captain Craft said, "we are going to get along just fine." He winked at me and slapped me on the back. "Nav, boomer, you got any questions?"

"No," TC said, still brooding.

The boom operator shrugged his shoulders. "Same old, same old."

"Fine," Captain Craft said. "I'll see everyone tomorrow at 0430."

We took off the next morning with another tanker a mile in trail and headed east over the Atlantic to wait for our two bombers. We got to the air refueling control point on time and set up an orbit. As soon as the bombers hit the air refueling initial point we turned to meet them. Our tankers did not have any sort of long-range navigation system other than the navigator, who controlled a needle on a sterile black compass card that the pilot attempted to keep centered.

"Nav," Paul said, "you sure about this heading?"

"Yeah."

"It's ten degrees further left than the last leg," he said.

"You want to turn ten right, pilot? You go right ahead." Paul turned ten degrees right. Once we rolled out on the correct heading I shifted my gaze and saw what I needed to see.

"Tally two bombers," I said, "eleven o'clock. They look close. Shouldn't we be turning?"

"Well turn," the navigator said, "geez."

"Turning." Paul whistled to himself and gave me a wink. My job was to keep an eye on the receivers in the turn but I lost sight of them. "They are going to be low, Eddie. We started our turn late."

"I got em," I said, "I think they are going to underrun us." And they did. It took about thirty minutes of S-turning by the bombers to finally join up. If it were a check ride, we would have busted as a crew. After the bombers finally got their fuel we headed back to base, using only the navigator's headings. It wasn't technically an "oceanic coast in," since we were flying "out and back." But we were over the ocean and we were coasting in. I pulled out my plotter and tuned in the nearest VOR, Halifax, Newfoundland. I plotted a line from the station and circled our position according to the ground station, not where we should have been. I handed the chart to the pilot. "Nav, let's come left a bit," Paul said.

"Sure," he said, "sounds good."

Paul winked and moved his heading bug to the left. "You're going to be fine, Eddie," he said. "Just remember to keep an eye on everyone and everything."

Flight Lessons 1: Basic Flight

Plotting

When is Plotting Required? [Advisory Circular 91-70A, ¶3-6.a.]

Turbojet Operations. All turbojet operations, where the route segment between the operational service volume of ICAO standard ground-based NAVAIDs exceeds 725 NM, require plotting procedures.

Turboprop Operations. All turboprop operations, where the route segment between the operational service volume of ICAO standard ground-based NAVAIDs exceeds 450 NM, require plotting procedures.

Where did these numbers come from? They appear to be arbitrary. The original version of this advisory circular came out September 6, 1994 and has the same 725 and 450 nautical mile requirements. There does not appear to be an ICAO specification, most international regulations recommend plotting procedures and North Atlantic regulations appear to assume they are being used.

Plotting Latitude Example

Locate the nearest five degree line in the general area of your point, e.g., 30° N. Locate the five degree line just above your latitude, e.g., 35° N.

If your chart has one degree markings locate the nearest degree below your point, otherwise count the degree lines, e.g., 33° N.

Count the tick marks between degree lines on the chart you are using. In our example there are six so we conclude each tick mark represents 10 minutes of latitude. Counting up four tick marks we identify 33°40' N latitude.

Notice that a line connecting 33°40' N 150° W and 33°40' N 160° W does not cross 33°40' N 155° W, it runs high. That's because the chart is a Lambert Conformal Projection which bends toward the poles. To get a more accurate position, we need to find the 33°40' point on the scale closest to our position.

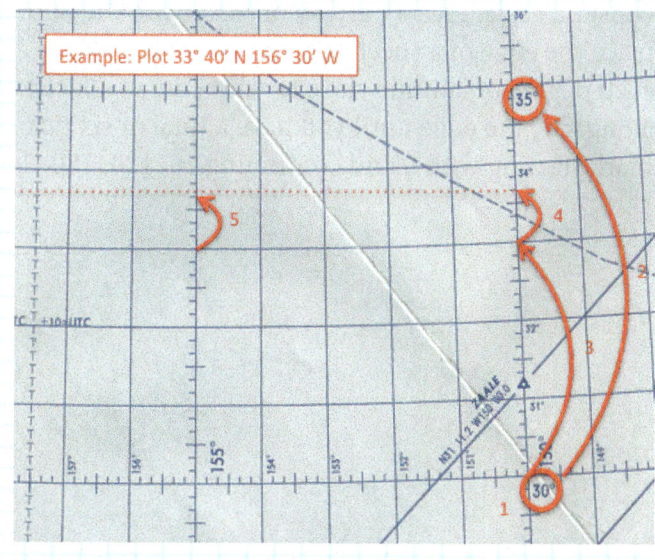

151

Plotting Longitude Example

When dealing with longitude, we look for the nearest five degree line under our desired position, e.g., 155° W. Then we look for the nearest five degree line greater than our desired position, e.g., 160° W. We can now locate the nearest degree under our position, e.g., 156° W. Counting the tick marks, we see there are six so 30' of longitude will be three greater. Unlike latitude, lines of longitude appear parallel between lines of latitude, so we can draw a line at 156°30' W between tick marks and it will remain accurate. We then transpose our mark identifying 33°40' N to this line of longitude and viola, we have our position.

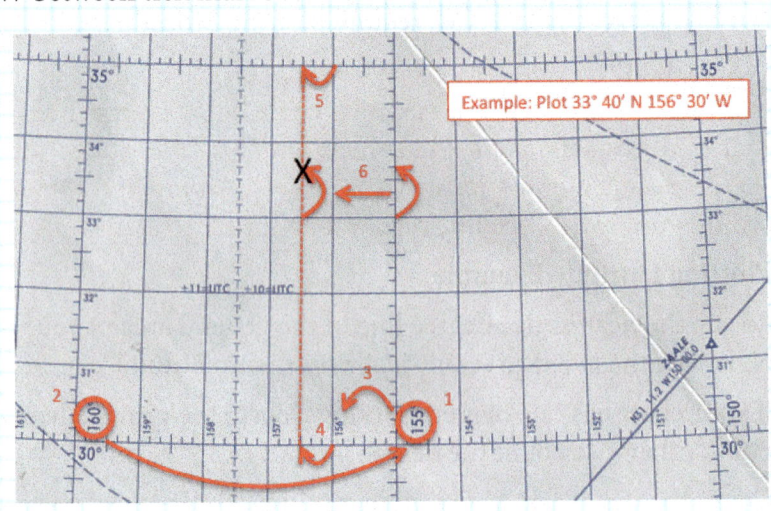

Plotting Distance

One of the disadvantages of the Lambert Conformal chart is the lack of a constant scale. Pick a parallel of latitude in the middle of your course and place the edge of a sheet of paper along side. Place a tick mark along side an even degree of latitude close to your course. Place tick marks every degree along side the edge until you have a total of six tick marks. Label each tick mark starting with 0 and continuing 60, 120, 180, 240, 300, and 360.

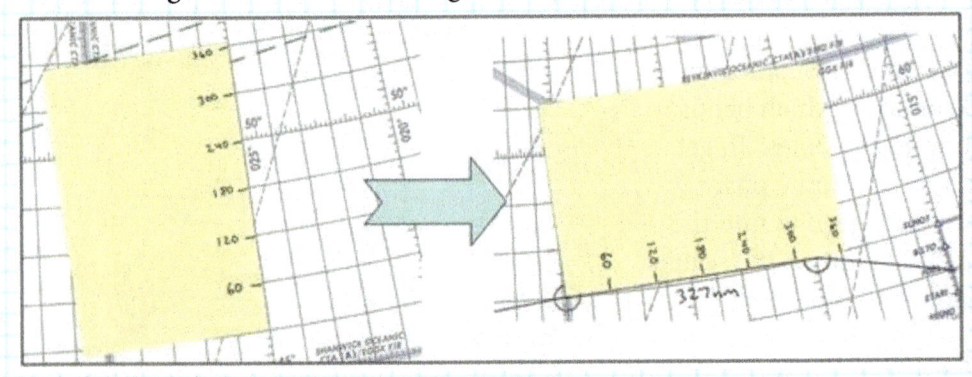

Flight Lessons 1: Basic Flight

Measuring True Course [AFM 51-40, Page 5-4.]

An angle is measured by placing the vertical line (that line containing the small hole) on a meridian, and aligning the base of the plotter with the line to be measured as shown in the illustrations. The angle measured is the angle between the meridian and the straight line.

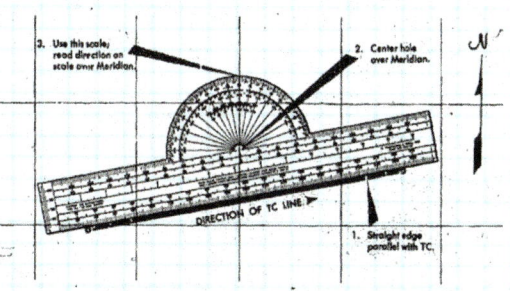

Converting True Course to Magnetic Course

To determine the magnetic course, you will need to add or subtract the variation: Look for the nearest lines of magnetic variation on the chart before and after the midpoint and interpolate if necessary. If the variation is West, add this value to the true course to determine magnetic course. If the variation is East, subtract this value from the true course to determine magnetic course:

TC + West Variation = MC

TC - East Variation = MC

Start / Mid / End Point Differences

Your plotting chart is based on a Lambert Conformal projection, the lines of longitude converge near the poles. Except for the equator, the lines of latitude are not straight, they curve toward the poles. The measurement of your true course depends on where you place the center of your plotter and it does make a difference. In the figure shown, flying from 33°N 160°W to 33°N 150°W should, intuitively, require a 090° true course. The actual course, however, depends on what you want: the starting, mid, or ending course.

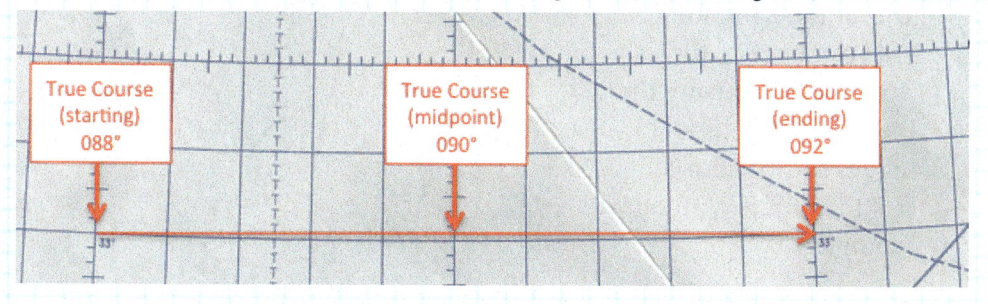

True Course (starting) 088°

True Course (midpoint) 090°

True Course (ending) 092°

153

VOR/DME Plotting

There are many ways to turn a VOR radial/dme into a latitude and longitude, the best of these may very well be inside your FMS. If you need to do this on a plotting chart, this method works well:

1. Place the plotter hole over the VOR in question and your pencil point in the hole to hold the plotter centered over the VOR. (CON in our example.)
2. Find the nearest line of variation. 6° West in our example.)
3. Rotate the edge of the plotter to 360° in the northern hemisphere, 180° in the southern hemisphere, and then rotate toward the magnetic pole by the amount of the variation. (Rotate 6° to the west, in our example.)
4. Move your pencil from the center hole to the straight line of the plotter that describes the line to the magnetic pole, move the plotter so the straight edge connects that point to the VOR. Draw a line with a flag on it from the VOR in the direction of the pole. Label this line "360° Mag" if you like. (In our example the flag points slightly left.
5. Now return the plotter center hole to the VOR and rotate it in relation to your 360° Mag line by the number of degrees in the VOR radial. Draw a line as you did earlier by placing a tick mark, moving the plotter, and drawing the line. (In our example the line is 15° clockwise from the Magnetic north line.)
6. Determine the distance using the Distance Measuring techniques shown earlier. Place a tick mark on the VOR line. (015°/85 DME in our example.)
7. The latitude and longitude can be read directly from the chart using the Plot a Position techniques shown above. (55°15'N 8°25'W in our example.)

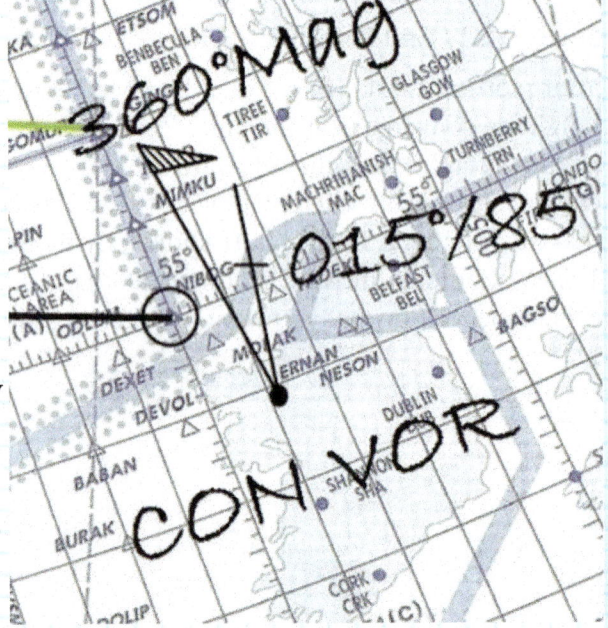

24: Found

Riding the Bomb (Dr. Strangelove - Public Domain)

"I heard you guys got lost last week," the squadron commander said while returning my salute. "That and you nearly blew the rendezvous." It was fortunate that I had been warned to never speak unless spoken to when being dressed down by Lieutenant Colonel Kendal Kong. It was also fortunate that I had been warned not to make sport of his unfortunate name. When I first saw his name on my orders to Loring I immediately thought of Major Kong riding the nuke down to his target in the sixties movie "Dr. Strangelove or How I Learned to Stop Worrying and Love the Bomb."

He was a dark haired caricature of a squadron commander, straight out of any 1960's Air Force training film, perhaps just like the movie. He was working on what would soon be a horseshoe of hair, the bald spot about a quarter of the eventual march from the front to the back of his scalp. I anticipated he would be an expert at one-half of the communication process, so I was prepared to be silent.

"The crew is the thing," he continued, his eyes circling every spot of the room except the spot where I happened to stand. "Not every navigator is at the top of his game all the time. When somebody screws the pooch doing something mission critical, the world doesn't fall apart because the crew picks up the pieces. You understand, lieutenant?"

"The crew is the thing," I said.

"Damned right," he said. He lifted his gaze to mine, for the first time. "So good job then. Have you met Rick Stiles yet?"

"No, sir."

"Well you are on his crew. I want you to prevent him from breaking any of my airplanes. First you got to pass EWO certification. I'm counting on you. Dismissed."

The squadron commander's office led out to a secretary's office, which led out to the squadron scheduling office. The scheduler sat behind a desk that faced a wall-to-wall grease board. On the left column there were names broken down into crews, starting with E-101 and the crew of four assigned to it. About halfway down I found S-105 composed of Stiles, Haskel, Neavis, and Ardmore. The top row had three months of days, looking one month back and two months forward. Scanning to the right I saw the next two days of my life. "EWO STUDY" on Tuesday and "EWO CERT" on Wednesday.

The next morning I reported to the command post at the appointed time and was ushered into a vault where stood a large table next to a map of the northern hemisphere. A captain with pilot's wings handed me four satchels, each marked "Top Secret."

"Your crew will probably show up a little later," Captain Black said. "This is just an annual for them so they probably don't need to study as much as you. You might as well get started."

I sat down and opened the first satchel and started reading. From the look of things, I was expected to become an expert in the U.S. – Soviet Union Cold War with an emphasis in delivering hydrogen bombs to various locations in Russia. As a tanker copilot, I knew without any reading I had a minor role to play in the ending of the world. But I had things to do and know, so I studied.

The navigator showed up after lunch, followed by the boom operator. "You can expect ten questions," Lieutenant Ben Neavis said, "unless we get the

Flight Lessons 1: Basic Flight

wing commander himself. He rarely does tanker certs, but I think he has to do one now and then just to prove he isn't focused only on the bomber."

I renewed my study on what appeared to be a tanker copilot's top concerns: initial takeoff performance, getting the cockpit sealed in case there was a nuclear blast, listening for a coded broadcast on a high frequency radio, and offloading fuel to a bomber. It didn't seem that tough. About 1500 the door to the vault opened and in walked the new boss, Captain Richard Stiles.

"So Eddie," he said while shaking my hand, "we finally get to meet." He was cast out of the movie Frankenstein, easily 6-foot, 7-inches and probably in the 250-pound weight class. "You got any questions?"

"What can I expect to be asked?" I said.

"Oh," he said. "I might as well let everyone know. Colonel Burkel is giving us our cert tomorrow." The navigator and boom operator groaned. "So we will probably fail," Rick said, "but we should at least go down swinging. So study hard. I'm getting some coffee."

Rick left the vault with Sergeant Hans Ardmore, the boom operator. Ben picked up a book from one of the satchels. "Shame to bust your first cert," he said, "but there's nothing to be done about it."

"Why is busting a foregone conclusion?" I asked.

"Because Colonel Burkel can't stand 'S' crews," he said, "and he eats new copilots for lunch." Ben explained that crew "S-105" was only an 'S' crew because we didn't have the minimum level of experience and accomplishments to be an 'E' crew. We were only standard. Expert crews got to be 'E' crews because each of their crewmembers had a minimum level of experience and had each passed all of their Emergency War Order certifications and airplane check rides without busts. Captain Stiles had several busts in both categories. Besides, he had a second lieutenant copilot. "Rotten luck," he added.

"What can he possibly ask a copilot that is so tough?" I said, perhaps to myself.

"You might as well get an easy question wrong," Rick said, reentering the vault with a cup of coffee and a stack of glazed donuts. "If you answer everything right he'll keep digging until he finds something you don't know. Last year he asked me a ton of navigator questions. I went down in flames. But you bust, they retrain you, and off you go. You only have to recertify to Captain Black so it really isn't a big deal."

"Except it goes on your permanent record," Ben said.

"It isn't so bad," Rick said. "They just want your butt on alert and nothing we do tomorrow is going to stop that."

Navigator questions? The toughest job the navigator had, I thought, was conducting the point parallel rendezvous with the bomber. The B-52 flew toward us while we orbited in a holding pattern. It was up to the navigator to ensure we had enough pattern offset so that when we rolled out from our turn we would do so right in front of the receiver. Knowing when to turn was the second mystery. I knew from my three months of training that offset and turn range were why we needed the navigator to go to war.

The offset was easy enough; it was just twice the turn radius. According to my aeronautical engineering text, radius was just the true airspeed squared divided by the quantity 11.26 times the tangent of the bank angle. With a book of math tables and using 25 degrees for the bank angle, I could approximate high altitude turn radius by squaring the true airspeed in nautical miles per minute and dividing by nine. So 420 KTAS is 7 nm/min, squared is 49, divided by 9 is about 5 and a half.

That was easy enough. But what about the turn range? The tanker and bomber had a closure rate of 840 knots! And during the tanker's turn the closure rate wasn't constant. No wonder the navigator was needed!

If I assumed the tanker rolled out exactly abeam where it initiated the turn, I no longer needed to consider the closure rate, only the bomber's speed. To find out how much territory the bomber covered while the tanker was in the turn, I needed only to find out how much territory the tanker covered in its half turn, their speeds were equal. The circumference of a circle is $2\pi r$ but I only wanted half the circle. So the distance of the half circle would be πr, or $\pi(5.5) = 17.28$ nm.

Of course this was the distance the bomber covered getting to the 3 nm roll out range. The offset range was the hypotenuse of this triangle, a larger number. With a little help of Pythagoras, I had my answer, turn range was the square root of the sum of (17.28 + 3) squared and (11) squared, 23 nautical miles.

So armed, the next day I waited my turn. Colonel Burkel was as intimidating as forecast and had already humiliated the pilot and navigator. The pilot missed a bit of breaking news about the Soviets on the Polish border.

"You have command of one of my crews," Burkel said. "They are looking to you to have all the answers. I am looking to you to at least have a goddamned clue about geopolitics! Do I make myself clear?"

"Yes sir," Rick said.

He asked Ben about aircraft endurance once refueling was complete. That question should have been sent my way.

"I'd ask the copilot," the nav said.

"You would ask a butter bar about something you should know?"

The nav stood at attention, in silence. Our crew was getting crushed. The cost of total failure would be a blemish on our permanent records: "failed nuclear certification."

Finally it was my turn. Rick introduced me as "our new superstar fresh out of copilot school, a distinguished graduate!" Burkel gave me the standard copilot questions and I gave him the standard copilot answers.

"Loo ten ant," he said while giving me a sideways glance, not bothering to pay complete attention to me standing at attention in front of a map of the Soviet Union, "let's say you get the thermal nuclear curtains installed, just the way you say you would. You pull out your standard issue flashlight to check your work and it doesn't work. Now what?"

"The curtains don't work?" I stammered.

"No, the flashlight!" He was yelling at me for some reason. "The thing Uncle Sam gave you on day one of pilot training and you've been using ever since. You click it on and there's nothing."

Now I knew where he was headed and I obliged him, disguising my joy at what was to come.

"Sir, I would borrow the navigator's."

"Very good," he said changing from anger to happiness in nothing-flat. "You look over and he's face down on his charts in a pool of blood."

"I would administer first aid, sir."

"He's dead."

"That's unfortunate, sir."

"It may be unfortunate for you, but he's dead." I stared into the wing commander's eyes and said nothing.

"The war effort means you are going to have to take over his duties, son." He let his words sink in. "You still have a point parallel rendezvous to perform or those bombers aren't going to get their gas and if they don't get their gas, my boys are going swimming and not bombing the way we promised Mother SAC they would. We can't have that, now can we? What is the purpose of our existence here?"

"Nuclear combat," I said, "toe-to-toe with the Rooskies."

He smiled. "Yes, so how we going to war if your navigator is dead."

"I will move his corpse aft and I will execute his duties."

"How the hell are you going to do that, son? You wouldn't know how to set up a point parallel if your life depended on it."

"I've seen a few," I said. "I believe I can pull one off."

Burkel chortled with glee. "Talk me through it, boy." Then, almost sotto voce, "this ought to be good!"

"Sir," I began, "first I will convert our indicated airspeed to true using the indicated temperature and my CPU-26 Alpha circular slide rule. The speed tends to range from 400 to 440. Using the formula in the "Aerodynamics for Pilots" manual I know that high altitude turn radius can be found by squaring the true airspeed in nautical miles per minute and dividing by nine. So 420 knots true is 7 miles per minute, squared is 49 and divided by 9 that comes to," I pretended to do the math in my head, though I had already figured it out the night before. "That comes to 5 point 44. Of course that is radius so we have to double it. So offset in that case would be 11 miles. Next we have to figure turn range."

I talked for about ten minutes. He just sat there and listened. He started to look a bit dejected. When I was done talking he almost didn't react. But then he recovered.

"Loo ten ant," he said, "sit down. We are done here." With that, he got up and left.

The rest of the crew just stared at me. Silently, we gathered our things, checked in our secrets, and we too left. The next day we found out we passed and the squadron was buzzing with the play-by-play. The next week we were on alert.

Turn Performance

Mathematical Proof

[ATCM 51-3, pg. 178]

The horizontal component of lift will equal the centrifugal force of steady, turning flight. This fact allows development of the following relationships of turning performance:

Turn radius

$$r = \frac{V^2}{11.26 \tan \theta}$$

Where:

r = turn radius, ft

V = velocity, knots (TAS)

θ = bank angle, degrees

Turn rate

$$ROT = \frac{1091 \tan \theta}{V}$$

Where:

ROT = rate of turn, degrees per second

V = velocity, knots (TAS)

θ = bank angle, degrees

Rules of Thumb

A standard rate of turn is 360°/2 minutes, or 3°/second. You can solve the radius and equation formulas to determine that a standard rate turn with less than 25° bank is only possible below 170 knots TAS. And:

A standard rate turn is possible up to 170 knots TAS and has a radius is equal to nm/min divided by 3.

A 25° bank angle turn will be needed above 170 knots TAS and has a radius equal to (nm/min)² divided by 9.

James Albright

[ATCM 51-3, figure 2.29]

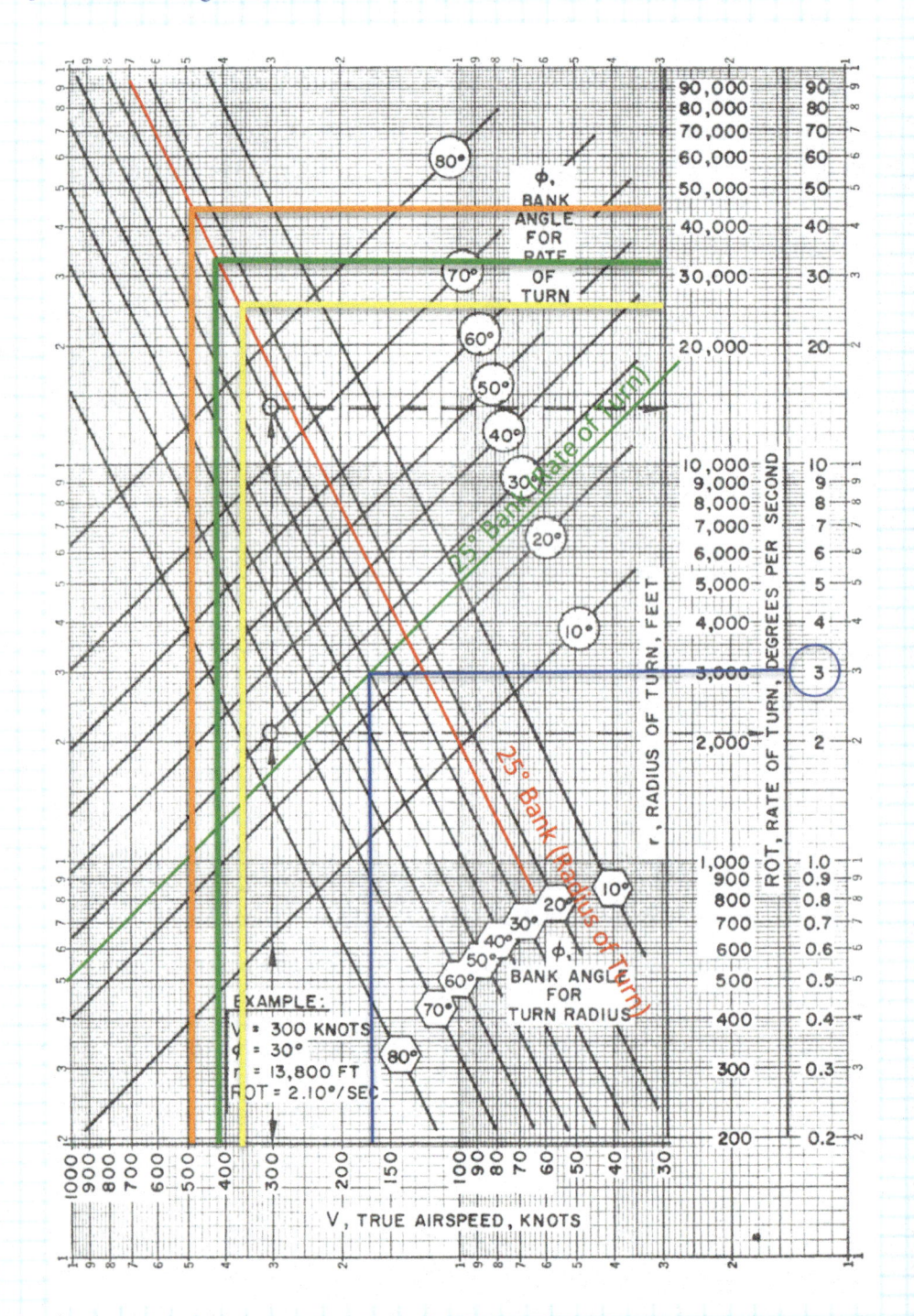

25: Limitations

Loring Alert Force (Gary Schenauer, courtesy of VetFriends.com)

Each alert crewmember was issued a Tactical Aircrew Alerting Network radio, or TAAN. The pocket size radio would buzz to life and announce: "For alert force, for alert force, klaxon, klaxon, klaxon." And that meant we would either be going to war or it was just another drill. I was just settling down with a good book for my first night on alert when there was a knock at the door. "Lieutenant Haskel?"

"Yes, sir."

"I'm Captain Daryl Schoen," he said, "senior tanker copilot this week. You have the first night of hall security duty."

"Really?"

"I wouldn't joke about something so serious," he said. "You will have to walk the length of each hallway in the facility, on the hour, every hour. Then you press the top button of the TAAN and report in with your name, the hallway designation, and the word 'secure' or 'non-secure.' Any questions, lieutenant?"

"The TAAN," I said, "is a receive-only radio. You know that, don't you?"

163

"You getting smart with me?" He looked a bit peeved.

"Apparently," I said, deliberately omitting the "sir."

"I don't want any sass from a second lieutenant," he said, "you got your orders." I slept soundly that night.

The next morning I saw Captain Schoen at breakfast, seated in front of a tray of eggs and toast. It was all covered with white, greasy ooze peppered with black specks of mystery meat. I sat across the table from him and quietly ate my pancakes, daring him to say something about my dereliction from his direct order. After the last bit of ooze was gone, he got up and left. Ben Neavis took his place.

"Surprised to see you sitting next to that asshole," Ben said.

"I wanted to see if I could get him to admit to that fact," I said.

"I heard about it," Ben said. "You blew him off. That means you passed your initiation. You would be surprised how many FNG's fall for it." I looked at him without saying anything. "Fucking New Guy," he explained.

"Oh." I thought between bites of pancake. "You would think this place is bad enough without us making it worse for each other."

"Welcome to Loring," Ben said.

My first flight with crew S-105 was the following week: a simple training sortie from Loring to Loring with an air refueling thrown in for good measure. Captain Stiles would fly the first takeoff and I would execute copilot duties. If he were to follow procedure, he would push the four throttles to their approximate takeoff engine pressure ratio, or EPR, and I would fine-tune them to the exact setting prior to the airplane reaching 50 knots. EPR measures the air pressure coming out of the engine and divides that by the pressure of the air going into the engine. On our KC-135A, that number was usually 1.83. Sitting below the four EPR gauges were a bunch of other gauges that told us when an engine was turning too fast, was using too much fuel, or was just too hot. The copilot's job on takeoff was to keep all those dials out of the red. The red is where I found myself during my first takeoff with Captain Stiles.

"Whoa," I said with my left hand full of throttles, "over temp on one and three." I pulled them back and Captain Stiles happily nodded and continued the takeoff. We lumbered into the air and the engines got us to altitude without complaint.

Flight Lessons 1: Basic Flight

"Should we write up the engines, sir?" I asked after the flight.

"No," the good captain assured me, "these engines were designed to take a little abuse and engineers always include a fifty percent fudge factor on all limits. We don't need to concern the maintenance folks that the engines were pushed a few degrees beyond their design limits." Of course the fifty percent fudge factor is hogwash. But I was new to the tanker, I told myself, and the captain had been doing this for twelve years. I resolved to listen and learn. Besides, Stiles hadn't pushed an engine to failure yet.

We had eighteen tankers up at Loring and we, crew S-105, were assigned to fly any of them on a random basis. We rarely saw the same airplane twice in a month. In fact, in my four months at Loring, I had yet to repeat an aircraft. Until our first trip to the Pacific, that is. We were assigned KC-135A 56-3637, an airplane that came out of Boeing Field, Washington the same year I was born. I would, for the first time in my two years as an Air Force pilot, fly the same airplane on every sortie for a month.

Day One. We flew from Loring AFB, Maine to March AFB, Riverside, California on 2 Sep 1980. As per usual, Captain Stiles pushed all four throttles to the forward stop and I pulled them back as quickly as I could. The number three engine EGT – exhaust gas temperature – flashed red and the needle made its way half way through the red zone before I arrested its progress. After 6.7 hours we were in Riverside, California. The next day would be my first ocean crossing.

"Number three got really hot, sir," I said while filling out the flight log. "Is this engine going to be okay crossing the pond?"

"No problem," Captain Stiles said, "they do that all the time. Besides, the EPR was just fine." Curious, I thought. The EPR gauge didn't have a red zone. I looked it up in the book and it was true. There were no EPR limits in the flight manual but we had definitely pushed past the exhaust gas temperature limit. EGT was important because of turbine blade creep. Creep is actually an engineering term to describe the slow but inevitable movement of metals in reaction to high temperatures over time. I knew, from Purdue, that even the strongest alloys were subject to creep when subjected to very high temperatures. The KC-135A engine, the Pratt & Whitney J57-P43W, had 16 stages of compressors and 3 stages of turbines where the metal blades were rated to 650°C degrees. On 2 Sep 1980, I saw an engine reach 660°C.

Day Two. The takeoff out of March AFB was just like the day prior, except this time number three reached 680°C. I decided those extra 20 degrees were because of the higher pressure altitude of the airport, not my slowing reflexes. In just a few minutes over six hours, I was home.

Day Three. The very next day we got to depart using the reef runway at Honolulu International. I had always wanted to do that. This time number three only made it to 670°C, but that was still 20 degrees higher than its design limit. But at least I was getting better.

Day Seven. The good folks at the Guam tanker task force gave us four days off before we flew our first mission. That was on somebody else's airplane, 63-8007 – the newest tanker I had ever flown. Its engines seemed to like Captain Stiles better and there were no red lights on takeoff.

Day Nine. We were back to our airplane, 56-3637, the airplane that was as old as me. It looked much worse for wear. The skin was wrinkled from nose to tail, the paint was tired, and the cockpit looked old and tired too. But it was our airplane and I was happy to see her. The flight for the day was to be my first maximum weight takeoff. Captain Stiles decided it was time for me to check that off my list of things to do. We would load her up to 297,000 pounds of gross weight. He would taxi her to the end of the runway and we would both stand on the brake pedals. He would push all four throttles to their mechanical stops, and I would dive at them to bring them back into the green. He would direct me to start the water injection system that would raise us from around 9,000 pounds of thrust per engine to just over 12,500 pounds of thrust.

They taught us in tanker school that the water served to cool the engine and allowed it to run at a higher RPM without exceeding any temperature limitations, therefore we got more thrust. My engineering texts, of course, had a more technical answer. A jet engine produces thrust by accelerating a mass of air and fuel aft. Sir Isaac Newton's Second Law of motion tells us a force acting on a mass causes the mass to accelerate, the proverbial $F=Ma$. His Third Law of Motion tells us that for every action (air and fuel shooting aft) there is an opposite and equal reaction (jet shooting forward). Adding water to the air increases the mass of the propellant, so more thrust. Of course the fuel doesn't burn as completely so you also get more black smoke.

With the water injection system doing its thing, the aircraft commander would count us down --- "three, two, one" – and we would release the brakes. And then we would thunder down the runway. At 80 knots he would say "your aircraft," and I would answer "my aircraft." At 150 knots or so, I would

Flight Lessons 1: Basic Flight

slowly pull back on the yoke and we would lumber into the sky. It was going to be great.

We were the last airplane in a twelve-ship formation. The first six airplanes were B-52 bombers on their way to the Indian Ocean. The next six were KC-135 tankers following closely behind. The interval between bombers was 12 seconds, between the last bomber and the first tanker would be 30 seconds, and 12 seconds again for each following tanker. At the runway's midpoint was a fleet of base cars; the wing commander in the lead. This was a big inspection for the base. At last I could hear the wing king's voice on the command post frequency. "This is Alpha, you are cleared to launch. Make us proud."

As each airplane crossed the runway threshold and pushed forward, their engines and water injection filled the sky with black smoke. By the time we got there, it was all Captain Stiles could do just to keep the airplane on the runway. He jammed all four throttles to their forward stops while I was mesmerized by all the noise, smoke, and vibration. I grabbed at the throttles, all four sporting red temperature lights, and brought each into the correct zone. At 80 knots I heard, "your aircraft."

I tightened my grip on the yoke and placed my feet on the rudder pedals. The ailerons and elevators were buffeting a bit from the wake turbulence and jet exhaust from the eleven airplanes in front of us, but that was to be expected. The acceleration wasn't breathtaking but we were gaining speed. I had seen a maximum weight takeoff twice before, both times in the cold Maine climate where the engines had denser air to turn F and M into A, and the wings had a fighting chance to turn the coefficient of lift into actual lift. Today, in Guam, it was nearly 100 degrees. The airplane consumed half the runway and we were nowhere near decision speed.

Once we got to decision speed, we could no longer abort the takeoff and were committed. The rest of the world called decision speed "vee one," vee being short for velocity and one being the first of several key velocities. In the Strategic Air Command, it was S-1, S for speed. After S-1, we could no longer abort.

"Ess one," I heard Stiles say just as a bright flash of light passed the aircraft on my right and then I heard the explosion. The airplane pulled, gently at first, but then more noticeably to the right. I corrected with left rudder. Stiles stayed quiet as I concentrated on keeping the airplane straight and waited for rotation speed. It wasn't coming.

With about a thousand feet of runway to go, Captain Stiles announced, "Rotate." I glanced at the airspeed indicator and saw we still needed another twenty knots. Back to looking outside, we had a thousand feet of runway left. No choice, I rotated.

The tanker flight manual says you need to rotate 3 to 4 degrees per second up to the target attitude of 8-1/2 degrees. It also says that if you rotate too fast and speed is critical, you risk stalling the wing and it will never end up flying. I pulled back ever so gently. We made it to 8-1/2 degrees and the airplane reluctantly left the earth's grip. But it didn't do much after that. For seconds, long agonizing seconds, the airplane seemed to mush along at 600 feet, the elevation of the runway.

"Clear to dump," I heard on the radio and from the corner of my eye I saw Captain Stiles flipping switches on the fuel panel to get rid of all that gas that was meant for a B-52 but now would find itself as a thin membrane atop the Pacific Ocean. As the thousands of pounds shot out the ass end of the airplane, the nose end started to respond to my coaxing. At last we were gaining altitude. With another few minutes I was able to dip a wing below the horizon without fear of having the rest of the airplane follow it. In another thirty minutes we were on the ground.

As we climbed down the crew entry ladder we each raced over to the number three engine only to be stopped by the fire crew. It was still smoldering and the once gray cowling was now black from soot and flames. Every colonel on base came by to shake Captain Stiles' hand for ably dealing with a heavy weight engine failure. Each time he pointed to me. Half the colonels then reached to shake my hand. The other half looked at the butter bars on my shoulders and walked away.

When we got back to Loring there was a commendation waiting for each of us on the crew. Captain Stiles was as happy as I had ever seen him. Me? Not so much. I knew the cause of the engine failure.

Thrust Measurement

Test Stand Measurement

Jet engines are commonly rated in terms of static thrust. The engine is restrained from moving and the "push" is measured with scales. In actual use, the true thrust is normally less than static thrust, since V_2 tends to be constant and V_1 increases with aircraft velocity, so the acceleration goes down. There are no scales to measure this.

Engineering Solution

We can measure drag in a wind tunnel and when the aircraft is in steady flight we know thrust equals drag and can therefore be approximated.

Engine RPM

Engine thrust can also be approximated by the engine's number of revolutions per minute, RPM. These numbers are converted to a percentage of a rated value for ease of reading. For twin spool engines, the inner spool is often connected to the most forward and aft sections and is called N_1, the outer spool is called N_2. Thrust normally does not vary in a linear relationship with RPM. In a typical engine thrust can be idle around 50%, a quarter of maximum at 90%, half at 95%, and maximum at 100%

Engine Pressure Ratio

A common method of presenting the pilot with an approximation of engine thrust is EPR, engine pressure ratio. In its basic form, pressure probes are positioned at the inlet and outlet, the outlet pressure is divided by the inlet to determine EPR. This number is not an accurate representation of thrust because the pressure pattern of the exhaust tends to be higher in the center and lower in the outer portions of the airflow. It is, however, good enough since it gives the pilot a way of telling relative power settings from idle to maximum.

Later engines use ambient air pressure instead of air inlet pressure, since it is close enough. Many engines do not measure outlet pressure because the temperatures tend to shorten the lives of probes. Instead these engines choose intermediate stages of pressure, such as aft of the compressor. EPR, then, has very little to do with pressure ratios and is nothing more than a fictitious number designed to give pilots an idea of relative thrust levels.

26: Hands Full

KC-135 Crew (NATO Photo)

"Well done," Lieutenant Colonel Kong said when he first saw me after we returned from the Pacific. "Eddie, now that we know we can count on you, we are putting you on a new crew. The aircraft commander is a retread so you will have your hands full, no doubt about it. But you've faced death before, so I am sure you will do fine." The squadron rule was to never say anything to Colonel Kong unless he asked you a direct question. I kept my mouth shut. "I guess we'll never know why that engine blew up, will we?"

"I know, sir."

"You do?" Kong looked genuinely puzzled. "Well, if you know, spit it out. Why did that engine fail?"

"We over-temped it on all but one takeoff leading up to the failure. Sir."

"Why did you do that?" he asked.

"Captain Stiles tends to fire wall the throttles on takeoff," I said, "I just couldn't get them pulled back fast enough."

"You are ratting out your boss, Eddie. That isn't very loyal."

Flight Lessons 1: Basic Flight

"You asked, sir."

"You have a lot to learn about officership," he said. "But the orders are cut. Maybe Major Diepetro can teach you some manners. I'm not sure you will ever be ready to upgrade. Maybe you should take a few lessons from Daryl Schoen. He's a model officer." I let his words hang. "Dismissed," he said, finally.

Major William Diepetro was a staff retread, meaning he left the cockpit on the first possible opportunity so as to ensure his promotion. Now he was a major with fourteen years of service coming up on his first flying time gate. If a pilot doesn't have at least seven years of flying by the fifteenth year, they have to be actively flying to get flight pay. Diepetro had spent twice as many years behind a desk as behind a set of controls in a cockpit.

"Call me Billy," the major said. "I heard you're a pretty good pilot who needs some seasoning and maybe a few lessons about officership. I think we can take care of that!"

Major Billy was a political animal. When he showed up on base he had never lived in a northern climate, never smoked, never hunted. After a day in the squadron ready room, talking with his fellow aircraft commanders, Billy fit right in. He bought a snow mobile, started chomping on stogies, and bought himself a rifle. He did a two-week refresher to relearn the airplane and they presented him with crew S-108.

The best thing about Major Billy was that he knew his limitations. He was overly cautious, which at first bugged me because we had a low likelihood of being assigned an airplane and actually making it off the ground. "I don't like the looks of number four," he would say, and we would sit on the ground working with maintenance until it was too late to launch and a spare aircraft had to take our mission. At first it infuriated me. But after a few close calls in the air, I decided being stuck on the ground might actually beat being in the air with him. After my first few actual trips away from base with Major Billy, I realized his biggest issue was being away from his wife. He talked incessantly about missing her; it was embarrassing. Whether it was an abundance of caution or a reluctance to spend the night away from his own pillow, Major Billy didn't like being on trips. In any case, I wasn't getting a lot of flying time working for Major Billy.

Still, I needed the flying time to upgrade and find my way out of Northern Maine. So when we got tasked to airline down to Alabama to pick up a depot bird, I was ready to go. These depot deliveries were a bit of a pain. You showed up, waited for the depot boys to finally release the airplane they had been working on for six months, and then you flew home. The rules said the return flight had to be done in daylight and the aircraft commander had to do the flying. It wasn't a good deal for the copilot. But at least it was flying.

"What did they do to the airplane?" I asked the operations officer when he handed me the orders.

"I don't know, lieutenant. Just pick up the damned airplane and bring it home."

The airline trip to Montgomery was pleasant enough. The hotel was passable and had a working air conditioner and a television that got five channels, two more than what we got up in Aroostook County, Maine. I flipped through the channels. I stopped on a shot of an airline captain with the obligatory four silver stripes on this shoulders talking with a model of a DC-8 beside him. He had a grim look to his face and was talking about the scariest landing of his life.

"We were carrying a load of cattle," he said, "each in a small pen to keep them from moving about. You can't have cattle walking about the length of the airplane, the CG change would overwhelm the airplane's horizontal stabilizer."

Cows and center of gravity? I was hooked.

"So each cow is in their own pen, but they are standing. Or they were standing. We hit the runway so hard that all twenty-five cows broke each of their four legs. They all had to be destroyed." The captain fought back tears.

He went on to describe his DC-8, an older cargo version that had just been upgraded with an inertial navigation system. He had never used one before, but was fascinated by its ability to report the airplane's ground speed instantaneously. I had never seen an INS at this point in my short career, but I understood the principles. Three spinning gyroscopes equipped with force meters could detect aircraft movement. You ended up with very accurate heading and speed information.

"We were on approach to runway three-one-left at JFK," he said, "and the copilot and I bugged 150 on our airspeed indicators. That number was a little higher than usual, but we were heavy. Everything seemed normal, but the INS said our ground speed was only 100 knots. I wondered how that was possible. The tower reported the winds were right down the runway at 25 knots. It seemed to me we were missing 25 knots." Sometimes those electronic gizmos don't work so well, I thought.

"Well," he continued, "at least it was right down the runway. So I continued what I was doing, keeping the airplane flying down the ILS." This airline captain appeared to be in his fifties, was very well spoken, and had a grave calm about him. "Right around 300 feet, I felt the airplane start to sink. The airspeed indicator was falling fast. I pushed the throttles forward a little at first, and then a lot. By the time we were at fifty feet I had them to the firewall but it was too late. I managed to get us to brick one of the overrun, but we hit hard."

The airplane was heavily damaged, but flew again. The cattle didn't make it.

"I've done a lot of soul searching after that," the captain said, "and I started to wonder about those missing 25 knots. What if the wind that day was greater a few hundred feet up than it was on the surface? When we lost all that headwind, wouldn't that have caused the sudden sinking?"

That made perfect sense, I thought. But it was a revolutionary thought. I had never seen such a wind shift before, in fact I'd never heard of anyone experiencing it.

"So I thought," the captain concluded, "if you know the magnitude of your headwind on the runway, and if you know the magnitude of your headwind in the air, why not come up with a minimum acceptable ground speed on approach?"

It was brilliant. I added it to my notebook, thinking that when I got to be a gray-haired captain in my fifties, I might find it useful.

The next morning we showed up at the plant at 0900, just like the orders said, and were told our KC-135A would be ready soon. They let us onto the airplane about 1200, but the paperwork wasn't ready so we had to wait. They let me into the cockpit to stow my gear and I spotted two new boxes, one on each side of the cockpit. I recognized them immediately, inertial navigation systems. In a box in the cargo compartment I found a 100-page instruction manual and while we waited, I read. It was good stuff.

By the time the paperwork was done it was 1500. "Major, we have to land in the daylight," I half asked, half stated, "don't we?"

"That's been waived," Major Billy said, "we're going home tonight."

I hopped into the right seat and turned the INS to "align," and punched in the latitude and longitude. As the inertials started to count down their alignment I could hardly wait.

"Hey," Major Billy said as he entered the cockpit, "we haven't been trained to use those, turn them off."

"I read the manual," I said, "I want to use it."

Major Billy said nothing, so I left the thing on.

By the time we made it off the ground, it was already pretty late. The INS's were counting up the latitude and longitude as we made our way northeast. I didn't figure out the waypoint system yet, so all I had was the orange glow of the lat/long on one side of the cockpit, and an instantaneous readout of our magnetic course and ground speed on the other. Still, it was pretty cosmic.

About an hour south of Loring, I got the weather via HF phone patch. "It sounds bad," I told Major Billy. "They are saying the winds are 350 at 40, ceiling is 200 feet, right at minimums. Forty knots of wind, I don't think I've ever seen that before."

Major Billy said nothing. He just sat in his pilot's seat thinking. Finally he keyed the interphone. "I think it's time for some copilot training tonight, you want the landing co?"

"Sure!" I knew the rule said the pilot had to fly the aircraft from takeoff to landing on these depot deliveries, but somehow his idea sounded better to me. As we got closer the automated weather report started coming in. The winds were still reported to be down the runway but now they were up to 50 knots.

The command post frequency, UHF 311, was usually reserved for the pilot. But I toggled the mike any way. "Has anyone landed recently?" I asked.

"Just one," they reported, "another tanker. He's taxiing in right now."

I got permission to speak to that tanker directly. It was Captain Paul Craft, probably the best tanker pilot I had ever flown with. "How was the approach and landing with all that wind," I asked.

"You gotcher hands full, buddy," he said, "those winds are pretty strong tonight."

I wasn't really sure that added anything to my knowledge. Fifty knots of wind! At least they were right down the runway, no crosswind controls required. But fifty knots!

Around 5,000 feet, turning south to align with the ILS, I was at 250 knots

Flight Lessons 1: Basic Flight

getting ready to slow for the landing gear. My normal timing cues were not working. It was taking forever to get to the glide slope intercept point.

Why were things happening in slow motion? I looked down to my INS and saw the answer: our ground speed was only 110 knots! How was this possible? I was still cruising along at 250. I didn't know the INS could give a wind readout—I hadn't read that far into the manual—but if I was indicating 250 knots and my ground speed was 110, the winds at 5,000 feet must have been 140 knots. I was going to lose 90 knots somewhere between 5,000 feet and the runway.

The airline captain on television said you should never let your ground speed get below the expected ground speed crossing the runway threshold. What does that mean? I couldn't put it all together while hand flying the airplane with all that wind.

Finally at glide slope intercept I extended the landing gear and let the airspeed decay to 200 knots. My ground speed was only 60 knots. It should have been 150 knots based on the tower-reported winds. What would that DC-8 captain have done? He would have added the difference, that's what.

I couldn't add 90 knots to my speed; I wouldn't be able to get the flaps down. The limiting speed for our full complement of flaps was 180 knots. Mother SAC wouldn't allow us to land with anything less than all the flaps unless there was an emergency situation. This wasn't an emergency, was it?

I decided to fly the approach and landing at 180 knots, 45 knots faster than normal. That should be enough. Major Billy said nothing about my hyper approach speed.

I was stable on glide path and on course, 180 knots, about four hundred feet above the treetops. At 300 feet I spotted the first set of approach lights and then felt a sinking sensation. The airspeed indicator was unwinding so fast I thought it was broken. Then, I firewalled all four engines.

We continued to drop but the airspeed slowed its plummet and as the wheels kissed the runway the airspeed stopped at 120 knots. We were on the ground so I pulled all four throttles to idle.

We were silent in the cockpit until the navigator keyed his interphone mike.

"Copilot, nav."

"Go ahead."

"When my son is born, I'm naming him after you."

The next day Major Billy asked to be reassigned to the command post, his flying days over. The squadron commander gave me another stern lecture about my faults, followed with another "well done," followed by another warning about my new boss. I was being sent to the Leper Crew.

Windshear

Windshear Defined

[Flight Safety Foundation, Approach and Landing Reduction Tool Kit]

Windshear is a sudden change of wind velocity/direction.

- Vertical windshear (vertical variations of the horizontal wind component, resulting in turbulence and affecting aircraft airspeed when climbing or descending through the shear layer); and,
- Horizontal windshear (horizontal variations of the wind component (e.g., decreasing head wind or increasing tail wind, or a shift from a head wind to a tail wind), affecting the aircraft in level flight, climb or descent).

Microbursts present two distinct threats to aviation safety:

- A downburst that results in strong downdrafts (reaching 40 knots vertical velocity); and,
- An outburst that results in strong horizontal windshear and wind-component reversal (with horizontal winds reaching 100 knots).

Recognition

Timely recognition of windshear is vital for successful implementation of a windshear recovery procedure. The following are indications of a suspected windshear condition:

- Indicated airspeed variations in excess of 15 knots;
- Groundspeed variations (decreasing head wind or increasing tail wind, or a shift from head wind to tail wind);
- Vertical-speed excursions of 500 fpm or more;
- Pitch attitude excursions of five degrees or more;
- Glideslope deviation of one dot or more;
- Heading variations of 10 degrees or more; and,
- Unusual autothrottle activity or throttle lever position.

Recognition – Airmass Thunderstorms

[Advisory Circular 00-54, Appendix 1.]

Precipitation signals the beginning of the mature stage and presence of a downdraft. After approximately an hour, the heated updraft creating the thunderstorm is cut off by rainfall. Heat is removed and the thunderstorm dissipates.

Recognition – Frontal Thunderstorms

Frontal thunderstorms are usually associated with weather systems like fronts, converging winds, and troughs aloft. Frontal thunderstorms form in squall lines, last several hours, generate heavy rain and possibly hail, and produce strong gusty winds and possibly tornadoes. The principal distinction in formation of these more severe thunderstorms is the presence of large horizontal wind changes (speed and direction) at different altitudes in the thunderstorm.

The downward moving column of air, or downdraft, of a typical thunderstorm is fairly large, about 1 to 5 miles in diameter.

Recognition – Symmetric Microburst

Downdrafts associated with microbursts are typically only a few hundred to 3,000 feet across. When the downdraft reaches the ground, it spreads out horizontally and may form one or more horizontal vortices right around the downdraft. The outflow region is typically 6,000 to 12,000 feet across. The horizontal vortices may extend to over 2,000 feet AGL.

Recognition – Asymmetric Microburst

Microburst outflows are not always symmetric. Therefore a significant airspeed increase may not occur upon entering the outflow, or may be much less than the subsequent airspeed lost experienced when exiting the microburst.

Recognition – Dry Microburst

Microbursts have occurred in relatively dry conditions of light rain or virga (precipitation that evaporates before reaching the earth's surface).

Flight Lessons 1: Basic Flight

Recovery

[Flight Safety Foundation, Approach and Landing Reduction Tool Kit]

Before V_1: The takeoff should be rejected if unacceptable airspeed variations occur (not exceeding V_1) and if there is sufficient runway remaining.

After V_1: Disconnect the autothrottles and maintain or set the throttle levers to maximum takeoff thrust; rotate normally at V_R; and, follow the FD pitch command if the FD provides windshear recovery guidance, or set the required pitch attitude (as recommended in the aircraft operating manual.)

During initial climb: Disconnect the autothrottles and maintain or set the throttle levers to maximum takeoff thrust; closely monitor the airspeed, airspeed trend and flight-path angle (as available); allow airspeed to decrease to stick shaker onset (intermittent stick shaker activation) while monitoring the airspeed trend; do not change the flaps or landing-gear configurations until out of the windshear condition; and, when out of the windshear condition, increase airspeed when a positive climb is confirmed, retract the landing gear, flaps and slats, then establish a normal climb profile.

During approach and landing: Select the takeoff/go-around (TOGA) mode and set and maintain maximum go-around thrust; do not change the flap configuration or landing-gear configuration until out of the windshear; allow airspeed to decrease to stick-shaker onset (intermittent stick-shaker activation) while monitoring airspeed trend, closely monitor airspeed, airspeed trend and flight path angle (if flight-path vector is available and displayed for the PNF); and, when out of the windshear, retract the landing gear, flaps and slats, then increase the airspeed when a positive climb is confirmed and establish a normal climb profile.

Minimum Ground Speed Technique

Caveat: This technique was once published in various Air Force manuals, such as AFM 51-9, Aircraft Performance, but has since fallen in disfavor as too risky. The technique remains valid for a shear caused by one air mass sitting atop another. It should not be employed when dealing with convective activity, especially a microburst, where the magnitude of the speed loss or gain can be unpredictable.

Approach Speed (V_{APP})

Actual Ground Speed (V_{GS})

Tower Winds (HW/TW)

Minimum Ground Speed (V_{MIN-GS}) = V_{APP} - HW

The Technique

Convert tower winds to a headwind or tailwind component

1. Determine aircraft approach speed (V_{APP}) for configuration crossing the runway threshold
2. Compute Minimum Ground Speed (V_{MIN-GS}) by subtracting the headwind from the approach speed or adding the tailwind
3. Once the airplane is in approach configuration, monitor actual ground speed
4. If actual ground speed goes below V_{MIN-GS}, add the difference to your target approach speed
5. If actual ground speed goes above V_{MIN-GS}, be aware of a possible loss of wind which will cause a sudden sink rate, or if the wind continues a long landing.

27: The Leper Crew

KC-135A Water Injection Takeoff (Courtesy of Photographer Martin Pole)

It was bad enough that the 407th Air Refueling Squadron had a Leper Crew. Worse yet, I found myself on it. The aircraft commander was Captain Don "Narco" Nelson, a once obese officer who lost nearly a hundred pounds of flab. When I first heard the name I thought he might be a drug abuser but was told "Narco" was for narcoleptic. The navigator was Lieutenant Calvin "Wrong Way" Wong who was known for confusing north with south. The boom operator was Senior Airman Artemis "Article 15" Hough. An Article 15 in the Air Force is one step short of a court martial and Airman Hough had somehow collected four of them in four years without getting thrown out. And then there was me.

"Welcome to the Leper Crew," Narco Nelson said. "We're going to have to come up with a name for you, we'll see how it goes on our first flight."

I resisted the urge to tell the new boss "Lieutenant Haskel" or "Eddie" would do me just fine. I was shocked to hear the squadron commander use "Leper" when describing one of his nine crews. I was doubly shocked to find the crew's leader either proud of the name or oblivious to the historical import of it all. Our first mission together was more than likely to be a ground exercise; we were to be spare aircraft number eleven. Our day began with the largest mission briefing I had ever attended: sixteen tanker crews.

"You men are probably wondering why we've got eleven spares tonight," Colonel Burkel said at the conclusion of the briefing, "when we normally only have one spare aircraft per mission." We sat silently.

"We are scrambling five tankers and eleven spares because sixteen aircraft is all we got right now." There was some laughter. Oh, it was a joke. "The mission is that important. But I don't want you spares thinking you aren't going to fly tonight. Everyone has to be thinking they are flying, we have to put five airplanes in the sky no later than 2016 tonight and that means you've got to be ready to fly when the time comes. That goes for sortie six, the first spare, all the way down to sortie sixteen. Even the Leper Crew has to be ready!"

Now there was some genuine laughter. Our squadron mates knew we were the Leper crew, but the brass wasn't supposed to call us that in public. "Now go get 'em," the wing commander said. "Make Loring proud."

We came to attention as the wing commander left the stage in front of us. From my peripheral vision I noticed Don was seated. I jabbed his shoulder. "Huh," he said, startled. More laughter. Narco Nelson came to attention.

An hour later I was nestled into the copilot's seat of Sortie 16 with my trusty Woolworth's clipboard on my knee. I had two sets of takeoff data, my radio log, my fuel log, and my Strategic Air Command codebook within the clip. Underneath that I had my Technical Order 1KC-135A-1-1 green book, a hundred pages of charts that turned the airplane's weight and our outside weather conditions into takeoff data, the information we needed to set our throttles and know what speeds to fly. Each set of data took me about ten minutes to produce, not bad for a new copilot. But I was working to get those times down.

At 1930 everyone got the signal to start engines and by 1940 everyone, all sixteen of us, were on our way to the end of the runway.

"All sixteen got started," Don announced on interphone, "we ain't going nowhere tonight, boys."

Don lined us up on the parallel taxiway and set the parking brake. He tilted his ball cap over his eyes and reclined, as best he could. I started the stopwatch to my right and measured the time from ball cap to the first sign of sleep. It was one-minute, twenty-seconds before the first gentle snore. Impressive. The boom operator was fast asleep too. Behind me Wrong

Flight Lessons 1: Basic Flight

Way Wong was reading a magazine. The temperature was dropping and my takeoff data was only good plus or minus five degrees Celsius. I pulled up my clipboard and started on two sets of data for ten degrees less temperature.

The KC-135A was an old, underpowered airplane. The engines were incredibly anemic and at warmer temperatures couldn't lift the airplane off the ground at some weights. So the wizards at Boeing installed a system to inject water into the engines that increased the power from nine to twelve thousand pounds of thrust per engine. Our airplane tonight was carrying six thousand pounds of water. I had to figure my takeoff data based with the water injection system, or assuming the water injection system failed (which it often did), without it.

"Sortie 1, time is twenty-hundred," the command post announced, "cleared for takeoff." Two miles ahead of us I saw a plume of black smoke kick up. A few seconds later I saw the first airplane race down the runway. By the time it was abeam us the nose rotated and off it went. One down, four to go. I hacked my stopwatch and looked ahead for the second plume of smoke. "Sortie two, negative water, aborting."

"Why can't he go dry," I said to myself, "he should have takeoff data for that." I double-checked my takeoff data just to be sure. Scanning the thirty or so entries on each page I realized the answer to my stupid question. The dry data - the takeoff data computed without water injection - was based on dumping the water overboard. The dry data was based on an airplane that weighed six thousand pounds less. It took fifteen minutes to dump the water. We didn't have fifteen minutes.

"Sortie three, negative water, aborting." Another!

"Expedite off the runway," the wing commander himself stepped onto the tower frequency, "we're fighting the clock here." I nudged Don who sprang to life and closed the gap between us and Sortie 15. I pulled out a blank takeoff data form and started a new set of numbers. Five minutes! I completed a set of data in five minutes!

"Sortie seven, away!" We now had two airplanes in the sky. "Sortie eight, engine fire, aborting." One-by-one, the next four airplanes aborted. Sorties thirteen and fourteen made it. Now we just needed to get one more airplane airborne. Don was paying attention now. The tanker in front of us taxied onto the runway and we saw the power come up. Seconds later there was black smoke billowing behind the airplane, but not the normal huge cloud.

"Sortie fifteen, no inboard water, aborting."

"Takeoff checklist," Don announced, "we are on stage." I turned on all the aircraft external lights, switched the transponder to transmit and waited as Don brought all four throttles to the dry power limit. "Start the water," he commanded. I wrapped my left hand around the guard just forward of the panel and pushed the switch to the up, "START" position. The "dump" light came on. The switch was wired upside-down.

"Damn!" Don yelled and brought the throttles back.

"No," I yelled over the interphone, "We can go."

"What?"

"I figured dry data, we can go."

"We're out of time," Don said pointing at the cockpit clock, "twenty-sixteen was the last minute, we don't have time to dump the water."

"No," I snapped back, "I figured the takeoff with dry power without dumping the water. We can go."

"You did?" Don hesitated, smiled, and pushed the throttles forward again. "Cool!" And off we went. It wasn't pretty, but we had the necessary speed at the end of the runway and rotated. We skimmed the treetops for a few miles but eventually joined the formation and completed our air refueling. On our way home I checked in with command post and gave our coded status report, expecting the normal sterile coded reply. Instead I got a message "in the clear," which would be a first for me.

"The pilot and copilot are directed to report to the wing commander after landing," the voice on the radio said, "immediately after landing."

I followed Don to wing headquarters and we waited in the outer office. It was a spacious affair with wood paneling, lush carpeting, and furniture that matched. Finally the wing commander's secretary opened the inner office door and gestured us in. Don marched in and I followed. He saluted and reported, "Captain Nelson and Lieutenant Haskel reporting as ordered, sir."

"Captain," Colonel Burkel bellowed, "if you think getting off the ground with seconds to spare makes you a hero you got another thing coming!" He stared Don right in the eye and was yelling while just inches away. He yelled about officership, integrity, regulations, and cowboy antics. I stood rigid, at attention with my eyes caged forward. But in the periphery I could see the wing commander's finger jabbing at the air in front of Don as he raged on. I could see rivers of sweat flowing from Don's scalp. I think he was trembling.

"What gives you the right?" The wing commander stepped back, as if to take a breath. "What gives you the right to gamble with the lives of your crew and with my million dollar airplane?"

At last I figured out what the issue was. "Sir?" I interrupted.

"And you," the wing commander spun on his heels and faced me for the first time. "We put you on the Leper Crew to keep an eye on the Leper! We gave you specific instructions to keep the Leper Crew safe. You're the lieutenant who could stand up to any captain, or so we thought. How could you let this Leper takeoff with dry power before dumping the water?"

"We had the performance," I said calmly, "sir."

"No you didn't, you goddamned liar!" Now the wing commander was giving me both barrels and that dagger-like finger was at my nose. I tried to remain expressionless and wait my turn. While I was the least experienced officer in the room, I knew a lieutenant couldn't win an argument with a colonel. "Any copilot knows it takes fifteen minutes to dump the water!" He gulped for air. "And I was there! I saw the power come up, come back, and up again. You didn't dump the water."

The wing commander's face was beet red and he was out of breath. As his shoulders started to slump I bent over to reach into the leg pocket of my flight suit. "Sir," I said while finding the correct page, "I did six sets of data, including one for taking off without water injection and without dumping the water."

"Bullshit!" He snapped the papers out of my hands and fell into his desk chair. He studied the papers and compared the numbers on all six pages. He sat back in thought for a minute. Or maybe it was five minutes. Don's breathing started to take on a normal rhythm again. The steady flow of sweat down his temples had stopped, but his flight suit was soaked. "Why did you do six sets of data, lieutenant?"

"When Sortie Two aborted," I answered, "it seemed like the thing to do."

"Good job, men." He didn't smile, but the pained look on his face was gone and he seemed, well, relaxed. "Dismissed."

The next Monday I was ordered to report to the squadron commander. "I don't like it when my guys get called into the wing commander's office," Lieutenant Colonel Kong said. "It makes the squadron look bad. When the squadron looks bad, I look bad." And then, as if an afterthought, "it makes all of us look bad."

He didn't ask me a question so I kept my mouth shut. "You just think about what you did, lieutenant. Dismissed." The next week a commendation medal appeared in my mailbox. No fanfare, no ceremony. "Lieutenants don't get commendation medals," I was told when I asked the squadron executive officer. I showed her the medal and certificate. "Well I'll be," she said, "I guess they do. What'd you get that for?"

"Takeoff data."

"Well mister commendation medal," she said, "the boss just issued the new upgrade rack and stack. You are on the bottom."

"Oh well," I said.

"That explains it," she said.

"What?"

"Your name," she said. "The crew is calling you 'Easy Eddie.' I thought that was strange compared to the others."

"It could have been worse," I said.

Flight Lessons 1: Basic Flight

Water Injection

Theory

Water is normally injected either at the compressor inlet or in the diffuser just before the combustion chambers. Adding water increases the mass being accelerated out of the engine, increasing thrust, but it also serves to cool the turbines. Since temperature is normally the limiting factor in turbine engine performance at low altitudes, the cooling effect allows the engine to be run at higher RPM with more fuel injected and more thrust created without overheating. The drawback of the system is that injecting water quenches the flame in the combustion chambers somewhat, as there is no way to cool the engine parts without cooling the flame accidentally. This leads to unburned fuel out the exhaust and a characteristic trail of black smoke.

Example [T.O. 1C-135(K)A-1, pg 1-7]

A water injection system provides thrust augmentation by allowing water to be sprayed into the air inlet and diffuser section of each engine. Water injected in this manner serves to increase the density of inlet and combustion air allowing increased thrust.

In the case of the KC-135A, 5,000 lbs of heated water boosted the thrust of each engine from around 9,000 to 12,000 lbs of thrust. The plumbing was complicated and prone to failure.

Obsolescence

The primary advantage of water injection was the ability to obtain higher compression ratios at the cooler temperatures needed by aluminum blades. Newer alloys have allowed higher temperatures, and therefore higher compression ratios, without having to resort to water injection.

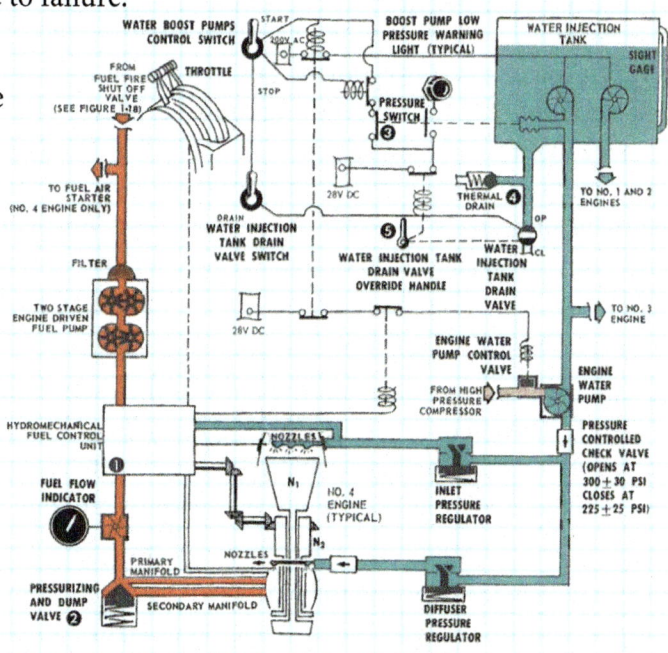

28: A Practiced Calm

KC-135A Air Refueling F-4C (USAF Photo)

Everything else was ops normal, except for Don. He was a bit reserved and appeared to be taking everything more seriously. The Leper moniker seemed to have bite now; he was determined to kill it. During our next mission we were number five of a five-ship formation over the middle of the North Atlantic heading back to North America. These "fighter drags" had us escorting and refueling a squadron of fighters to the halfway point where a flight of tankers based in England took over. We then made a one-eighty and came home without the fighters.

It was just past midnight but the glow of the radar by my left knee kept things illuminated. Set to its furthest range I could see the line of thunderstorms the navigators were chatting about. T. C. Blow was navigating the lead ship and Wrong Way Wong was with us, tail end Charlie.

"Formation, turn left new heading two, four, zero." I recognized Daryl Schoen's voice over the formation frequency; it appeared he was being prepped for upgrade to the left seat. Don waited until the first four airplanes

Flight Lessons 1: Basic Flight

started their turns and dutifully slid us into our number five position.

"When we turning west?" I asked.

"When lead tells us to." I looked at my fuel log again and again. Another ten minutes, I told myself.

"Formation," the radio crackled, "turn left new heading two, zero, zero." Don busied himself with the change while I looked at the radar again. Its green glow showed a line of something to our right, maybe fifty miles. The line started at the bottom and extended beyond the top.

"Where's this line end?" I left my seat to look at the navigator's scope for reassurance. His scope was ten inches wide to my scope's paltry three inches.

"Don't know," Wong said. He had an advantage over me; he had been formally trained on how to use the radar. My training consisted of reading the manual and wondering how it all worked.

"You got the tilt too low," I said. "Calvin let's see what it looks like with less tilt."

"I don't tell you how to fly," Wong said, "leave my stuff alone."

"Don't worry about it, Eddie." Don gestured me back into my copilot's seat. "There are four airplanes out there looking at this too. We can't break formation." I was embarrassed to admit

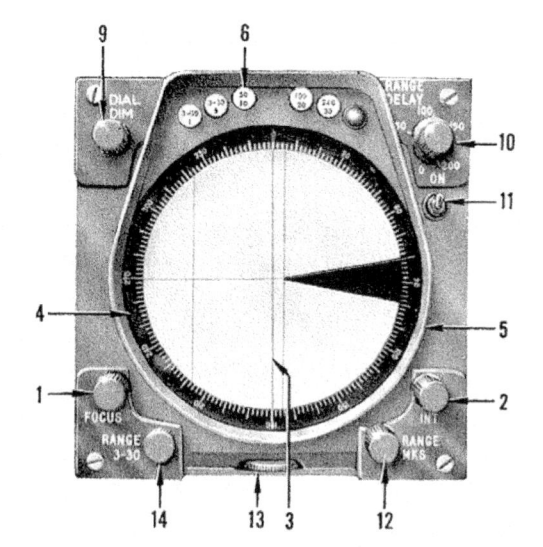

NAVIGATOR'S SEARCH RADAR INDICATOR

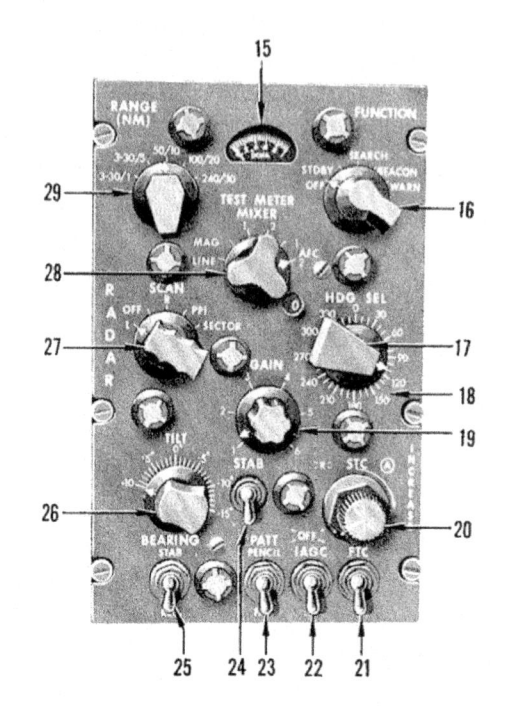

KC-135A Radar Control (1TO-KC-135A-1)

I didn't have a clue about the radar and felt even worse that my life was now in the hands of two navigators I didn't trust. I had no choice but to return to my seat and worry about fuel. Every way I computed it, the gas didn't add up. I took our fuel on board, subtracted the difference from the fuel log and the expected fuel burn and came up with a very small number. Then I took the fuel flow rate on the engine gauges and multiplied that by the ETE and came up with negative numbers. Nobody seemed to care.

"Formation," the lead aircraft announced again, "turn left new heading one eight zero."

"What?" Now I knew the world was mad.

"Don," I said while pulling my fuel logs out with the navigation chart on top, "at this heading do you know where the next land fall is?"

"The Antarctica?"

"Yup." I said. "If you want to go swimming I'm there. But I'd rather spend another night in Colonel Burkel's office. It was so much fun the first time."

"You are right," Don said. He clicked off the autopilot and banked sharply right.

"Number five," he announced calmly on the radio, "is out of gas and heading for home."

"You're doing what?" we heard from multiple voices on the frequency. The screaming on the radio was, in one sense, pretty intense. But in another sense it was funny. Don sat in his seat and took it all in, never once betraying any worry. Not even our second-ever in-the-clear message from the command post: "Both pilots will report to the wing commander."

"We're getting good at this," Don said, smiling.

We sat in the wing commander's outer office, just as before, except this time we could hear the command post radio crackling. We had been on the ground nearly an hour and the formation was still airborne. Number two broke formation next and made it back to base, with two engines flamed out due to fuel starvation. Finally the formation threw in the towel and headed back. We landed right at legal fuel minimums an hour ago. How much fuel could they have now?

The formation headed for Gander, Newfoundland. Don sat motionless, mesmerized by the radio. Finally word came, the last two airplanes made Gander, each with two engines flamed out. "We're the only ones to land with four,"

Flight Lessons 1: Basic Flight

Don said happily, "I guess we did good."

The radio fell dead and the wing commander walked out with his coat on. "What are you two doing here," he asked.

"We're the guys who broke formation first, sir," Don said while coming to attention. "We landed over an hour ago and you asked to see us."

"Oh," he said, blushing. "Well, good job guys. Good job. Dismissed."

It was three a.m. as we made our way to the wing headquarters parking lot. I wasn't at all tired. "You were right, Eddie." Don was happy.

"Yeah," I agreed, "formation integrity isn't all it's cracked up to be."

Don stopped and turned to face me. "Oh no, not that. When you first came on the crew I asked about the engine blowing up on you in Guam. You told me then that 'a practiced calm will always serve you well.' That's what I was thinking about."

I let his words hang. Perhaps I was too cavalier about heading for Antarctica and it was more serious than I thought. The KC-135A's engines were each individually fed by their own fuel tanks but the gauges were notoriously inaccurate. The fact that no airplane lost more than two engines was a stroke of luck.

"The thought of meeting the wing commander used to terrify me," Don said. "I wasn't worried at all this time; before, during, or after."

I knew the pressure of being the aircraft commander – the big kahuna – was still years away for me and would continue in the category of something I didn't know for quite a while. But it was part of the meaning of it all and would require my attention sooner or later. I decided it would be a subject for later since there was still much to learn about the mysterious radarscope at my knee.

Radar

How Radar Works: Distance to Target

How Radar Works: Distance to Target

- Control Unit → Transmitter → Radar Antenna → Radar signal out
- Reflected signal back → Radar Antenna → Receiver → Signal Processor → Display Unit

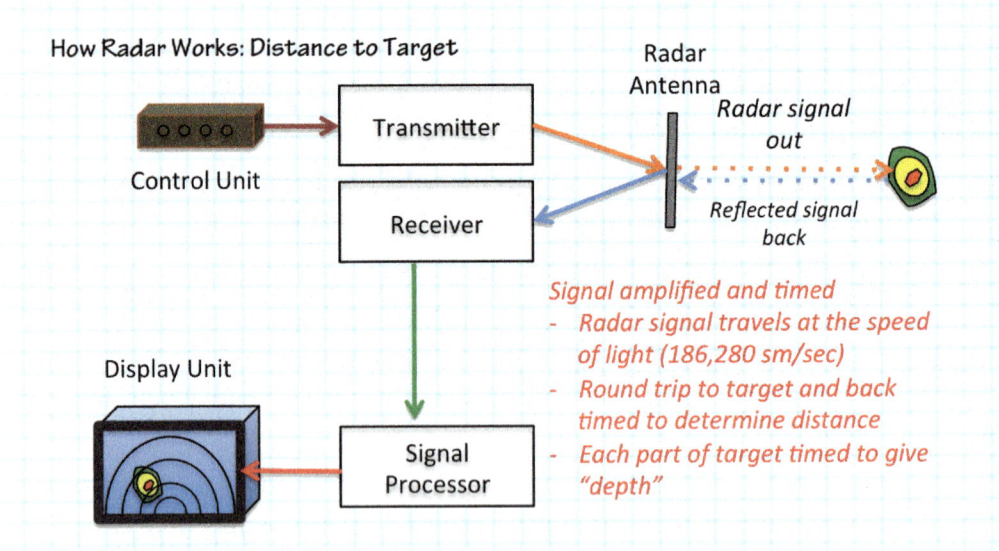

Signal amplified and timed
- Radar signal travels at the speed of light (186,280 sm/sec)
- Round trip to target and back timed to determine distance
- Each part of target timed to give "depth"

How Radar Works: Direction to Target

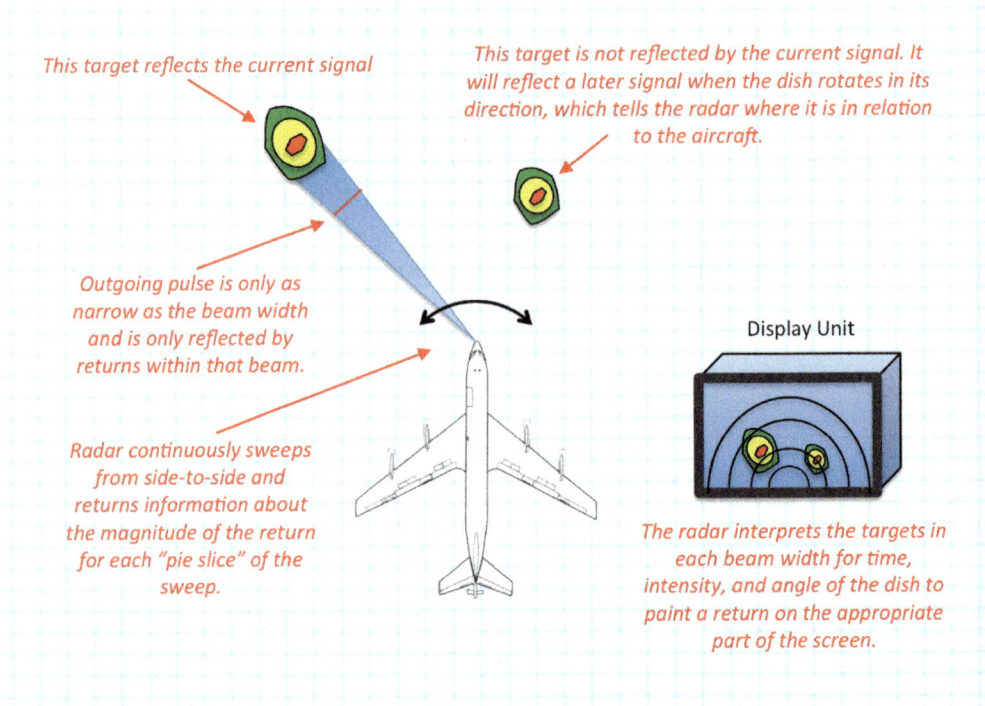

This target reflects the current signal

This target is not reflected by the current signal. It will reflect a later signal when the dish rotates in its direction, which tells the radar where it is in relation to the aircraft.

Outgoing pulse is only as narrow as the beam width and is only reflected by returns within that beam.

Radar continuously sweeps from side-to-side and returns information about the magnitude of the return for each "pie slice" of the sweep.

Display Unit

The radar interprets the targets in each beam width for time, intensity, and angle of the dish to paint a return on the appropriate part of the screen.

How Radar Works: Amplitude of Target's Return

The radar signal processor evaluates each return for intensity and round trip time. The data is then converted to distance and intensity. Varying intensities are color coded. Reflection and attenuation are very useful to the signal processor.

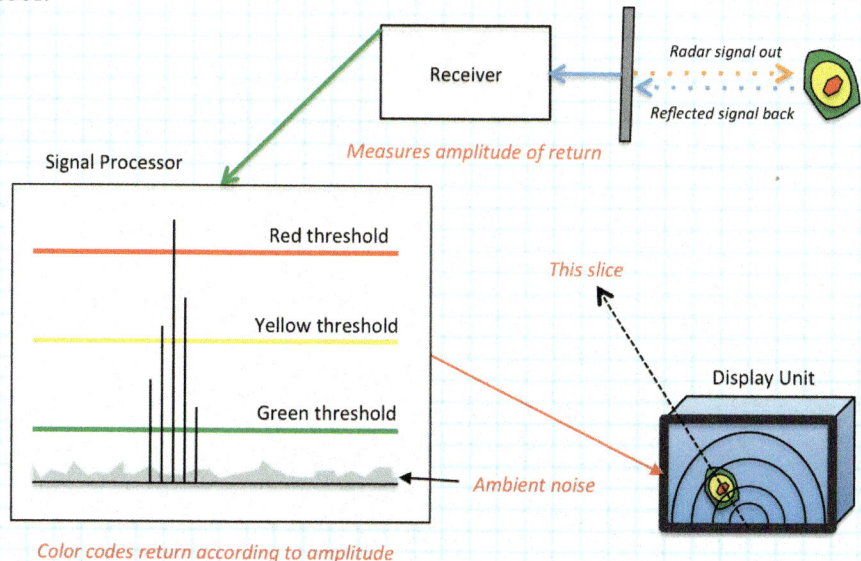

Radar signal out
Reflected signal back

Receiver

Measures amplitude of return

Signal Processor

Red threshold
Yellow threshold
Green threshold

Ambient noise

This slice

Display Unit

Color codes return according to amplitude

How Radar Works: Beam Width Focus

Radar plate size determines beam width:
- 10" antenna typically has 10° beam
- 12" antenna typically has 7.9° beam
- 18" antenna typically has 5.6° beam
- 24" antenna typically has 4.2° beam

Regardless of beam width, energy is most intense at center:

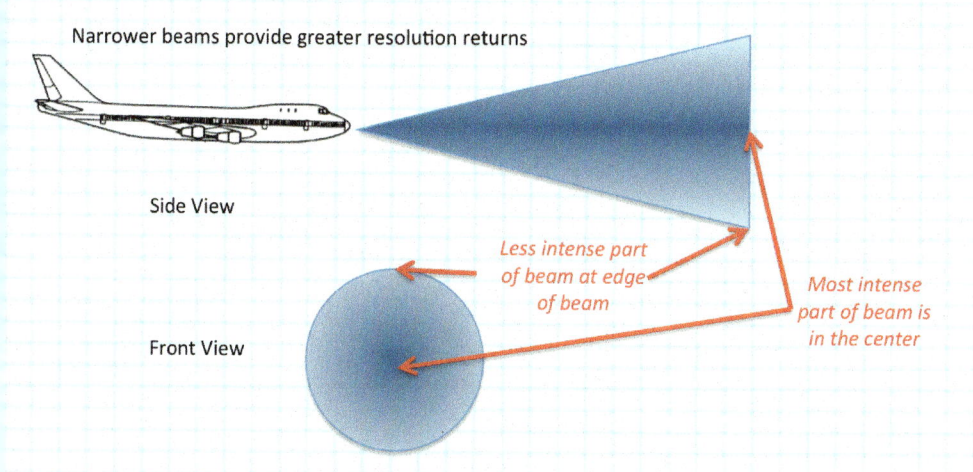

Narrower beams provide greater resolution returns

Side View

Front View

Less intense part of beam at edge of beam

Most intense part of beam is in the center

How Radar Works: Reflection and Attenuation

If the beam is aimed to the most intense part of the storm and the gain left in "calibrated" mode, the colors should provide useful storm information. Each target lessens the signal strength (attenuation). If the signal is attenuated to zero, a shadow results, possibly hiding more weather.

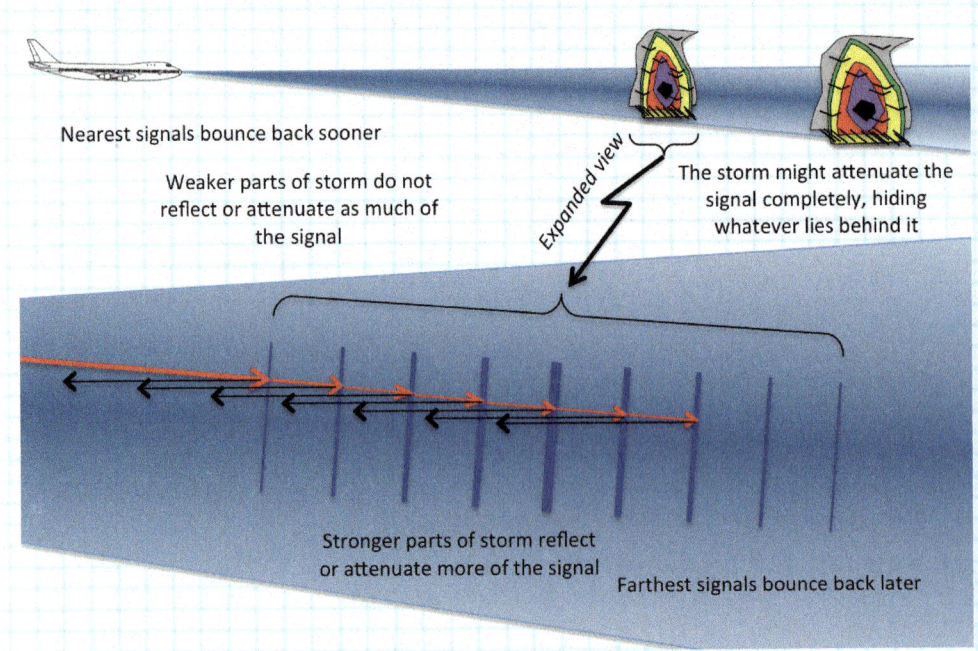

Nearest signals bounce back sooner

Weaker parts of storm do not reflect or attenuate as much of the signal

Expanded view

The storm might attenuate the signal completely, hiding whatever lies behind it

Stronger parts of storm reflect or attenuate more of the signal

Farthest signals bounce back later

Tilt: Adjusting for Beam Width

The radar paints more than just a point at the end of the beam, it includes everything in the width of the beam. In the case of a 24" radar:

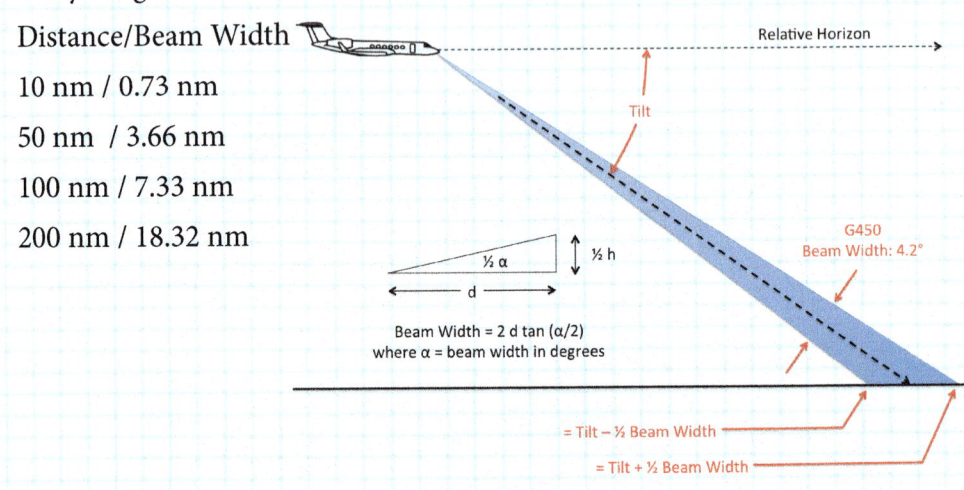

Distance/Beam Width

10 nm / 0.73 nm

50 nm / 3.66 nm

100 nm / 7.33 nm

200 nm / 18.32 nm

Relative Horizon

Tilt

G450 Beam Width: 4.2°

Beam Width = $2 d \tan(\alpha/2)$
where α = beam width in degrees

= Tilt – ½ Beam Width
= Tilt + ½ Beam Width

Flight Lessons 1: Basic Flight

Thunderstorm Levels

[Advisory Circular 00-24B, Thunderstorms, ¶6.]

To standardize thunderstorm language between weather radar operators and pilots, the use of Video Integrator Processor (VIP) levels is being promoted. The National Weather Service radar observer is able to objectively determine storm intensity levels with VIP equipment.

- 1 "weak" and 2 "moderate" — light to moderate turbulence is possible with lightning
- 3 "strong" and 4 "very strong" — severe turbulence is possible with lightning
- 5 "intense" — severe turbulence, lightning, hail likely with organized surface gusts
- 6 "extreme" — severe turbulence, lightning, large hail, extensive surface gusts

Radar Calibration

Most modern radar manufacturers have adopted these levels with a color code. With the radar set to a preset gain, you can expect the following:

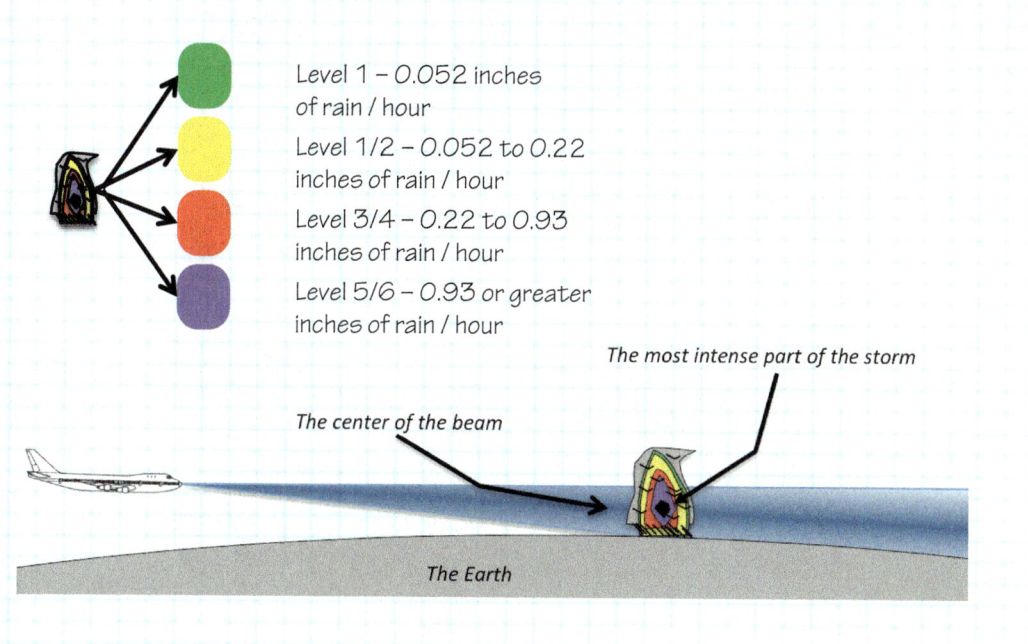

Level 1 – 0.052 inches of rain / hour

Level 1/2 – 0.052 to 0.22 inches of rain / hour

Level 3/4 – 0.22 to 0.93 inches of rain / hour

Level 5/6 – 0.93 or greater inches of rain / hour

The most intense part of the storm

The center of the beam

The Earth

Gain: Calibrated Setting

Most modern aircraft radars have calibrated gain settings that ensure the colors you see on the radar display reflect standard intensity levels. On some the setting is noted as "AUTO" and still others may default to calibrated settings and allow the pilot to switch to "Variable." It is vitally important to leave the gain in its "Preset" position. There is only one exception . . .

Radar Shadow Technique

The best way to detect a thunderstorm is to aim the tilt down far enough to paint lots of ground clutter and then look for returns. The entire beam needs to fall into the weather. A large return with no shadow can be a city, a lake, a tall mountain, or a thunderstorm. Compare the map of the return to the map of the terrain.

The photo shown is headed east to Boston. Notice the ground clutter disappears behind the large thunderstorm.

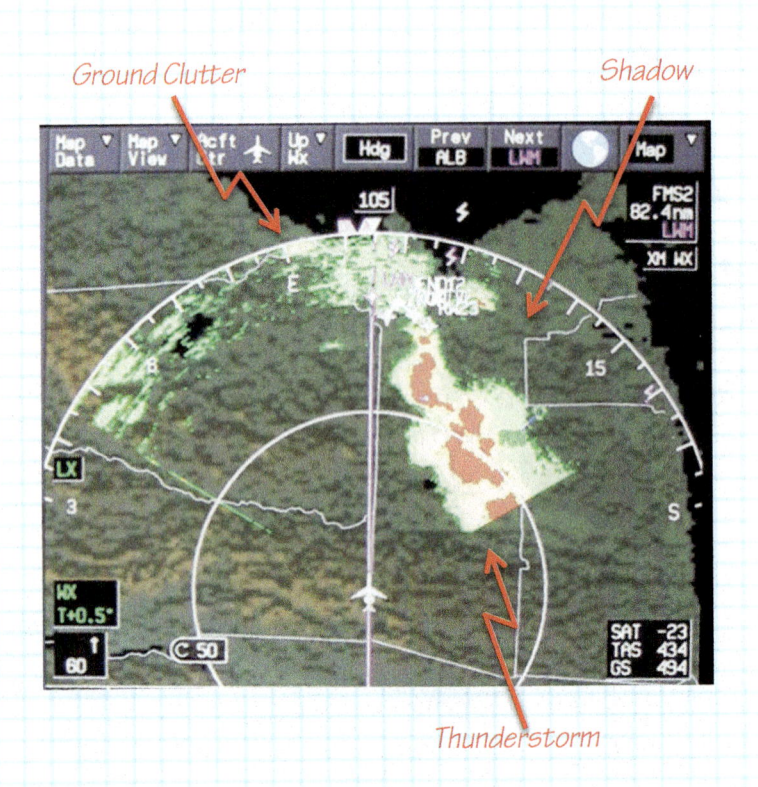

Flight Lessons 1: Basic Flight

Gain: Looking for Shadows

Lowering the gain tends to make weather seem less intense than it is, and that can decrease the radar's ability to "poke" through weather. The result could reveal a shadow:

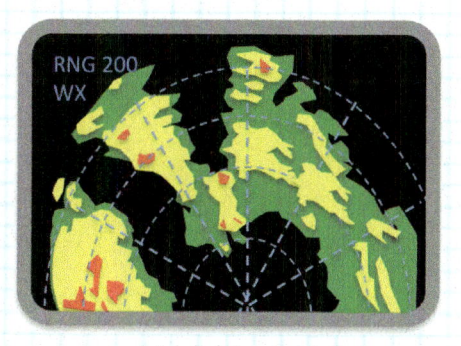

Only the lake and the thunderstorm at 11 o'clock are casting shadows. Are there any other thunderstorms nearby?

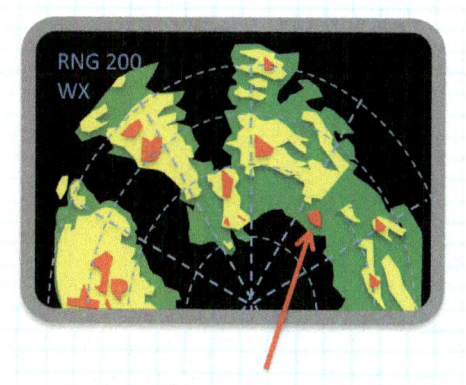

Lowering the gain has turned much of the yellow into red (the colors no longer reflect calibrated values). This reveals a previously hidden shadow at 2 o'clock.

Tilt: Looking for Shadows

Adjust the tilt until you paint the ground or a good portion of the weather. Low hills and cities do not cast shadows. Bodies of water do not reflect radar beams directly and can appear to be shadows, having good situational awareness will detect these. Large thunderstorms cast shadows – that tells you the thunderstorm is real, large, and dangerous. You have no idea what lies behind the thunderstorm in the shadow.

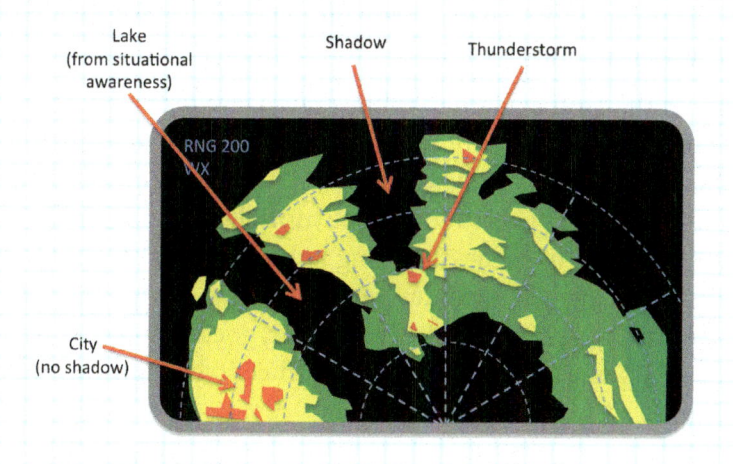

Lake (from situational awareness)

Shadow

Thunderstorm

City (no shadow)

29: Magic

At Minimums (From Eddie's collection)

The Lovely Mrs. Haskel and I took the next two weeks off to explore the scenic part of Maine, five hours to our south. When I showed up for alert our entire world had changed. Lieutenant Colonel Kong was gone and a new squadron commander was sitting at his desk. The lead pilot from the lost over the Atlantic mission was now working at the command post and his navigator, Captain Blow, had decided to separate from the Air Force. The list of promotions from captain to major were on the base, but was being kept very secret. It was a subdued alert force I found myself joining.

"It isn't normal at all," Don explained to the crew as we drove out to our alert bird. "When you change commanders, you have a change of command ceremony. The old boss gets to say goodbye and wish the new boss the best of luck. Then the new boss gets to introduce himself. But that's not what we got. One day Kong is in his office, throwing lightning bolts at whomever he happened to hate that day, the next day we got a new guy who marches in at 0700 every morning, fires a pilot or a navigator, goes to some wing staff meeting, and at 1700 marches right out of his office to his house on colonel lane. It isn't right."

Flight Lessons 1: Basic Flight

"Colonel lane?" I asked.

"That's where all the brass live," Don explained. Northern Aroostook County was so poor that just about everyone assigned to Loring lived on base. Including, it would seem, the colonels.

"Why does he want to see you, Eddie?" Calvin asked.

"Me?" I hadn't heard that.

"It's just all wrong," Don said. After we preflighted our alert aircraft I pulled our alert truck in front of the facility to let the crew out while I parked. Crew S-109 had the worst parking spot of the alert force, part of our penance for being the Leper crew. Though it seemed nobody was using that term anymore. Pity, I thought, I was starting to like it.

Haskel: Meeting CC 0900

The note next to my name on the scheduling board drew everyone's attention. "I'd hate to be in your shoes, Eddie," the scheduler said. "Everyone he's met at 0900 since he's taken over ended up demoted, fired, or both." The congregation in the scheduler's office all nodded in agreement. They would hate to be in my shoes.

"Lieutenant Haskel," the new boss's secretary said, "Colonel Francis is ready early if you are." I marched to my fate, all eyes in attendance following what all expected to be my last steps. I was a copilot and a second lieutenant. How could I possibly be demoted? I marched into the familiar office with the unfamiliar officer behind the desk, and saluted. Lieutenant Colonel Francis returned my salute, smiled broadly, and gestured me to sit down.

"Good to meet you Eddie," he said finally. "Your promotion orders came in last week. You can pin on the silver bars tomorrow. Congratulations."

He reached to shake my hand with what looked to be genuine happiness. The promotion to first lieutenant was almost automatic, around ninety-five percent for pilots. There was rarely any ceremony involved and this was more than I had expected.

"I've been going over your file and noticed half the aircraft commanders think you are a pain in the butt," he said. "What do you think of that?" He accentuated the "that" as if making a joke.

"I might have a talent for provoking strong feelings," I said, "one way or the other."

"That you do!" Again, he accentuated the last word. It was all very funny to him. "Well good news for you," he continued, "most of the squadron really appreciates the job you do and as it turns out you are the most requested copilot we have. But it isn't going to be that way for long because I took a look at Colonel Kong's upgrade rack and stack and think he's got it exactly backwards. You are number one on the list. Our next upgrade slot is in May. What do you think about that?" Again, the accentuated last word.

"I don't know," I said, "I guess that sounds like an honor."

"You bet it is! Not only that, I am sending your crew to Hawaii for a week. We got a slot to support one of the V.I.P. units there and I am sending crew S-109. So have a good time, don't get sunburned, and see you when you get back!"

Word of the upgrade rack and stack shocked the squadron as much as the three fired aircraft commanders. Half the squadron rose up to congratulate me, the other half started giving me more distance. It was as if I had some kind of magical power that needed to be feared. A week later I was an hour out of Honolulu with Don Nelson happily humming to himself as I strained to hear the weather report.

"It's pretty bad," I said, "especially for Hawaii. The airport has heavy rain and visibility is at minimums. The forecast is for it to stay that way all night. Our alternate airport just closed."

"How's the fuel?" Don asked.

"Not good," I said. "I think we can make one approach and hope for the best. Or we could head for Maui right now and not worry about it."

"Mother SAC will have our collective ass," Don said, "if we put this thing down any place but Hickam." Hickam Air Force Base shared the runways at Honolulu International, our destination. Our alternate was a Naval Air Station but it was closed. Landing a KC-135A at a purely civilian airport would be a big problem. We didn't have the correct radios to talk to the tower and they didn't have the correct ground equipment to support us. But it beat swimming.

"You're just going to have to fly the best ILS of your life, Eddie."

"I can do that," I said. Flying over Diamond Head we got more bad news. "We've lost radar," the approach controller said, "proceed direct the Honolulu VOR and fly the entire procedure."

"Roger," Don replied, "execute full procedure." I gave the approach plate a

Flight Lessons 1: Basic Flight

second look and memorized the altitudes, headings, and inbound course. I would have to fly west from Honolulu on a 259 degree course, turn left 45 degrees for a minute and a half, make a right 180 degree turn and intercept the instrument landing system localizer beam inbound. From that point it would be a simple ILS. Easy.

It was just like in the simulator except for the turbulence. Sure it was eight p.m. but usually you could see Oahu for miles. We saw nothing. I made the turn outbound to a 214 degree heading, level at 3,900 feet, and hit my stopwatch. At ninety seconds I turned right to a heading of 034 degrees. Once wings level I began my descent.

"Not yet," Don said, "you gotta be on course first."

"Yikes," I said, pulling the nose back up. How could I make such a stupid mistake? From this direction there was nothing but water underneath, but if the course needle didn't come up there were mountains on the other side. The rules say don't descend until you are on course. I pushed the thought out of my head: make a mistake, correct, move on. You have to concentrate on keeping the airplane right side up and on course.

Finally the needle came alive. I turned inbound and happily saw the localizer beam center. I brought each of the four throttles back a knob-width and allowed the altimeter to wind down to 2,000 feet. After another minute the glide slope needle started its march from the top of its case. "Gear down," I said, "before landing checklist please."

Don got busy with these chores and I made a mental note to leave the throttles alone as the glide slope needle centered and I ensured the added drag of the gear and flaps forced the airplane into a gentle 700 feet per minute descent. At 1,500 feet everything seemed to be in order though the speed was bouncing up and down a good fifteen knots. The trend of the needle seemed to be about five knots too high. My initial pitch was too low, causing us to dip below the glide slope. Oh yeah, I thought, all this headwind means lower ground speed. Maybe 600 feet per minute will do it. I pulled back on the yoke just a little, made note of the new pitch setting, and left the throttles alone.

"A thousand above," Don said. And then, with a faux German accent, "I see nutting." He often lapsed into Sergeant Schultz mode when he was nervous. The glide slope behaved itself but the localizer needle was on a journey to the right. We were heading 104 degrees, a good 25 degrees of drift. I dipped the right wing a few degrees. As the localizer needle reversed its movement I dipped the left wing to turn to a new heading of, let me see, we'll try 108.

"Five hundred feet," Don said, "needles are centered, on speed, but nothing outside."

We had to see the runway by 200 feet. We had 300 feet to go at 600 feet per minute. We had thirty seconds. The localizer needle started moving again. The winds must be dying off down low. I wiggled the wings to the left. The needle found its way home.

"A hundred to go," Don said, "nothing yet." The needles were centered. I left everything alone.

"Lights," Don said, "I got lights." I lifted my head from the instruments and saw nothing. Crosswind, I reminded myself. I turned my head to the left and there was the runway. We were crabbed a good 20 or 30 degrees into the wind. I added a healthy dose of right aileron and left rudder and landed the airplane.

At 100 knots I relinquished control of the airplane to the aircraft commander and reverted to being a copilot again. As Don taxied us off runway 8 left at Honolulu International I was overcome with a sense of pride. My mom would not have approved of my internal smugness but still I was happy. I looked back to the navigator, also a Hawaiian native, only to see him reading a magazine. I guessed it wasn't as impressive as I had thought.

The base gave us a twenty-year old sedan to make it to visiting crew quarters. I dropped the pilot and navigator off at officer's quarters and the boom operator at airman's quarters. Then I headed directly to the in-law's house, knowing I could use the excuse of having to see my own parents for the first time in a few years. It would give me the perfect escape clause while keeping the lovely Mrs. Haskel happy way back in Maine. Yes, dear, I did visit them.

It was still raining at the airport but as I climbed the mountains of Aiea in my rickety crew car I soon reached clear air. The in-law's house normally had a view of Pearl Harbor, the airport, and just a bit of Waikiki, but not tonight. It wasn't that they were rich or anything — they were not — but back then just about everyone had a view of some sort.

I pulled into the driveway and noticed the always-present glow of the black and white television. One day they would have color, I knew, but not anytime real soon. I rapped my knuckles on the metal part of the screen door, shaking the entire house, and was greeted by a sea of in-law faces.

Flight Lessons 1: Basic Flight

"You made it?" came from more than one in-law.

"Of course," I said, "how could I not make it?"

In-law Bruddah Numba One pointed to the south, where the airport should have been. "It's been raining all day down there."

"Sure," I agreed, "but it isn't too bad."

"How you can see the runway when it's raining?" In-law Bruddah Numba Two asked. I explained how the localizer antenna broadcasts two frequencies, left and right of centerline, and how another two antennas broadcast a glideslope. Then I explained how the aircraft had special receivers to interpret those into needles for the pilots. For me.

"But don't you have to see the runway before you land?" the remaining in-law Bruddah asked. I tried again, trying to equate the electrons into something more day-to-day, but the looks on their faces told me I wasn't doing a good job. I thought back to the old pilot training explanation, "it's magic." But they would think I was making fun of them and that would only get me in trouble with the Lovely Mrs. Haskel back in Maine. Then I came up with it.

"I have really, really good eyes," I said.

"Ah," they said as one, "we knew it."

Later that night I got no such cross-examination from my own parents. "How goes the search?" My dad asked. He had long since stopped mocking my search for the meaning of it all. I began to suspect he was on a search of his own.

James Albright

Instrument Landing System (ILS)

ILS: How it Works [Illustration from: AFM 51-37, figure 16-2]

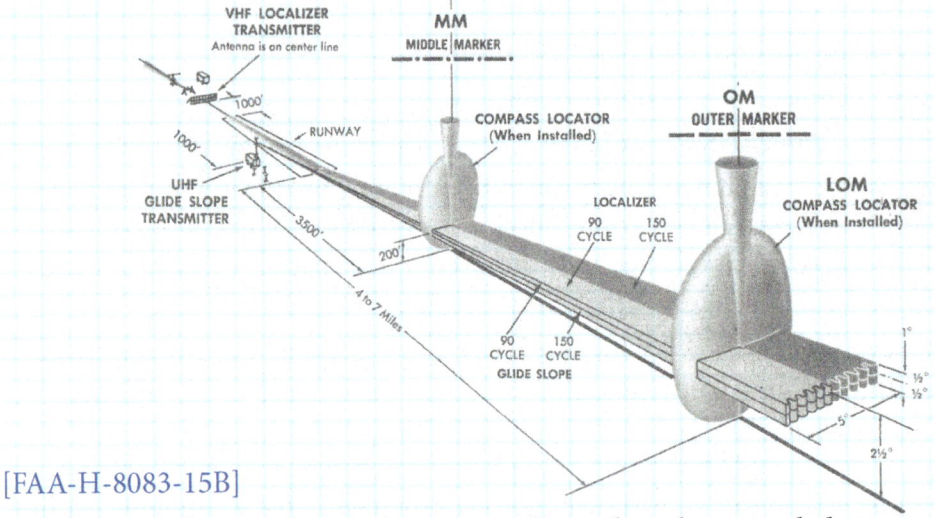

[FAA-H-8083-15B]

Localizer. The localizer ground antenna is located on the extended centerline of the runway. The localizer provides course guidance, transmitted at 108.1 to 111.95 MHz, from 18 NM from the antenna to 4,500 feet above the antenna site. The localizer course is very narrow, normally 5°. This results in high needle sensitivity. With no more than one-quarter scale deflection maintained, the aircraft will be aligned with the runway.

Glide Slope. The glide-slope equipment is housed in a building approximately 750 to 1,250 feet down the runway from the approach end of the runway, and between 400 and 600 feet to one side of the centerline. The course projected by the glide-slope equipment is essentially the same as would be generated by a localizer operating on its side. The glide-slope projection angle is normally adjusted to 2.5° to 3.5° above horizontal, so it intersects the MM at about 200 feet and the OM at about 1,400 feet above the runway elevation. At locations where standard minimum obstruction clearance cannot be obtained with the normal maximum glide-slope angle, the glide-slope equipment is displaced farther from the approach end of the runway if the length of the runway permits; or, the glideslope angle may be increased up to 4°.

Unlike the localizer, the glide-slope transmitter radiates signals only in the direction of the final approach on the front course. The glide path is normally 1.4° thick. At 10 NM from the point of touchdown, this represents a vertical distance of approximately 1,500 feet, narrowing to a few feet at touchdown.

Flight Lessons 1: Basic Flight

ILS: Coverage Limits [FAA-H-8083-15B, figure 9-36]

Unless otherwise noted, the localizer is only good out to 18 nm. Surface vehicles or airborne aircraft can disrupt the signal. False courses are possible if receiving the signal at too high a vertical angle.

The glideslope is normally good to 10 nm. Snow in front of the antenna can deflect the glideslope upwards beyond the maximum glide slope angle for some categories of aircraft.

ILS: Obstacle Clearance [TERPS, Vol 1, Ch 9, para 903]

The primary area has a perpendicular width from runway centerline = 0.10752 (D-200)+ 700, where D is the distance in feet from the runway threshold.

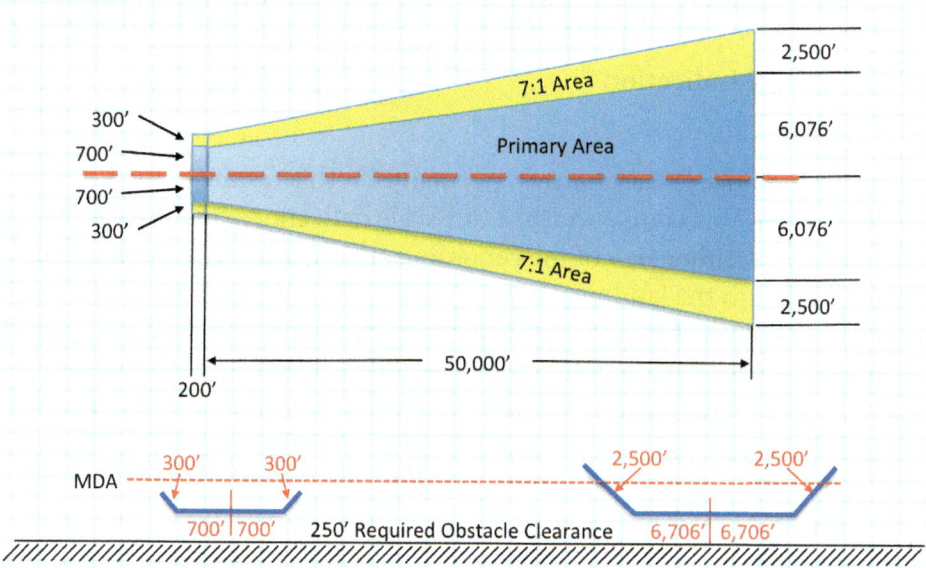

Sloping Obstacle Clearance Surface [TERPS, Vol 1, Ch. 2, para 203]

The vertical distance between the glidepath and the OCS is ROC; i.e., ROC = (glidepath height) - (OCS height).

OCS Slope = 102 ÷ glidepath angle; or glidepath angle = 102 ÷ OCS slope.

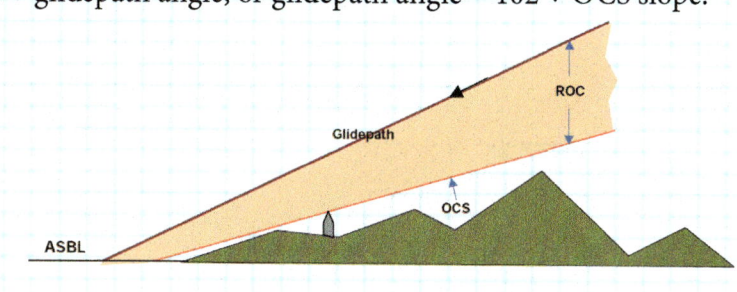

The OCS slope is "run over rise" – opposite convention. For a 3° glide path:

Distance (nm)	Distance (feet)	Glide path height	OCS height	ROC
1	6076	318	178	140
2	12,152	637	356	281
3	18,228	955	535	420
5	30,380	1,592	891	701

If an object penetrates the OCS, the glide path must be raised to raise the OCS. There is a limit to this, the maximum allowable glide path angle under TERPS is 3.1° for Category D/E, 3.6° for Category C, and 4.2° for Category B.

ILS: On Course Indication

[FAA-H-8083-15B, pg. 9-37]

The localizer course is very narrow, normally 5°. This results in high needle sensitivity. With this course width, a full-scale deflection shows when the aircraft is 2.5° to either side of the centerline. This sensitivity permits accurate orientation to the landing runway. With no more than one-quarter scale deflection maintained, the aircraft will be aligned with the runway. Generally speaking, if you are on a segment of the approach and have less than full scale deflection, you will have the required obstacle clearance when descending on an ILS glide path.

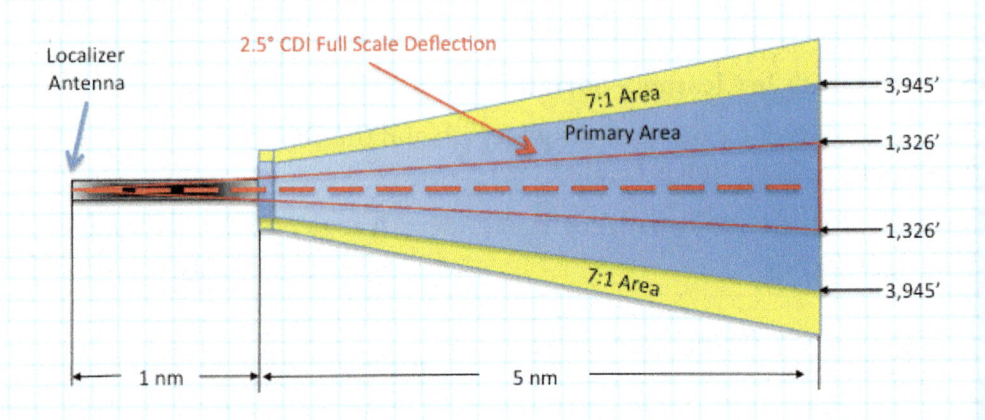

30: The Big Sky Theory

Honolulu International Runway 8R (Ron Reiring - Creative Commons)

It was to be a week in Hawaii, three days of which were devoted to air refueling aircraft from the 9th Airborne Command Control Squadron. They had four EC-135J aircraft, Boeing 707's outfitted with lots of communications equipment, passenger seating, and the plumbing that made them receiver aircraft. On day one of our visit the squadron commander singled me out from the crew.

"You Eddie Haskel?" Lieutenant Colonel Johansson asked. "I got your folder on my desk. The personnel center says you are number one on the list to come here if you pass the interview. Why don't you interview this week?" Why not? I spent my first day off meeting with squadron members and playing the proverbial "Twenty questions about flying" game. Everyone seemed to have come from a higher caliber of human being than we had back at Loring. The questions were intelligent and respectful. I volunteered for the assignment as a way of coming home. Now I wanted the assignment as a way of becoming a better pilot.

The interview included a flight in the jump seat of an EC-135J to see what refueling looked like from the receiver end and to spend some quality time with a couple of squadron pilots. The aircraft commander was Major Dan Greco, the squadron's chief of standardization.

The airplane was newer, cleaner, and sexier than our drab tanker. Painted in white and gray, it had a presence I had not enjoyed since the T-38. The cockpit was familiar, but filled with strange and new gizmos.

Major Greco taxied the aircraft from the left seat while copilot Captain Mark Christ read from the checklist and negotiated with Honolulu Ground Control to get us into the line of airliners waiting for their turn on the reef runway. "Takeoff briefing," Mark said over the interphone, holding his finger on the appropriate line in the checklist.

Dan spouted off the noise abatement procedures for the airport, which involved an immediate right turn at half bank. He covered the five immediate action emergency procedures and ended with "all members of the flight deck are responsible for traffic clearing procedures, we don't believe in the big sky theory." Looking at me over his right shoulder he added, "that includes you, lieutenant."

I nodded from the jump seat and Greco turned his attention to pulling up behind the next aircraft, waiting our turn for takeoff. I thought about "the big sky theory," the idea that the sky was big enough for everyone and there was no need for vigilance. The 9th Airborne Command Control Squadron did not subscribe to the big sky theory.

Finally we got our clearance. Mark called out each item on his checklist, placed the checklist on the floor between his seat and the center console, and placed his left hand behind the throttles and his right on the yoke. Greco pushed the four throttles forward and Mark fine-tuned them from below. At decision speed Dan removed his right hand completely. At rotation speed Dan pulled back on the yoke, called "gear up," and banked gently to the right. I looked over Dan's left shoulder to see Keehi Lagoon disappear behind us.

A few seconds later Dan called "flaps up" and steepened his bank. Mark moved the flap handle up and reached to his left for his plastic-bound checklist. Dan, still flying the airplane with his left hand, reached over with his right and grabbed the checklist from Mark. With a flick of his wrist he threw the checklist backwards. I ducked just in time and heard the booklet whoosh over my head. I turned around and saw that with the deck angle of the aircraft helping, the checklist ended up almost halfway down the aircraft aisle.

Flight Lessons 1: Basic Flight

"Your eyes," Greco barked, "belong outside right now." I sat upright and made sure I too had my eyes glued outside.

After the flight, Major Greco debriefed his crew and filled the room with cigarette smoke. I did my best to restrain a cough and listened quietly. His critique points were very good and it was one of the best debriefs I had ever heard. Still, none of that made up for the flying checklist. Mark and I left the office and he let me in on a squadron saying I would hear many times in the years to come: "Greco sucks."

The next day, my last before returning to Maine, the squadron commander asked to see me one final time. So far every part of the interview process seemed low key and more about getting to know each other than any formal, ritualized interrogation. Lieutenant Colonel "Call me Jim" Johansson was about as easy going a colonel as I had ever met.

"So, Eddie," he said with a strange pause before my name while gesturing me to sit, "whadda ya think?"

"I like the squadron," I said, "I like the airplane, and I like the people."

"Even Dan?" he asked.

"He has a very strong personality," I said, "but the points he makes are very good. I will never forget the flying checklist, but I will never forget to keep my eyes out of the cockpit either."

"Dan does that," Johansson said. "He lost a squadron mate in the traffic pattern once, two perfectly good jets flew right into each other. He harps on the big sky theory but I godda admit that's important at this airport."

I sat quietly, hands alongside the chair arm rails. I was conscious of leaving the hands unclenched, casual but not too casual. Perhaps I was overthinking things.

"So, I godda ask you one last question," he said. "What is the meaning of it all?"

"Sir?"

"I like to ask that question at all interviews," he said, "gives people a chance to talk about whatever and gives me a chance to listen."

Was it a trick? I hadn't used the "meaning of it all" phrase during our week in Hawaii and didn't think anyone on our KC-135A crew would have either. I was starting to drop it from my normal conversation because the reaction I got from most people wasn't too positive. As a teenager it was fun to provoke peers. As an Air Force officer? Not so much. Maybe it really was a legitimate question. Hurry up, I told myself. Thoughtful delay is okay, but minutes of confusion is bad.

"I have been in search of that very thing for many years," I said, deciding to play it straight. "When you start to think about becoming a pilot you dream of the airplane dancing through clouds or pulling a loop in front of an air show crowd while inches away from your wingman. But they are dreams about the airplane, not the mechanics of what makes the airplane obey your stick and rudder inputs. It isn't until you've actually flown fingertip formation or flown an instrument approach to minimums that you really get to appreciate there is more to it than just the end result of the airplane doing what it is supposed to do."

Johansson sat quietly, appearing to be genuinely interested. I pressed on.

"After we lost a few airplanes in pilot training and after the last two losses in the tanker world I've started to think about the differences between pilots you can trust and those who seem to be cruising through on luck. Mr. Boeing builds a fine airplane but we in the military often task the airplanes with doing things they weren't designed to handle. And even when flying missions the airplanes were meant to do, we are flying them years past their life expectancies. Add to all that, we as pilots often have imperfect information and have to make decisions based on faulty data."

"It sounds pretty serious," Johansson said. "I might need to recheck my life insurance policy."

"Maybe," I said, "but maybe not. I've come to the conclusion that the meaning of it all depends on your way of thinking things through. I guess this might be the engineer part of me invading the pilot part of me, but you can tell how someone thinks or feels about something by the way they behave. I've noticed that the better pilots all have this way of thinking in common."

"Attitude?" Johansson said, "they all have the same attitude?"

"Yes!" I said, realizing that one word encapsulated what I was thinking. "Sir that is exactly right. Mr. Boeing makes a great airplane but he couldn't think of everything. Even if he did, his airplanes weren't designed to fly as long as we have been flying them. Too many pilots strap on the jet and assume everything will work out, until it doesn't. The best pilots learn their jets inside and out, know their procedures, know the airspace, memorize the rules of engagement. Then, if things go south on them, they can make the best decisions possible with the information on hand. Major Greco's Big Sky Theory is another example. Technically, we are on instrument flight plans and have the right of way. But all it takes is for someone else to make a mistake and we end up dead, right of way or not. Keeping your eyes out of the cockpit not only answers the problem of the Big Sky Theory but it gives the pilot another tool for survival. An intelligent pilot uses all the tools available. For me, the quest to know the meaning of it all has led me to that. We as pilots have to understand that our attitude towards learning will determine our fates."

"Attitude determines altitude," Johansson said. "In more ways than one."

My smile was genuine, it was the answer I had been looking for.

The Big Sky Theory

The Theory

The sky is big enough for everyone, the chance of one airplane hitting another are so small you really don't need to worry about it.

The Reality

In 1986 a Piper Cherokee flying VFR blundered into the approach path of a DC-9 that was flying on an IFR flight plan in radar control just minutes away from landing. The weather was clear and visibility was 14 miles. All 70 aboard both aircraft and 15 more on the ground were killed.

Technology

TCAS and ADS have definitely made things safer and the number of midair collisions has decreased. But the problem still exists. Visual scanning techniques must still be employed.

Limitations of the Eyes: External

[Collision Avoidance, EASA Leaflet GA-1, Jan 2010] Vision, is vulnerable to many things including dust, fatigue, emotion, germs, fallen eyelashes, age, optical illusions, and the effect certain medications. In flight, vision is influenced by atmospheric conditions, glare, lighting, windshield deterioration and distortion, aircraft design, cabin temperature, oxygen supply (particularly at night), acceleration forces and so forth.

Most importantly, the eye is vulnerable to the vagaries of the mind. We can 'see' and identify only what the mind permits us to see.

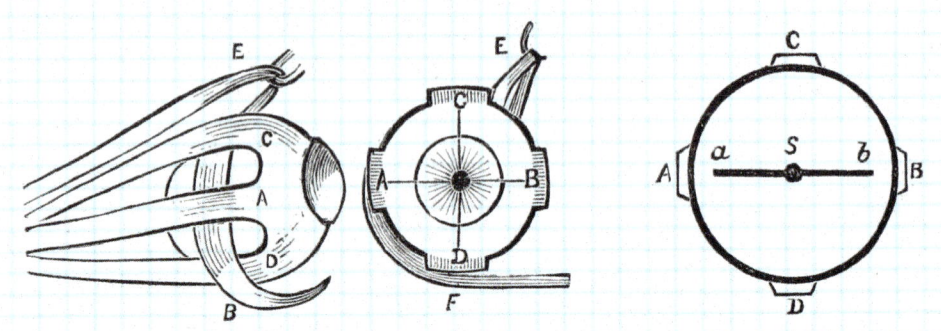

Illustration: Muscles controlling eyeball movement (Popular Science Monthly 1912)

Limitations of the Eyes: Accommodation

[Collision Avoidance, EASA Leaflet GA-1, Jan 2010] One inherent problem with the eye is the time required for 'accommodation' or refocusing. Our eyes automatically accommodate for near and far objects, but the change from something up close, like a dark instrument panel, to a bright landmark or aircraft several miles away, takes one to two seconds.

The eye has nothing to specifically focus on, which happens at very high altitudes, but also at lower levels on vague, colourless days above a haze or cloud layer with no distinct horizon, people experience something known as 'empty-field myopia', and opposing traffic entering the visual field is just not seen.

To accept what we see, we need to receive cues from both eyes (binocular vision). If an object is visible to only one eye, but hidden from the other by a windshield post or other obstruction, the total image is blurred and not always acceptable to the mind. Therefore, it is essential that pilots move their heads when scanning around obstructions.

Although our eyes accept light rays from an arc of nearly 200°, they are limited to a relatively narrow area (approximately 10 – 15°) in which they can actually focus on and classify an object. Anything perceived on the periphery must be brought into that narrow field to be identified.

Limitations of the Eyes: Day Versus Night Vision

[US Army Aeromedical Training for Flight Personnel, Chapter 8] The retinal rod and cone cells are so named because of their shape. The cone cells are used principally for day or high-intensity light vision (viewing periods or conditions). The rods are used for night or low-intensity light vision (viewing periods or conditions). Some of the characteristics of day and night vision are due to the distribution pattern of rods and cones on the retina. The center of the retina, the fovea, contains a very high concentration of cone cells but no rod cells. The concentration of rod cells begins to increase toward the periphery of the retina. The night blind spot occurs when the fovea becomes inactive under low-level light conditions. The night blind spot involves an area from 5 to 10 degrees wide in the center of the visual field. If an object is viewed directly at night, it may not be seen because of the night blind spot; if the object is detected, it will fade away when stared at for longer than two seconds. The size of the night blind spot increases as the distance between the eyes and the object increases.

Effective Scan Patterns

[Collision Avoidance, EASA Leaflet GA-1, Jan 2010]   Glancing out and moving your eyes around without stopping to focus on anything is useless; so is staring out into one spot for long periods of time.

Concentrate your search on the areas most critical to you at any given time. In the circuit especially, always look out before you turn and make sure your path is clear. Look out for traffic making an improper entry into the circuit.

During final approach stage, do not fix your eyes on the point of touchdown, but scan all around.

In normal flight, most collision threats will come from an area within 60° left and right of your flight path. You should also scan at least 10° above and below the projected flight path of your aircraft.

Effective scanning is accomplished by a series of short, regularly-spaced eye movements that bring successive areas of the sky into the central visual field. Each movement should not exceed 10°, and each area should be observed for at least one second to enable detection.

USAF Techniques

Eyes where you are headed. Spend 90% of your visual scanning time on where the airplane is going and that isn't always straight ahead. We are often turning, climbing, and descending. That's where your focus needs to be.

Pick a far object, jump around from there. Pick something at a distance, a cloud or an object on the ground, and give your eyes a second or two to clearly see it. Then jump from spot to spot where you expect the threat to be, keeping your distant focus intact.

Head on a swivel. A stationary object on the windscreen is headed right for you but you have the least chance of seeing it until it fills your windscreen. Improve your odds by moving your head. The motion and change in perspective could produce the motion your eyes need to see.

Look askance. Include your peripheral vision, especially at night. Realize you have a blind spot directly in front of view at night.

Flight Lessons 1: Basic Flight

Target Acquisition Performance Test
[NTSB Aircraft Accident Report PB87-91409]

The Massachusetts Institute of Technology evaluated the ability of pilots to spot other aircraft patterned off the 1986 Piper/DC-9 mid-air. The chances of spotting the other aircraft was higher in the slower moving Piper but was still probable in the jet at close range. With only one pilot looking, the DC-9 crew's odd were less than 50% until the aircraft had closed to within a half-mile, giving them less than 5 seconds to react.

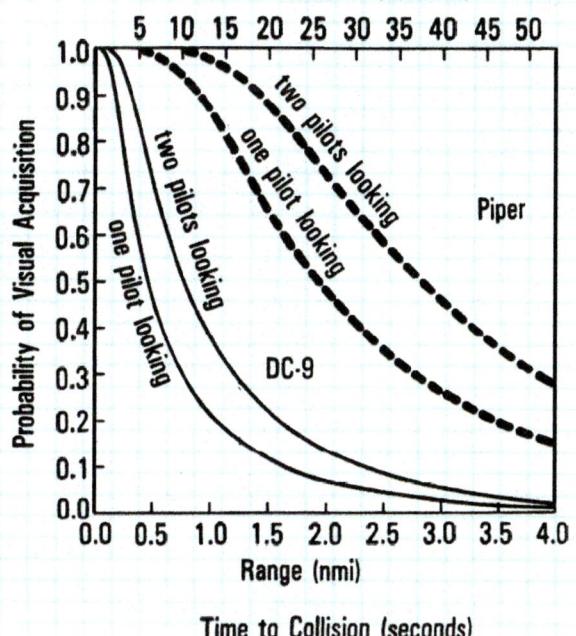

If armed with TCAS and alerted to the presence of the other aircraft and given an approximate position to begin scans, the probability of acquiring the other aircraft visually greatly improved.

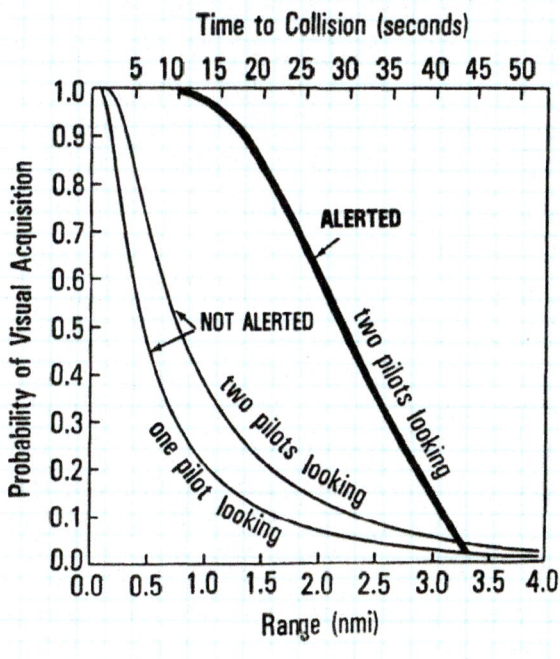

Going Forward

Loring AFB Main Gate from Rearview Mirror (Alan Wisniewski)

We got back to Loring just as it was getting cold again, having missed the week of summer allotted to northern Maine. The base was in an uproar over yet another crisis that nobody could differentiate from the previous crises. The squadron copilot population was still in a state of panic over the inverted rack and stack; and that was made only worse when my orders to Hawaii showed up.

"Dumbest thing you could do," the squadron commander said. "In SAC you are a part of a family and the family takes care of its own. You know why they call Hawaii a special duty assignment? Because it is special, there are only a handful of EC-135J pilots and nobody knows them. You won't get promoted and you won't get a good assignment out of there. In SAC, you have a home." I promised to think about it, knowing that my mind was already made up. Everyone in the squadron had an opinion but the one I trusted most had the best advice of all.

"Leave this madhouse while you can," Captain Paul Craft said. "SAC doesn't take care of its own, SAC eats its own. At least in Hawaii you will have a

Flight Lessons 1: Basic Flight

whole new world open up to you. In SAC, once you fall off the favored few list, you are banished to alert hell for the rest of your career. That is if you make it to twenty. Chances are you won't."

It was as glum as I had ever seen Paul. I signed my orders and saw my name crossed off the scheduling board. Captain Rick Stiles congratulated my escape and revealed the rest of the unfolding puzzle.

"I got passed over," he said, "I get one more try and they throw me out. No pension, no thank you, not even a gold watch. We didn't promote a single aircraft commander, Eddie. The only tanker pilots on base who made it aren't really tanker pilots. Like Tommy Black, that toad."

"Captain Black got promoted?" I asked.

"Major-select Black to you and me," he said. "I remember when he got thrown out of the squadron because he nearly lost it in the flare. An aircraft commander who can't handle Dutch roll! So he's too dangerous to fly an airplane and he has to fly a desk. Now he's doing something the rest of us aren't, teaching us schmucks emergency war orders. So he gets promoted and guys like me and Paul get passed over."

"Captain Craft?" I asked.

"Yeah," he said, "Paul got passed over too."

I always knew that being a good pilot wasn't enough to get promoted in the Air Force. But Captain Craft was the best tanker pilot of them all. Getting out of the tanker, I felt more certain than ever, was the right thing to do.

I left Maine in February of 1982 a better pilot for the 22 months I had spent there. I had learned to deal with the stress from failures of aircraft, commanders, peers, and subordinates. After three years flying jets I still had much learning to do, but I felt my basic flight instruction was complete.

The meaning of it all begins and ends with the search for knowledge. You cannot know everything and even those things you are certain of can change. Of greatest danger to pilots are those things we don't know that we don't know. You don't know what you don't know and those things tend to be the most consequential. As pilots we must always be in "learn mode" and must always be willing to challenge "the way we've always done it." That attitude determines our fates as pilots. Attitude truly determines altitude.

References

Code of Federal Regulations, Title 14, Part 1: Aeronautics and Space, Definitions and Abbreviations, Federal Aviation Administration, U.S. Department of Transportation

Code of Federal Regulations, Title 14, Part 25: Aeronautics and Space, Airworthiness Standards: Transport Category Airplanes, Federal Aviation Administration, U.S. Department of Transportation

Advisory Circular 00-24B, Thunderstorms, 1/20/83, U.S. Department of Transportation

Advisory Circular 00-54, Pilot Windshear Guide, 11/25/88, U.S. Department of Transportation

Advisory Circular 91-70A, Oceanic and International Operations, 8/12/10, U.S. Department of Transportation

Aeronautical Information Manual, U.S. Department of Transportation

Air Force Manual (AFM) 51-9, Aircraft Performance, 7 September 1990

Air Force Manual (AFM) 51-37, Instrument Flying, 1 December 1976

Air Force Manual (AFM) 51-40, Air Navigation, Flying Training, 1 July 1973

Air Training Command Manual (ATCM) 51-3, Aerodynamics for Pilots, 15 November 1963

Air Training Command Regulation (ATCR) 51-4, Primary Flying, Jet, 15 October 1988

Air Training Command Regulation (ATCR) 51-38, Advanced Flying, Jet, 15 October 1988

Creative Commons, "free to distribute in any medium or format, providing attribution is made"

Davies, D. P., Handling the Big Jets, Civil Aviation Authority, Kingsway, London, 1985

Department of the Army Field Manual 3-04.301, Aeromedical Training for Flight Personnel, 29 September 2000

Dole, Charles E., Flight Theory and Aerodynamics, 1981, John Wiley & Sons, Inc, New York, NY, 1981

European Aviation Safety Agency (EASA), <u>Collision Avoidance, Methods to Avoid the Risk</u>, Safety Promotion Leaflet, GA-1, Jan 2010

FAA-H-8083-15B, <u>Instrument Flying Handbook</u>, U.S. Department of Transportation, Flight Standards Service, 2012

Flight Safety Foundation, <u>Approach and Landing Accident Reduction Tool Kit - Wind Shear</u>, August-November 2000

Hurt, H. H., Jr., <u>Aerodynamics for Naval Aviators</u>, NAVWEPS 00-80T-80, Skyhorse Publishing, Inc., New York NY, 2012

NTSB Aircraft Accident Report, AAR-87/07, Collision of Aeronaves de Mexico, S.A., McDonnell Douglas DC-9-32, XA-JED and Piper PA-28-181, N4891F Cerritos, California, August 31, 1986

Technical Order 1C-135(K)A-1, KC-135A Flight Manual, USAF Series, 25 April 1957

Technical Order 1T-38A-1, T-38A/B Flight Manual, USAF Series, 1 July 1978

United States Standard for Terminal Instrument Procedures (TERPS), Federal Aviation Administration 8260.3B CHG 25, 03/09/2012

Index of Flight Lessons

Aerodynamic Force 58

Angle of Attack 83

Basic Navigation 128

Big Sky Theory 212

Climb Performance 145

Control and Performance Concept 32

Course Intercepts 73

CR-3 / CPU-26 (Computer Side) 38

CR-3 / CPU-26 (Wind Side) 50

Critical Mach 110

Crosswinds 78

FAA Holding 105

Fix-to-Fix 87

Ground Effect 100

Instrument Landing System (ILS) 204

Jet Engine 101 46

Mechanics 9

Radar 192

Region of Reversed Command 96

Stability 138

Thrust and Drag 91

Thrust Measurement 169

Turn Performance 161

Unusual Attitude Recovery 64

V1 (Decision Speed) 118

Water Injection 187

Windshear 177

About the Author

James Albright is an average pilot with average stick and rudder skills, but has an above average desire to learn and instruct. He spent twenty years in the United States Air Force as an aircraft commander, instructor pilot, evaluator pilot, and squadron commander. After retiring as a lieutenant colonel, he went on to fly for several private and commercial operators as an international captain, check airman, and chief pilot. His logbook includes the T-37B, T-38A, KC-135A, Boeing 707, Boeing 747, Challenger 604, and the Gulfstream III, IV, V, and 450.

His website, www.code7700.com attracts a million hits each month and his articles have appeared in several magazines, most notably Business & Commercial Aviation.

While he claims to be devoid of ego, that can hardly be true of someone willing to write a five volume set of flight lessons based on his own experiences.